TRAINS UNLIMITED

IN THE 21ST CENTURY

TRAINS UNLIMITED
IN THE 21ST CENTURY

TIM FISCHER

ABC
Books

The ABC 'Wave' device is a trademark of the Australian Broadcasting Corporation and is used under licence by HarperCollins*Publishers* Australia.

First published in Australia in 2011
by HarperCollins*Publishers* Australia Pty Limited
ABN 36 009 913 517
harpercollins.com.au

HarperCollins*Publishers*
Level 13, 201 Elizabeth Street, Sydney NSW 2000, Australia
31 View Road, Glenfield, Auckland 0627, New Zealand
A 53, Sector 57, Noida, UP, India
77–85 Fulham Palace Road, London W6 8JB, United Kingdom
2 Bloor Street East, 20th floor, Toronto, Ontario M4W 1A8, Canada
10 East 53rd Street, New York NY 10022, USA

National Library of Australia Cataloguing-in-Publication data:

Fischer, Tim, 1946–
  Trains unlimited in the 21st century / Tim Fischer.
  ISBN: 978 0 7333 2834 3 (pbk.)
  Railroad trains.
  Railroads.
385

Cover and internal design by Natalie Winter
Cover images: Tim Fischer courtesy *Border Mail*; remaining images by shutterstock.com
Internal images except where indicated by Shutterstock.com; Atocha Madrid by rubyphoto/Shutterstock.com; Delhi Metro by Paul Prescott/Shutterstock.com; Union Station Washington by Jason Mehl/Shutterstock.com. Picture section images except where indicated by Shutterstock.com; TGV running alongside trucks by André Klaassen/Shutterstock.com; ICE at Cologne by Regien Paassen/Shutterstock.com; Eurostar after engine problems, 2008 by Baloncici/Shutterstock.com; Shinkansen bullet by Dr_Flash/Shutterstock.com; Union Pacific Freight train in Berea, Ohio by StonePhotos/Shutterstock.com; Grand Central Station from the outside by sepavo/Shutterstock.com.
Typeset in 11.5/15.5pt Minion Regular by Kirby Jones
Printed and bound in Australia by Griffin Press
70gsm Classic used by HarperCollins*Publishers* is a natural, recyclable product made from wood grown in sustainable forests. The manufacturing processes conform to the environmental regulations in the country of origin, Finland.

5 4 3 2   11 12 13 14 15

Part of my royalties from this book will be donated to Caritas Internationalis, as well as to rail heritage operations, to recognise individual excellence in service by a volunteer under the age of 25. This reflects my desire to give something back, and the fact that I was indirectly assisted in the final stages of this writing task — a task undertaken mainly on weekends — by having a work station based in Rome.

— Tim Fischer, 2011

Dedication: To my wife, Judy, sons, Harrison and Dominic, and my late father, Julius Ralph Fischer, of Boree Creek, who first introduced me to real trains. When did he do this? In the middle of last century.

Inspiration: Many factors have motivated me to write this book — firstly, to help build a broader understanding of modern rail; secondly, to provide another avenue to answer queries from the listeners of ABC Radio's Great Train Show *who want to know more about the successful side of rail. Above all else, in a small way it's a salute to the railway engineers, designers, surveyors, financiers, general workers and project managers, along with the odd political leader, who have made rail happen around the world over 20 extraordinary decades of development and now more.*

CONTENTS

FOREWORD
by Lord Richard Faulkner

Writing in his novel *Sybil* in 1845, Britain's Prime Minister Benjamin Disraeli correctly predicted, 'The railways will do as much for mankind as the monasteries did.' It is therefore entirely appropriate that this Foreword should appear in a book about railways in the 21st century written by the current Australian Ambassador to the Holy See.

Tim Fischer demonstrates how much Disraeli's prediction has proved to be correct, though there have been periods in the recent past when those of us who care about the railway were in despair about whether governments would ever be prepared to take on and defeat those forces who wished to concrete over the countryside, building one new motorway and airport runway after another.

Certainly there were times in Britain in the '70s and '80s when it looked as though the forces of darkness in transport policy terms would succeed in drastically reducing the size of the UK's railway network, forcing more freight onto our increasingly congested roads, and driving passengers into their cars or onto environmentally disastrous short-haul flights.

While we in Britain were debating whether we needed a modern railway at all, our Continental friends in France, then Germany, followed by Spain and Italy, were investing massively in brand-new high-speed railways. As Britons travelled abroad, they realised that not only had railways a future, they were by far the most comfortable, most environmentally friendly, and often the fastest form of transport. The argument for trains has now largely been won. It is almost inconceivable that a major advanced nation would embark on a program of railway closures and cuts of the sort carried out in Britain in the '60s and '70s post-Beeching [Dr Richard Beeching, chair of the British Railways Board who oversaw savage cuts to the British rail network]. How public opinion was turned around is the subject for another book.

I am delighted to celebrate the renaissance of the railway, described with such prescience and verve by Tim Fischer. Ambassador Fischer is an extraordinary phenomenon: a country boy and farmer from New South Wales, a Vietnam War veteran who became successively a legislative assembly member and then federal politician. He was leader of his party, and for three years Deputy Prime Minister in a Coalition Government. For all the time he has been such a distinguished public servant, Ambassador Fischer has kept alive and developed his passion for the railway, both ancient and modern, and most importantly, convincing others of his point of view.

Many of his successes are described in the book. And so too are the achievements of his beloved railways — from transforming urban and rural life in the nineteenth century, and making the Industrial Revolution possible, through to the development of high-speed rail in the late 20th and early 21st centuries. In many countries the railways' heyday was in the years leading up to World War II, to be followed by periods of retrenchment, contraction and doubt. Thanks to people like Tim Fischer their time in many countries has come again. Read this book and you'll see how this has happened, and enjoy with Tim the railway's superb architectural legacy, its extraordinary technological advances, his description of some of the finest lines, stations, and services around the world — and above all his message of hope for railway's future.

Tim Fischer is living proof of Nicholas Whittaker's comment in his book *Platform Souls: The Trainspotter as 20th-Century Hero*: 'Trainspotting has always been a democracy, embracing all men, from right scruffs to Right Honourables.'

* * *

Richard Faulkner (Lord Faulkner of Worcester) is a British parliamentarian who has served in a range of railway-industry roles, ranging from 20 years' service as an adviser to the British Railways Board, and chairing the Railway Heritage Committee (the statutory body charged with ensuring the preservation of records and artefacts which form an essential part of the nation's railway heritage), to eleven years' membership of the House of Lords. He has also been a trustee of the Science Museum in London and National Railway Museum in York, and has recently been reappointed to the First Great Western Trains Advisory Board, and become president-elect of the Heritage Railway Association. From 2009 to 2010 he was a minister in the British Government, speaking on transport in the House of Lords.

ALL ABOARD!

There are many ways to write about railways and with some enjoyment, but in a sense just two ways to run a railway, to quote a truly great editorial from the UK *Financial Times* on 11 December 2004 — early in the 21st century.

> *The Swiss model, essentially modern, is based on the idea that the railway timetable is literally true and that the trains will run at the stated times. Swiss trains are so reliable you can set your cuckoo clock by them. The British model, essentially postmodern, rejects the idea that railway timetables are capable of conveying a fixed meaning or universal truth, holding that train times can only be shifting, relative and provisional.*
>
> *Next to the simplicity and rationality of the Swiss model, British style dysfunctionalism may appear unsatisfactory. But there are enormous advantages in living with a rail system that simply cannot get any worse. Having no expectations that a train will ever appear on time, passengers are amazed and delighted when it does, and so life contains only pleasant surprises.*

The British model has staggered along through the first decade of the 21st century with plenty of further deterioration and delay. Parts of the UK railway system for both freight and passenger services not only got a whole lot worse, some closed down altogether.

To be fair, things can go wrong even in Switzerland, the land of the cuckoo clock and ever-punctual trains. In 2010, for the first time ever, I passed by overnight sleeper through Switzerland on the Rome–Paris Express. We were two hours late on arrival at Brig, from Italy, so we were punished and shunted away, around Martigny in southern Switzerland and again at Lausanne, to ensure we did not foul 'on-time running' for the morning peak-hour trains. By the time we left Switzerland we were four hours late, although domestic morning-peak trains probably all ran on 'cuckoo-clock time' that day.

Nevertheless, there must be a railway-inspired God, as at Dijon we were switched to a TGV, first class and free of charge. We made up two hours to arrive in a fast approach to Gare de Lyon, Paris.

Today the ultra modern Eurostar arrives in a fast approach to Gare du Nord, offering a two-hour fifteen-minute train service from London to Paris. This high-speed 'all the way' service was introduced in 2007, although in the Christmas week 2009 simple snow-generated condensation wiped out the service completely for three days. To be fair this was during record snow falls in northern France and apparently a destructive temperature difference occurred when the Eurostar train sets dived into the Chunnel (English Channel tunnel). Occasionally the most modern of rail equipment can break down.

In some places around the world the Swiss model dominates, especially on many well-run heritage tourist railways. But over the decades, both Australia and New Zealand have run closer to the British model than the Swiss model, with a culture of near enough to the optimum is good enough. Likewise at times in the USA, but on a grander scale, leading to railroad bankruptcies. Too often this slackness operates among senior levels of transport public servants and rail planners, through rail company

Boree Creek on Sunday, 6 February 2011, after deluge from post-cyclonic rains. The new Australian Rail Track Corporation (ARTC) bridge handled the flooding with ease on the very day the first grain train of 2011 was scheduled to run to Boree Creek. (Tim Fischer)

management to the train despatcher who must complete a smoko before giving the necessary clearance for a train to depart.

In this book just about every aspect and model of railway transport is canvassed, as I crystallise a lifetime of studying and writing about rail, following working visits to over 72 countries.

Its big difference from many other books about rail is the fact I write it from outside the dominant UK and USA railway cultures. It was mostly researched and written in the southern hemisphere but completed on weekends during a posting as Australian Ambassador to the Holy See, living in an apartment in Nomentana, Rome, near the six-track portion of the main line to Florence and the rest of Europe.

My interest in the subject did not arise from love of a model train set as a kid, but from going to meet the Monday night rail motor, a self-propelled single passenger carriage with engine on board but sometimes with a small freight van or extra carriage attached. My father would take me for the 4-kilometre (2.5-mile) drive from the family farm to Boree Creek, a tiny branch-line station in the Riverina District of New South Wales, Australia. First we would hear the rails hum, then the big bright headlight of the CPH rail motor would come rolling round the corner lighting up everything ahead; the rail motor would stop with a jerk and a couple of passengers would disembark along with bundles of prized newspapers and parcels.

Our purpose was to collect the much-desired Sydney Sunday papers, buying them on the platform — yes, 36 hours late which seems a little bizarre as viewed 50 years later. Today we complain if there are a few seconds' delay in downloading digital versions of newspapers from anywhere in the world to anywhere in the world!

My interest in rail matured through my schooling and then during a period as transport officer of the First Battalion, Royal Australian Regiment, at times having to organise troop movements by train to such 'delightful' places as Shoalwater Bay military training area in Central Queensland.

Later, after taking an honourable discharge from the army, having served nearly three years in Australia and Vietnam, I followed up on rail issues while serving both in the NSW State Parliament and the Federal Parliament. Often I used the neglected area of parliamentary committee work in a strategic way to build the case for rail and rail projects.

Just before the turn of the century, I was Deputy Prime Minister of Australia, Minister for Trade, and Federal Leader of the National Party. Against some odds, I was in fact Deputy Prime Minister to John Howard, during his first term and nine months of his second term as PM. As Prime Minister he drove forward the project to build the world's newest transcontinental railway — from Adelaide to Darwin. His role was truly decisive, not once but twice, when a top-up government funding injection was required during construction.

At one stage when the project was touch and go, a vital three-way telephone hook-up took place between the PM, Treasurer Peter Costello and myself. Extra funding for the Adelaide–Darwin railway, through the then South Australian Government, was being sought and straight away it was two to one in favour; eventually the Treasurer came on board and the project cleared another hurdle.

After stepping down from Federal Parliament in 2001, and after a brief, cleansing 'time out', I joined the board of Asia Pacific Transport (APT) FreightLink, the company operating rail to Darwin — which, despite the critics, can be considered a success. On the key criterion of 'trend in freight tonnages', the world's newest transcontinental, the Adelaide to Darwin, has had a fivefold increase in tonnage over the first four financial years of operation. While the original business case involved revenue projections which were too optimistic, the railway has made an operational profit each year since inception and is anything but a white elephant.

At the same time I served on several other boards, including the Australian Agricultural Company (AACo) for seven years; this was the company, as mentioned elsewhere in this book, that built Australia's first-ever railway — in Newcastle. In 2007 an unexpected invitation arrived to chair the Rail Freight Network Review (RFNR) of the Victorian State Government, then in 2008 an invitation arrived to host ABC Radio's *Great Train Show* broadcast across Australia. Our tiny ABC Radio team, based at Albury–Wodonga carved out a successful niche and learned a great deal more about rail, both serious and light-hearted. This in turn led to the writing of this book and a look at the past, present and the future of rail. Please enjoy. As I noted at the start, part of the net proceeds from sales of the book will go to rail heritage projects, including the famous Pichi Richi Railway in South Australia. The aim is to help provide training scholarships in heritage and tourism train operations for the next generation.

So all aboard — and to assist, there are four important acronyms to keep in mind while reading this book:

- HSR, which stands for high-speed rail passenger trains operating at or above 240 kph or 150 mph, such as the TGV (Train à Grande Vitesse — France) and ICE (Germany);
- RST, meaning regular-speed trains, travelling at around 110 kph maximum on a good day, and on many tracks this is what it has been since around 1850;
- DSFT, meaning double-stacked container intermodal freight trains; and
- RFT, or regular freight trains, be they mixed freight or unit train-loads (where the freight is all one type of commodity, for example steel or coal) or even intermodal containers.

See also the glossary of railway terminology that follows, and smile.

Rail is here to stay in the 21st century, faster and safer than ever before, at least in those railway realms in the world where it is allowed to operate efficiently. The various inefficiencies and brilliant efficiencies are all there to behold, as rail wobbles in some places but roars in others, into its third century of existence. The third century of 'modern' rail as a mode of transport on this planet earth will be the biggest century yet for rail worldwide, mark my written word!

GLOSSARY OF RAILWAY TERMINOLOGY

Herewith is an explanation of some of the key terms and phrases used in the construction and operation of railways over the decades. You will note it is in reverse alphabetical order, as I have done once before with the book *Transcontinental Train Odyssey*. There are three main reasons for this. First, the more colourful and interesting terms are towards the end of the alphabet and need elevating. Second, it is to counterbalance the order of the index, and so a gesture of salute to the 200th anniversary of reciprocating steam piston motion. Finally, in the churlish writing spirit of Mark Twain, who caught sixteen trains in Australia in 1895 and survived, this is a book on rail which is deliberately different from most others and hopefully entertaining, interesting and informative.

Zigzag: Used by railway engineers to rapidly gain or lose height by providing for tracks to literally zigzag up a mountain. A train crosses a set of points into a loop. The points are then switched and the train changes direction and reverses out of the loop, to continue its climb or descent. Zigzags are often used in mountainous areas. The best examples include the Zig Zag Railway in the Blue Mountains, Australia, and the Khyber Pass Railway in Pakistan.

Y points: A set of points laid out so that the centre line of the single section of track is different from but equidistant to the centre line of each of the double tracks, making the letter Y.

XPT: Express Passenger Train, the generic term used for regional passenger trains in New South Wales, which are usually, but not always, configured as locomotive, carriages, locomotive. The XPT was based on the high-speed train sets of Great Britain. It now runs interstate as well — Sydney–Melbourne and Sydney–Brisbane.

Whistle stop: Generally a tiny country station, such as Grass Valley near Northam in Western Australia, where trains stop very briefly, for the duration of one whistle blast, to pick up or unload parcels and passengers.

VFT: Very fast train. In Australia the term applied to the Melbourne–Canberra–Sydney high-speed train project developed by Dr Paul Wild in the 1980s. Loosely patterned on the French TGV, it was killed off by deeply negative elements in the then Federal Government.

Uniform loading specifications: Different national rail systems may well have the same rail gauge width between rails but different loading requirements for both size above rail and weight. Uniform loading specifications provide harmonised standards, such as the Berne loading gauge in many parts but not all of continental Europe.

TGV: The French TGV (Train à Grande Vitesse) has held the world speed record of 526 kph (326 mph) for many years, but on 3 April 2007 created a new record of 574.8 kph (357 mph), albeit with wheel and some other modifications. This all-electric train has a near-perfect safety record.

Steam locomotive: The steam locomotive took over from the horse as the main method of haulage in the first half of the nineteenth century. Many steam locomotives have names that have become legend over the centuries, including the *Rocket, Mallard, Sir Thomas Mitchell* and *3801.*

Rail track: The term applying to the two steel rails, sleeper or tie, clip or spike, pad and ballast. Today the head of each rail line is usually cantered in by about 1 in 20, to match the same canter, or slope, on the rail wheel surface.

Quagmire: Also called mud hole, this is a short section of track where the ballast has turned to powder or even been washed away, causing sleepers to drop down, thus creating an uneven ride which, if not fixed, can lead to derailments. Quagmires can even occur along tracks in desert locations and during drought.

Pacific Class: A class of steam locomotive with arrangement of wheels on the basis of four small, then six large and then two supporting wheels, 4–6–2, as opposed to all other combinations.

Oscillation: Also called hunting, this term describes lateral or sideways movement in carriages and wagons due to mismatch of wheel profile on railhead profile, or when the rail track is badly maintained and the gauge width actually varies by up to ½ inch (1.3 cm).

Near miss: An aviation term that also refers to trains being cleared onto the same pathway or track but not colliding. This can be in the same direction or worse still, in the opposite direction, risking a head-on crash. The US Congress has mandated Positive Train Control equipment by 2015 across much of the USA rail network, a move prompted by a deadly train collision near Los Angeles in 2008 and designed to preclude train collisions.

Motion sickness: More common in sea and air travel, but also experienced by train passengers, particularly when travelling on rough-riding trains on old tracks.

Lounge cars: These are generally located near the dining car or sometimes at the very end of a passenger train where they double as both a lounge car and an observation car. This is the case with the famous daily Colombo–

Kandy Intercity in Sri Lanka. Since lounge cars were introduced in the late nineteenth century, they have become more or less permanent in premium long-distance passenger trains, such as the Coast Starlight between LA and Seattle or the Ghan between Adelaide and Darwin. Some in Canada and the USA feature observation domes or even large full-length double-decker window lounges, with the lounge on the top deck.

Kitchenette: Not many are left on trains today, but the dining cars of the Blue Train, the Orient Express, the Indian Pacific and the Ghan all have stainless-steel kitchens producing gourmet meals from cramped quarters. There is a certain joy conferred by eating a meal that has actually been cooked on board.

Jump track: This occurs when rail wheels jump the track and derail, but the train remains vertical. This generally happens only when the derailment is at slow speed and on relatively straight track.

Inching forward: The process of coupling wagons, carriages and locomotives together under power.

Hump marshalling: Used in large freight yards. Wagons are pushed up a hump and then released through a set of computer-controlled braking pads and several sets of points at just the right speed to hook onto waiting wagons.

Gauge: The distance between the inside of each rail at its nearest point.

Frame: Used in mechanical signal-control boxes. A steel frame below the points and signal control levers prevents false moves being made, thus ensuring trains are not put on a collision path.

Express: This should denote passenger and freight trains that run without stopping, other than at major stations, from starting point to destination. It's a misused term in some railway systems.

Departure: In freight terminology this means when a freight train has been assembled and checked and has cleared the freight terminal onto the main line. For passenger trains it is the moment the train moves away from the platform. The time of departure has become more important, as today penalties often attach to delays.

Coupling: Today almost all couplings are heavy semi-automatic steel jaws and clasps designed to absorb jolting and prevent too much stretch. They are a far cry from the original hook-and-ring type.

Bogie: The set of rail wheels, axles and frame with a central pin attaching to the wagon/carriage or locomotive. At some break-of-gauge borders, trains are jacked up and bogies changed.

Arrival: Now a hotly disputed term. It is the moment a passenger train stops moving, having reached the destination platform. However, some railway systems have a five-minute period of grace on time arrival; others allow ten minutes. With efficient freight-train operations today, it is often the case that the first containers are coming off a train within 30 seconds of arrival at the freight terminal or siding.

INTRODUCTION

OFF AGAIN, ON AGAIN, GONE AGAIN

'Off again, on again, gone again!' This is a great catchcry from yesteryear discovered by ABC Radio's *Great Train Show* and arising from a frustrated stationmaster in Victoria, Australia, not long after the reign of Queen Victoria. It was of course a shorthand way of describing one of many frequent derailments in the Western District of Victoria, last century.

The Victorian Railways stationmaster had been chipped by HQ about the length of his reports on the various derailments of goods trains using the lightly ballasted Irish broad gauge system of 5 feet 3 inches (1600 millimetres). So he thought, in his best Australian manner, 'Stuff them!' and henceforth sent just these six words back to HQ every time a freight train departed the rails.

The phrase took off and was also used around Roma, in central southern Queensland, where a very light form of Anglo Cape narrow gauge of just

3 feet 6 inches (or 1067 millimetres) operated, and derailments on branch lines such as Roma-to-Injune and Warwick-to-Dirranbandi occurred ever so frequently. Unless it involved passenger trains, for a period the shorthand report sufficed.

Too often it might also be the catchcry of the railways of the world, as they reach the 200-year mark of their extraordinary activity.

It was George Stephenson more than any other person — more than the great engineer Isambard Kingdom Brunel, famed for his tunnels, bridges, viaducts and even steamships — who might be described as the 'founder of the modern railway'. Stephenson started devising, planning and building the first locomotive-hauled 'proper railway' around 200 years ago, leading to the opening of the Stockton and Darlington railway in northern England in 1825. Then, shortly after, as chief engineer he completed the first double-track all-purpose exemplar railway to the world: the Liverpool & Manchester Railway. It was officially opened on 15 September 1830.

In the USA, also in 1830, the Baltimore & Ohio Railroad led the way with the opening of a line westward from Baltimore to Ellicott City in Maryland. The original track is still a railway today, with excursion trains from the Baltimore & Ohio Railroad Museum running most Sundays a few kilometres along a tranquil corridor to the exact point where the main opening ceremony was conducted.

The first railway in France opened in 1830 near Lyon, while in Australia, the oldest private company with a continuing name, the Australian Agricultural Company (AACo), opened Australia's first railway in Newcastle, New South Wales, in 1831, for the haulage of coal over a distance of 3 kilometres. Conversely, Mauritania, in Africa, waited until as late as 1963 to establish its first (iron-ore haulage) railway.

Technically railways and their cousins the so-called plateways (cast-iron flat rails with an outside rim for guiding wagons) go back through the seventeenth century to around AD1500, when they were used in collieries in the north of England, but serious legislation on railways emerged on

1 May 1801, when the *Surrey Iron Railway Act* was passed by the British Parliament, and originally concerned horse-hauled railway. This changed when Cornish mine owner Richard Trevithick developed the first steam locomotive, in a fragile way, in 1804. It was the first-ever case of steam propelling a vehicle forward, a kind of road locomotive, but, alas, in celebrating its first moves, the crew became distracted in the local inn. They allowed the boiler to run dry and it exploded. However, notwithstanding the explosion, steam locomotion was on the move and over the next few years the modern-day railway began to emerge.

If the nineteenth century, the first century of the modern railway, saw massive expansion and development worldwide, the 20th century saw the near-death of the railway, with two world wars, the Great Depression, but more particularly the advent of the mass-produced motor car, truck and aeroplane taking effect. Railways fell off the pace, and only towards the end of the 20th century were two big breakthroughs obtained, guaranteeing their future. As a curtain-raiser along came the *Staggers Act* deregulating the railroad industry in the USA, and on its heels double-stacking of containers on trains, most notably in Australia, Canada and the USA, thereby nearly doubling freight transport productivity.

Secondly, in Europe and even earlier in Japan, along came very fast passenger trains, such as Japan's Shinkansen (Bullet train), the TGV in France, the AVE in Spain and the ICE (Intercity Express) in Germany. More flexible work practices and labour laws also contributed to improvement, as trade unions slowly but surely began to see the ever-changing and bigger picture.

Hence, I contend we are now at the start of the third century of the railway and in much improved shape, with massive increases in both passenger and freight. Although there have been some troughs due to recession in parts of the world, railways have continued to make gains in energy efficiency and by degrees in profitability.

It is a case of '21st Century Trains Unlimited' without a shadow of doubt, and this book will carefully lay out the case for a big future in rail, albeit one that learns from and builds on all that has gone before. The expression '21st Century Trains Unlimited' is a take on the famous luxury passenger train the '20th Century Limited', which operated on the water-level route between New York and Chicago from 1902 until 1967 and has nothing to do with travel companies of related name. It thus looks back to the past but emphasises the scope for the future. Railway is needed more than ever, and through the massive revamp of just about every aspect of the system over the last 50 years, it is set to deliver greatly to a congested, fossil-fuel scarce, polluted world.

This brings us back to 'Off again, on again, gone again!' It is a catchcry that still applies around the world, for there are always new challenges emerging.

To take the UK, the 'on again, off again, on again and gone again' project of renown has to be the very high-speed rail project for the main trunk route London–Birmingham–Manchester–Leeds–Newcastle–Edinburgh–Glasgow, along the spine of Britain. Over decades this has been mooted and dropped but has recently surfaced again with the completion and opening of the magnificently revamped St Pancras Station, as the London terminal for high-speed Eurostar trains from the Continent.

A few years back, the concept had been somewhat dammed in the massive Eddington Report on British infrastructure, headed up by Sir Rod Eddington, ex-head of British Airways and a West Australian of renown. To be fair and more accurate, the Eddington Report simply made no strong recommendation with regard to high-speed rail. The relatively small loading gauge in Great Britain — that is the height and width of rolling stock and locomotives using the Stephenson standard gauge — vis-à-vis, say, France or the USA, has always meant that whole new corridors and tracks would have to be found and developed for TGV-type operations, initially northwest then further north of London.

It took over a decade after the tunnel — or Chunnel — was completed under the English Channel in 1994 for the high-speed line from Folkestone to London to be eventually built. During this period, I recall vividly the acceleration upon leaving behind Ashford and the Southern rail system, with its antiquated third rail for power supply greatly limiting speed, speeding up into the Chunnel and travelling faster again on the French side past Calais. Now a two-hour fifteen-minute service prevails London to Paris, and 24 minutes less — an incredible one hour 51 minutes — London to Brussels Midi.

In the USA the Obama administration has unveiled a set of high-speed train projects as part of the 2009 stimulus package to help overcome the global financial crisis. Pro-rail Vice President Joe Biden has played a key role in this and so it will be interesting to see if and how many of these projects come to early fruition. There is more on this in the North America chapter (Chapter 6).

The large hub of Chicago has been a major zone of congestion over the decades for passenger trains in the past but now it is freight train congestion dominating. Mark Twain once wrote that a pig could pass through the Chicago train hub faster than a passenger. At last an 'off again, on again' project has emerged to provide extra key lines and more grade separation, including east–west rail pathways at a different level to north–south rail pathways, eliminating dreadful double or quadruple diamond crossings. The whole business is being given focus and some priority with an overarching project called CREATE.

CREATE is a good pointer to how to get big projects up across several layers of government, big business and a critical public. CREATE stands for Chicago Region Environmental and Transportation Efficiency program. Note the use of both the words 'Environmental' and 'Transportation Efficiency' to confer focus and leverage, along with community understanding of the project. This is a smart approach to help engender the right kind of media and momentum in the community and relevant legislatures.

Even with CREATE some mistakes have been made, such as allowing railway companies rights of veto and priority setting. As one of the key drivers of CREATE, John Rinard has pointed out this has meant the common overall good was derailed by degrees, or waylaid in favour of particular advantages for railroad company x or y or z.

In South America, modernisation of rail has struggled along, not helped by the fact that the huge economy of Brazil has a railway network in 5-foot 3-inch (1600-mm) Irish broad gauge, versus Argentina and Chile with imperial broad of 5 feet 6 inches (1676 mm) dominating, but even in these two southern neighbours, there are large distances of narrow-gauge networks. At least when another 'off again, on again' project is completed, namely the provisionally titled 'John Paul II Peace Tunnel' between Argentina and Chile through the Andes, at a much lower level than the existing disused narrow-gauge Mendoza Pass Tunnel, the main gauge in both these countries will be the same.

You might ask why gauge matters so much. There is more on this down the track but the massive cost of break of gauge matters a great deal and can influence history. One extra problem Hitler had on the Eastern Front was the delays and congestion in the supply lines created by the gauge breaks between Poland and Russia.

Australia has gradually removed the worst of its gauge breaks, with every mainland capital city now connected in Stephenson standard gauge, but almost all of Australia's main lines remain on steam-era alignment (that is, with the sharp curves and steep grades necessary in the era before big earth-moving equipment) still slowing down trains. Further, Australia is 'off again, on again' with high-speed rail, and do not mention the word 'metro', as Sydney juggles the prospect of matching its largely overground and overcrowded heavy-rail commuter system with some cut-through underground metro lines.

Asia has many projects on the board, with some excellent progress already made, such as high speed in South Korea from Pusan (or Busan) to Seoul, and in Taiwan, Taipei-to-Kaohsiung in the south. The Shinkansen leads the way on many fronts in Japan, but maglev (magnetic levitation) remains uncompleted on a direct route Tokyo-to-Osaka.

China is building more new railway double track than any other country in the world. It already has a maglev system operating over a short distance of 30 kilometres (19 miles) from Pudong International Airport to an odd location in the suburbs rather than the CBD of Shanghai. Maglev is not technically a railway, because it is a magnetic pathway hurling carriages forward guided by a raised concrete pathway, at speeds of over 500 kph. In short, maglev will have strictly limited application this century, mainly due to the enormous trackbed and energy costs required to operate.

There is another exciting approach under experimental development with no rollout as yet: it is a variation of maglev using magnets embedded in the trackbed to propel carriages carrying the reverse magnets attached underneath each the carriage, but with the weight of the carriage or wagon supported by conventional rail bogies, and normal steel wheels running on rails. Essentially this eliminates the need for any locomotive whatsoever. Imagine this! Watch this space as linear wheeled propulsion unfolds further.

Mooted are another two Greater Asia international railway projects: metre gauge from Singapore through Malaysia and Thailand and on to China (exact route to be finally agreed), then on to Lhasa, Tibet, down through the Sikkim Gap in the Himalayas, and connecting with the Indian Railway network, albeit with a break of gauge at the junction. And there is an extraordinary map in China today showing HSR routes from China through Myanmar to India, avoiding the Himalayas, and even China to Moscow and Berlin.

These routes are likely to continue in the 'off again, on again' category but may yet come to fruition in this extraordinary 21st century. As always, politics, both domestic and international, will play their part, along with the issue of climate change and diminishing oil supplies.

The truth is that the world stands on the cusp of another 'railway mania' phase, as happened in the mid-nineteenth century in Great Britain. However, do not expect revived branch lines operating to almost every town or village; rather there will be considerable hubbing with trunk railway lines dominating the landscape, but done in a way that is less obtrusive than expressways and freeways.

The fundamental advantage of rail — that when operated properly a steel wheel on a steel rail has one-seventh of the friction of a rubber tyre wheel on a bitumen surface — ensures that rail will be competitive.

Per tonne-kilometre, rail is way ahead of all other modes of land and air transport, even allowing for some caveats that will be discussed as we gather our own momentum in the chapters ahead, the largest being the simple fact that railway will only stack up if operated efficiently.

'Off again, on again, gone again' is a timely catchcry from the past; the trick is now to see if the start-stop-start-again mentality dominant in too many railway realms of the world can be left behind once and for all, with a forward strategic approach to now apply.

Finally, along this grand route of rail activity over five decades, I have been helped by many and I thank them all, especially my long-suffering family. From riding a steam train up the Khyber Pass on the Afghanistan–Pakistan border to riding the first-ever freight train and a fortnight later the first-ever passenger train from Adelaide to Darwin (on the only new transcontinental railway built this century), I have enjoyed a diversity of direct railway interface more than most, and I am grateful for it.

However, it is the colourful people of rail that add another layer of deep interest, from those long-gone founders such as George and Robert Stephenson and Isambard Kingdom Brunel to the many people well and truly alive today to be found beavering away in all corners of the globe, such as Ted Franco of the five-generation Italian-American-Australian rail engineer family, headed up originally by Lou Franco. Ted has merely worked on major rail projects in California, Alaska, Queensland, Puerto Rico and Western Australia; he now lives in Perth, Western Australia, when not facilitating rail projects around the world, such as in Libya (more on which later).

For the record Ben Franco was born in Italy in 1883 and went to work on the railways of the USA; his son Lou Franco was born 1914 and did likewise; then came Ted Franco in 1936 with his rail work detailed above. Ted had three railroad sons: Greg, born 1958; Ted, born 1960; and Adam, born 1968; before a grandson arrived in 1984 — Ted the third or Ted Franco Junior, Junior, and also working on railroad development. Clearly the Franco family, no relation to the Spanish dictator, has contributed to rail perhaps more than any other family in the world, across five generations.

We will meet many colourful people who have driven the progress of rail, including Cecil Rhodes, Mark Twain, and the redoubtable rail traveller and raconteur Peter Ustinov. All of these and many more were fixated by that mode of transport fathered by just one extraordinary Englishman, George Stephenson.

So once again, all aboard for the '21st Century Trains Unlimited' and a look at where the railway has been, what it is today and where it is going.

PART ONE

RAIL ARRIVES AND ACCELERATES

GAUGE MATTERS

How George Stephenson's gauge came to dominate the world

All roads led to Rome then and many do so now. In addition today, six trunk railway routes lead to or originate from Rome, two of these being high-speed direct lines to Florence and Naples.

On the matter of land transport in Italy over the centuries, at first there were pathways and walking trails, then roads of all descriptions and the Roman roads were built to last. Later canals were developed for transport purposes in parts of Italy, such as to the inland port of Mantova but also in many level parts of the world.

In the second half of the second millennium, rudimentary rail tracks, initially edge rail and plateways with an L-shape (flange) to guide wagons emerged. These were closely followed by rail as we know it today and the development of the locomotive. Common to all of these transport methods was the key aspect of width, an aspect determining capacity and cost. In the case of rail, the width between rails was known simply as the gauge. With the advent of the railway, in almost all circumstances the gauge was determined first, the track surveyed and construction commenced, then the locomotives were ordered and designed and built to fit the gauge. Perhaps only in Argentina was it a case of the UK-built locomotives arriving in a broad gauge and so the tracks were built to match the locomotives that had arrived. However, generally it has been a case of: determine the gauge for the railway network, then order the locomotives to match.

You do not put the cart or chariot before the horse and it has been thus since the advent of the Stockton and Darlington Railway in the UK in 1825, with a gauge still dominating today. In fact 175 years later, in China in November 2010, a regular HSR trainset reached a record breaking 478 kph (just short of 300 mph), on the very same gauge used by the embryonic Stockton and Darlington Railway. Gauge does matter and so let us deal with it first and look again at those Roman roads.

Two thousand years ago the road system was so good that Emperor Claudius was able to return to Rome from Colchester, east of Londinium, in just two weeks' travel time, to trumpet his famous victory at Colchester. Obviously Claudius, arguably up there with Julius Caesar and Augustus and Constantine as the greatest emperors of the Roman Empire, knew how to ride a horse and travel in a chariot. More importantly by then the Roman Empire was good at providing teams of fresh horses at staging stations, to ensure fast journey times along built-up roads.

How these roads relate to the important matter of gauge, the exact distance between railway tracks, is via the age-old contention that the common width of the ruts in Roman roads became the benchmark for the famous Stephenson standard gauge of 4 feet 8 ½ inches (1435 mm). Is this true or false?

The July 2009 edition of the US publication *Trains*, a journal of standing in the railway industry worldwide, ruled that when all aspects and evidence were carefully weighed, the link was not supported by the available evidence. Yet this tale (or furphy) continues to bounce around the internet, with more colour attaching to each burst of cyber on this issue. Many who rang in to the ABC's *Great Train Show*, for example, asked about gauges and their origin, often wondering if a width of a horses's arse in front of a Roman chariot influenced selection of gauge.

George Stephenson's link with railways went back to his early jobs in collieries in the north of England and in Scotland. He had already built various steam locomotives when, in 1821, he was given the job of building the railing for the new Stockton and Darlington Railway to connect various collieries near these places and the River Tees. But one of the things linking him to Roman roads is the fact of where Stephenson lived, just south of Hadrian's Wall, at the northernmost extremity of the Roman Empire at its zenith. But did he there pace out the exact distance between the old remnant Roman ruts in the cobblestone main roads, and then apply that exact distance to his new railway lines?

The answer is clearly no, yet curiously he ended up with a distance between rails, as measured inside to inside, that was not very different. Further, as Eric Harding in his book *Uniform Railway Gauge* states, there are horse-cart ruts in Pompeii around the 4-feet 8-inches width; indeed there are, but the majority I measured at Pompeii were a good deal less than that (by more than 4 inches/110 mm). The real explanation, I think, is that two other very practical, but unrelated, reasons were in play.

Many have noted that both the William Joseph 'edge rail' (in which each rail is shaped as an L) of the 1780s and the Killingworth tramway on which George Stephenson worked and for which he built his first locomotive were already about 4 feet 8 inches wide. However, that is only half the story. In fact locally at the time, many of the short embryonic railways in existence measured out at 5 feet from outside edge to outside edge. This was a rounded-out distance that was easy to recall and even easier to measure. Just put an inverted U-shaped piece of wood right across the top of both rails, turning down at each end at precisely the 5-foot mark.

Now the 5-foot benchmark tramway and railway tracks had a lot of use (although there were several narrower ones) around the collieries in the north of England throughout the last half of the seventeenth century and at the start of the eighteenth century. These early version railheads had a width of about 2 inches (51 mm), so subtract that twice from the 5 feet (or 1524 mm) and you get to very close to 4 feet 8 inches (1422 mm).

The second factor was driven by the existing blacksmith moulds for laying out the axles of the wagons doing all the coal carrying, and also for the larger horse-hauled general freight wagons. Clearly these axle lengths, providing the direct link from wheel to wheel, were around the 5-foot length to run on the early tracks. Further, for over 100 years, by Stephenson's time, blacksmiths and forgers had been creating axles of this length. Why step out of this parameter and craft a gauge forcing massive changes in the pouring of hot metal into moulds to make axles and so forth?

Now it could be argued that the moulds and lathes were broadly geared to those Roman chariots, but this is not exactly true, and in northern England, perhaps due to muddy conditions for many months each year, the axles were a good deal wider than the racing Roman chariot or even Roman cart.

Above all else, George Stephenson, along with his son, Robert Stephenson, found that their gauge worked and provided the necessary stability while permitting a reasonable curve along the track. Further, the track ties, in some countries called railway sleepers, laid horizontally and at right angles to the actual railway tracks, were more manageable than with, say, 7-foot or 8-foot gauges.

Between 1825 and 1830, George Stephenson then made his one big amending decision: to alter his initial standard gauge, which had been applied to the Stockton and Darlington Railway, the original 4 feet 8 inches (or 1422 mm), and expand it out some 0.88 per cent to create the renowned 4 feet 8½ inches (or 1435 mm). This was not a minor matter; it involved amending legislation in Westminster relating to approval of the creation of the new Liverpool & Manchester Railway and to provide for the ½-inch adjustment to the line. The practical side of a somewhat stubborn George Stephenson had come to the fore; he found that the trains needed the extra width, primarily to travel more smoothly along

First fatality of the railway

Sadly the opening day of the Liverpool & Manchester Railway produced one fatality, the former president of the Board of Trade, and local member for Liverpool, William Huskisson, who stepped back into the path of Stephenson's *Rocket*. He had been talking with the Prime Minister the Duke of Wellington, trying to ease recent tensions between the two, when the *Rocket*, running on a parallel track, loomed large.

In the confusion and panic Huskisson stepped back into its pathway and was skittled by the train as it hurtled along. The poor fellow died several hours later at a nearby manse, but not even this tragedy was allowed to stop the big opening of this section of famous railway, which has operated in one guise or another just about every day since.

curves. In other words, the flanged wheels, which were often rigidly locked onto the carriage frame, needed the extra space to run at a slight angle to the line of railhead, or top of rail, through curves, at least until the modern bogie emerged. By its intrinsic design the modern bogie allowed a more flexible and less distorting angle of the wheel relative to the trackhead, or railhead, and so greatly easing wear and tear and screeching wheels.

As that grand opening day of the Liverpool–Manchester track unfolded in the presence of the then Prime Minister, the Duke of Wellington, in 1830, few realised the worldwide exemplar of railway and railway gauge was being unveiled.

The first fair dinkum modern railway was away and running, and so was the Stephenson standard gauge of 4 feet 8½ inches (1435 mm). Not many at the time realised this was truly the start of something big. As Douglas J. Puffert has meticulously laid out in his excellent bible on gauge, *Tracks Across Continents, Paths Through History*, the concept of 'path dependency' then came into play.

Path dependency buildings

To the examples given elsewhere we can add the iconic domes of Rome: the Pantheon of nearly 2000 years of age through to the Michelangelo masterpiece of the cupola, or double dome, of St Peter's Basilica, over 500 years old and still going strong. Then there are so many look-alikes, such as the Bernini Dome at beautiful Castel Gandolfo, just south of Rome, and many more right across Italy.

The path-dependency factor has seen many architects adopt this workable and magisterial solution to providing strong roofing over large areas in a memorable way. So St Paul's, London, and the huge dome dominating the Washington, DC, Congressional Building followed down the path laid out brilliantly in the drawings of Michelangelo. The Utah State Capitol building in Salt Lake City is just one of many other examples across the USA.

There are nine major Australian parliamentary buildings, and due to boom and bust economic phases too often applying, not one of them has a big dome or cupola. One or two were meant to have domes, but the great gold rush in the 1850s and resultant economic boom was followed by the great bust in the 1890s and frugal times, even for big-spending feisty colonial state governments pre-federation. Australia eventually federated in 1901.

Still, some large railway stations built in the nineteenth century used domes to help roof large concourses, such as with the noble Adelaide Station in South Australia, but alas now in part a casino.

As with copycat domes, so with bridges, some taking a leaf from dome construction.

St Peter's Basilica, Rome.

The Causey Arch Bridge, near Durham, UK. (Wikimedia Commons)

This phenomenon extended to the best bridge designs around the world, going back to the classic Roman arches style of the historic Ponte Nomentana on the northeast entrance to Rome. Then came longer bridges with path dependency applying, such as the giant Golden Gate Bridge at San Francisco. The oldest remaining railway bridge still standing is the Causey Arch bridge, a classic single Roman arch near Durham and Newcastle in the north of England. It was double-track design when built back in the eighteenth century.

The point is that good design will dominate and be copied, from bridges to domes, all the more so where seamlessness is a factor. While the French Revolution introduced right-hand side road driving, and this now dominates the world, most Commonwealth countries plus Japan, drive on the left. At sea though, confusion about this difference would be outright dangerous. 'Path dependency' has ensured one rule worldwide: ships pass on the 'port' or left side of each other, unless locally specified.

What is meant by 'path dependency'? In short, it is the adherence to an earlier design or set of measurements because they worked, conferring an advantage of seamlessness; above all else to diverge or break away to a different yardstick or design requires extra costs and inefficiencies, which can rarely be justified.

The Puffert bible lays this out in detail and points to some excellent examples of path dependency over the years, such as the original QWERTY keyboard design, purchased by Remington around 1880, and the powerful Microsoft Windows tool, all continuing to dominate in the English-speaking world and beyond.

Path dependency, combined with the determination, energy and the enlightened leadership of both George Stephenson and Robert Stephenson, resulted in a most extraordinary statistic emerging in the year 2000.

As the new century and millennium arrived, no less than 609,200 kilometres of the 1,082,300 kilometres of railway in existence were in the gauge derived and developed around 200 years ago by just two people: George and Robert Stephenson. The gauge of the Liverpool–Manchester line was so close to optimum that it became the yardstick against which the vast majority of railways were built in exactitude or closely matching.

It was an outcome not guaranteed, however, because, as noted, there were many gauges used around Scotland and the north of England around the decade before and after 1800, and the great engineer Isambard Brunel had used a big broad gauge of 7 feet ¼ inch (2140 mm) on the powerful Great Western Railway from London to Bristol and on to Penzance and Land's End. It was also an outcome that could have lost momentum post the direct involvement of Stephenson father and son. In 1845 the Westminster Gauge Commission was convened to determine once and for all which was the best gauge for the UK — Stephenson standard or Brunel broad. Robert Stephenson gave evidence suggesting three important things — that more Stephenson than broad had been laid; that it was cheaper to convert broad to Stephenson than vice versa; and that curves could be tighter in Stephenson standard and thus follow terrain more closely — and eventually the commission confirmed Stephenson standard over all other gauges. Had the Commission gone for a broad gauge, Stephenson standard would have been much more limited in its usage.

As it was, by 1892 Brunel broad had been overwhelmed and completely switched to Stephenson standard gauge. Only at Didcot, not far west of London, at the excellent heritage Railway Centre is there a kilometre of Brunel broad gauge in operation today.

Stephenson standard was the main gauge to emerge and dominate, greatly helping the early success and profits of the Liverpool & Manchester Railway. Success breeds success, and good leadership can accelerate the spread of particularly successful designs and standards.

Belgium, Germany and Poland all started operating railways in 1835, and thanks to the early success and domination of the designs of George and Robert Stephenson, these three countries adopted the Stephenson standard gauge from inception. The entire central zone of mainland Europe went this

Broad gauge at Didcot. (Tim Fischer)

way, including large countries such as France, Germany, Italy and Poland; exceptions were (in part) Greece, Norway, Portugal, Russia and Spain.

Russia has stayed with its 5-foot (1524-mm) gauge to this day, adding to a total distance in this gauge, according to the reliable Puffert, of 154,200 kilometres. The only other gauge still in operation and exceeding 100,000 kilometres of track is the key narrow gauge known as Anglo Cape, of 3 feet 6 inches (1067 mm), but only just, coming in at 103,500 kilometres. Now, Puffert has based his calculations on *Jane's World Railways* and also the CIA's *World Factbook*, plus one or two other sources. With new high speed lines, but also many branch-line closures, these distances change by degrees each year.

However, the clear fact is that a majority of railways in the world in the 21st century are Stephenson standard gauge, and this proportion is likely to increase as the vast majority of very high-speed railway construction — the biggest game in town — is in Stephenson standard gauge.

The big votes of confidence in the continuation of Stephenson standard were the bold decisions since World War II by both Japan and Spain to depart from their existing main-line gauges and build their new-generation very high speed tracks in Stephenson standard gauge. Later Portugal also made the switch, with its plans to facilitate high-speed running from Lisbon.

George and Robert must be smiling down from above as they see these shiny new tracks appear in the very gauge they established about 200 years ago, not that different from Roman wheel ruts but arrived at for the practical reasons I have suggested.

The six great railway realms of the world, namely Africa, Australia and New Zealand, Europe, Greater Asia, North America and South America, have all used large quantities of Stephenson standard gauge. Likewise with the business of light rail or trams worldwide, many are run on Stephenson standard, with a couple of notable exceptions, such as one north–south line in Rome, and in the Balkans at places like Zagreb, where the large tram system is built using metre gauge.

God's wonderful railway: the GWR

The Great Western Railway, which was established in 1833 and operated its first trains in 1838 westward from London to Bristol and later to Penzance, was often nicknamed God's Wonderful Railway. It operated in Brunel broad gauge of 7 feet ¼ inch (2140 mm) from inception, when the GWR was created by legislation, until about 56 years later, in 1892, when the final switch to Stephenson standard gauge was made. Coincidentally, the GWR then operated for another 56 years until 1948 when the Attlee Labour Government nationalised virtually all railways in the UK, including the lingering GWR. So the big gauge switch was at the halfway mark of the legendary GWR company's existence.

Today there are two outstanding places to step back into the glory of the GWR. One is the Didcot Railway Centre, complete with a section of fully operational Brunel broad gauge track and the steam locomotive *Fire Fly* to go with it. Secondly, there is the superb Steam Museum of the Great Western Railway at Swindon. I commend both for a visit, at least a half day in each, and enjoy.

One other factor often determining gauge in countries previously without railways was the Stephenson locomotive construction capability. Many a railway started out by ordering Stephenson locomotives from Great Britain and, unless especially otherwise directed, these were built for the standard gauge the Stephensons had created. It made obvious sense to build the railways to match the width between flange and wheels. So Baltimore & Ohio Railway ordered Stephenson locos and built Stephenson standard gauge. With some exceptions this was the case across Europe, down to Egypt and across to Iran.

China went with Stephenson standard gauge from inception; even the conquering Japanese took the step of converting the Russian shortcut through China (Harbin to Vladivostok) from Czar broad to Stephenson standard gauge. Again a form of path dependency applied, as one of the very first proper and approved railways in China at Tangshan in 1880 was built by Claude William Kinder, an English engineer with considerable international experience. In fact he was the son of a master of the Hong Kong mint, had worked in Japan and studied railways all over Europe before moving to China with much-valued skills but, importantly, with a comfortable knowledge of the work of the Stephensons. He chose the obvious gauge, already dominating in Great Britain, namely Stephenson standard.

This 10-kilometre (6-mile) short line for coal traffic later became a main line from Beijing to Shenyang, and having already been used at the very outset, Stephenson standard was the gauge of choice in the huge expansion in railway construction in China from then to this day. So it was a case of one engineer of English connection in the middle of Asia, one familiar gauge to the fore. China has been well served by the choice made by Mr Kinder, who died in Churt, England, in 1936.

BREAK OF GAUGE

Gauge matters in many ways, but break of gauge has been the destructive 'kneecapper' faced by almost all railway nations at various early stages of development of their railways.

In fact, in too many countries break of gauge continues to apply by degrees to this day — for example in Poland with its Stephenson standard (except for one dedicated Czar broad gauge line) versus neighbouring Lithuania and Russia in Czar broad gauge. This particular break of gauge was to have an impact on two world wars; arguably it was a key blockage in German resupply that was enough to allow the Russians to hang on and eventually turn the German forces back in World War II.

Break of gauge was eliminated almost completely in the UK and USA around 1892, the Great Western Railway completing its final conversions right through to Paddington Station on one very busy weekend in 1892. However, break of gauge was still emerging in many other places, and is still being resolved in the 21st century.

Because of its dominance, break of gauge has almost always involved some broader gauge clashing with Stephenson standard, or occasionally a narrow gauge clashing, such as at the border between Queensland and New South Wales in Australia for so long. Australia dreamed about having just one railway gauge, a very sensible notion, which the UK Colonial Secretary had urged upon the six colonies, but instead the country ended up devising and operating 22 different gauges — a record for any one country — partly as a matter of state pride and partly because of what seemed suitable for the terrain or materials at hand. Five different gauges are each still operating a length of more than 40 kilometres today; indeed, four of the five operate well over 1000 kilometres each.

On his famous visit to Australia in 1895, Mark Twain travelled on sixteen different trains and gave lectures everywhere he went. It is worth quoting Twain's outburst in full when, in 1895, he encountered one of the worst examples of break of gauge. In the early hours of 26 September 1895, he lost his cool at Albury when he heard the shout 'All change,' due to the break of gauge at the NSW–Victorian border.

> *Now comes a singular thing: the oddest thing, the strangest thing, the most baffling unaccountable marvel that Australasia can show. At the frontier between New South Wales and Victoria our multitude of passengers were routed out of their snug beds by lantern-light in the morning in the biting-cold of a high altitude to change cars on a road that has no break in it from Sydney to Melbourne. Think of the paralysis of intellect that gave that idea birth; imagine the boulder it emerged from on some petrified legislator's shoulders.*
>
> *It is a narrow-gage [sic] road to the frontier, and a broader gauge thence to Melbourne. The two governments were the builders of the road and are the owners of it. One or two reasons are given for this curious state of things. One is that, it represents the jealousy existing between the colonies — the two most*

*important colonies of Australasia. What the other is, I have
forgotten. But it is of no consequence. It could be but another effort
to explain the inexplicable.*

What Mark Twain meant to say was that it was standard gauge in New
South Wales from Sydney to Albury on the border, and Irish broad gauge
on to Melbourne, forcing all passengers and all freight to change trains, a
saga that went on for eight decades before the Albury–Melbourne standard
gauge connection track was laid in the 1960s, eliminating the break of
gauge at least along this corridor.

All change!

The rich, powerful and famous all had to change at Albury's very long
interstate platform, where for 80 years break of gauge interrupted trips.
Dame Nellie Melba, the famous opera singer, changed trains alive often
enough, and even when dead, as her coffin came on a special funeral train
from Sydney to Albury and after the change on to Melbourne. So she had
the distinction of passing through Albury vertically and horizontally.

Australia's greatest stayer, Phar Lap, also changed trains at Albury and
was put in a stable for the night at Soden's Hotel near the station. His strapper
was peeved that no locals recognised the great Melbourne Cup winner and
cussed, 'The locals would not know a good horse if they saw one.'

Other famous passengers to change trains at Albury include first PM
Edmund Barton, cricket legend Don Bradman, ex train-driver PM Ben
Chifley, painter Russell Drysdale, ex PM Billy Hughes, first female federal
MP Dame Enid Lyons, US General Douglas MacArthur, first Australian
RC Saint Mary MacKillop, outstanding Australian general John Monash
on his honeymoon (twice), and record-serving PM Robert Menzies. I pray
for a plaque to salute this history to be erected at Albury Station soon.

The Victorian system met the NSW system at just two other locations, namely Oaklands and Tocumwal. In World War II these three break-of-gauge junctions became very busy, as huge flows of troops and equipment, along with munitions and other essential supplies moved interstate. The munitions tended to be put through the Oaklands junction, which was busy for years even after the end of the war, but in the 1970s the NSW rail access was cut off by closure of the Boree Creek–Urana–Oaklands section.

Talk continues to this day that this might reopen for a new coal mine near Oaklands, but meanwhile the branch line from the south — Benalla–Yarrawonga–Oaklands — was gauge-converted to Stephenson standard in 2010. So the real question becomes interstate competition. If the super coal mine goes ahead, will it be exported southwards to the key port of Geelong or northwards through the geared-up modern Port Kembla? But of course I remain neutral, and, yes, I declare I own a farm near Boree Creek.

The most hilarious of Australia's 22 gauges, in a sense, was 'mistake gauge', built at exactly 3 feet 8½ inches (1131 mm), all because the engineer wrote down a three instead of a four. It operated for many years near Bulli just south of Sydney for the haulage of coal.

Herbert Horatio Kitchener (British Secretary of State during World War I) came to Australia in 1910 to write a report on national defence and military structure, but ended up highlighting the rail layout and break of gauge which dominated at all state borders. He observed that the railways in Australia could not have been designed better for helping an enemy invade.

There is no doubt that the different rail gauges in each state of Australia bedevilled the flow of trade — not so much exports heading to ports but the internal flow of goods within the country for the domestic market. In some places it bordered on the absurd. From 1917 South Australia had all three major gauges operating, often in the same town, for example in Port Pirie from 1937, and later in Gladstone and Peterborough. Railway switches, or points, were made to handle Anglo Cape narrow, Stephenson standard and Irish broad gauge trains. This involved great complexity and huge tonnages of steel.

Buenos Aires, Argentina, has many claims to fame as a national capital city, such as grandest and largest Italian-style opera house in the world, namely the Colon. However, one unique claim is the fact it has three railway gauges operating into and through the city. There are three huge terminus railway stations on a grand scale; in the case of the Retiro complex both supreme metric and imperial broad 5-foot 6-inch gauges operate; out in the suburbs there is also a large Stephenson standard gauge terminus.

In the early phase of railways in each country, often a plethora of rail gauges existed, but the smarter countries deliberated quickly on the unfolding agony and inefficiencies of break of gauge and moved to eliminate same. Three good examples of the right leadership applying at an early stage can be found in the countries of Holland, New Zealand and the USA.

Holland's railway opened in 1839 with a 2000-millimetre gauge line from Amsterdam to Haarlem, across very level, low-lying lands. The Dutch soon observed that the gauge they used was an exception and unique, and in 1866 they converted to Stephenson standard and today are linked into the high-speed network.

Likewise New Zealand started out in the 1860s with several gauges, ranging from Irish broad to American narrow before correctly moving away from Stephenson standard gauge, deciding it was too large and costly for the Land of the Long White Cloud. On gauge matters it should always be remembered the narrower the gauge, the sharper the corners that can be safely engineered, thus making hilly terrain easier to conquer by rail. Wide gauge must run with no sharp curves, just moderate ones, requiring more earth to be moved to cut through hills and fill depressions, at greater cost than the terrain-hugging narrower gauges. Under the leadership of Sir Julius Vogel, initially Colonial Treasurer but just about everything else as well — a very powerful man in tiny New Zealand — rail expansion continued but he ordered the switch to Anglo Cape narrow gauge on both islands.

Six gauges in the USA in the early days of rail, ranging from Stephenson standard to a special broad gauge of a neat 6 foot, reflected the land of the free. The Civil War saw the dominant Czar broad gauge in the south ripped up and replaced by the Unionist armies with Stephenson standard, the gauge decreed by Congress after the Civil War for the big east–west transcontinental linking the US Atlantic Coast with the Pacific Coast. In fact, initially, in 1869, the western terminus of this line was at Sacramento, on the big river port. This terminus is still standing in the Californian capital with the original platform located near the enticing Californian State Railroad Museum, alongside a wide river leading straight to San Francisco Bay.

It was at 12.47pm on 10 May 1869 that the famous Western Union telegram went out from the meeting point of the two ends of rail at Promontory Utah with the one word, 'Done.' Celebrations started immediately in Chicago and elsewhere along the historic corridor. Alas, the Promontory part of the corridor has now been bypassed, but the joining-up place is much revered, with a memorial located there.

Except for some narrow gauge around the old gold mines of the Rockies, which are now mainly tourist train lines, the USA and neighbours Canada and Mexico have all stayed with standard gauge. This has helped greatly with the growing interconnection and volume of rail freight, thanks to the NAFTA (North American Free Trade Agreement) treaty.

If the world was starting again with rail, the best big gauge in my opinion would most likely be the Irish broad, at 1600 mm, and the best small gauge for mountains and light work would be the 1000 mm supreme metric metre gauge, both now possible thanks to the capability of earth-moving machinery to allow straighter tracks at lower cost along with slightly enhanced stability. Nevertheless, almost all new rail track being built in the world today is in Stephenson standard. Even the new metros in India at Bangalore, Chennai, Mumbai and Delhi are using

Stephenson standard. Recent comments by an official associated with the Delhi Metro explained that since metro alignments have to pass through heavily congested areas, the standard gauge scores over the broad gauge, as it permits sharper curves and requires less land. More on the stellar and profitable Delhi Metro later, but the fact remains standard is winning out, just about everywhere in the world.

The full list of main gauges is in the accompanying table, and for those who want more there are websites laying out every single rail gauge used in the world.

Given the multiplicity of gauges available and the jealousy between various European countries, it is amazing that there is so much harmonisation in rail gauge, allowing train travel from Rome and Vienna to Paris, and in recent years on through the Chunnel to London and Glasgow, without any break of gauge as such. For other reasons, no train is as yet running right through from, say, Brindisi, Italy, to Birmingham in the UK, but if operators wanted to, the tracks would allow it. In fact in October 2010 the German ICE3 high-speed train unit was allowed to make a special first-ever trip through the Chunnel to go on display at St Pancras in London, but regulations still preclude its regular operation in competition with Eurostar. This is changing with the lifting of the ban on distributive power being used in the Chunnel. This will allow the use of

Famous Roman wheel ruts at Pompeii did not add up as Stephenson standard when measured by the author mid-2011. (Courtesy Margaret Richardson)

electric engines on each axle under every carriage rather than just at each end with the locomotive design of TGV and Eurostar Alstom units to date.

There are two other snags to be overcome, however: the different voltages and current where overhead electricity is being used by locomotives; and various complex EU requirements that are meant to open up rail for competition but have often enough had almost the opposite effect.

All of this is not a bad achievement for the Stephensons. In fact, I contend that this is the greatest achievement of any father-and-son team in the world, although for those of Abrahamic Christian faith a rider should be added — at least since that first Easter in Jerusalem!

Two thousand years since that first Easter and 200 years since the first proper modern double-track railway and passenger train, George Stephenson's standard gauge rules supreme on planet earth. More importantly it stands ready to continue to be utilised in the massive high-speed expansion of rail, especially in China, but indeed with almost all of the new modern '21st Century Trains Unlimited'.

Three lines with four rails

It is a little known fact that George Stephenson had one other trick of the trade up his sleeve, although ultimately it did not prove to be all that practical. In a further example of his raw ingenuity, he actually built the gap between the two sets of tracks of the Liverpool & Manchester Railway at 4 feet 8½ inches (1435 mm). This meant freight trains carrying very wide loads in the middle of the night when no passenger trains were operating could run along the middle pathway, having entered the middle by special points or switches.

Soon enough more separation had to be created between the double tracks, especially as the loading gauge was expanded in width and height above rail. It was a one-off from one incredible George Stephenson and never replicated.

Tim Fischer's
GREAT AUSTRALIAN RAILWAY GAUGES
1831–2011

1. **IRISH BROAD** 1600mm (5' 3")
Vic, SA & NT ◆ □ ■

2. **STEPHENSON STANDARD** 1435mm (4' 8½ ")
now all mainland states/ACT/NT ◆ □ ■

3. **DELORAINE STANDARD** 1372mm (4' 6")
Mersey to Deloraine, Tas ◆

4. **STARVATION NARROW** 1219mm (4' 0")
Starvation Creek, Vic ◆

5. **MISTAKE NARROW** 1131mm (3' 8½")
Mount Pleasant colliery, NSW ◆ □

6. **OUTER SYDNEY NARROW** 1080mm (3' 6½")
El Caballo Blanco, NSW □

7. **ANGLO CAPE NARROW** 1067mm (3' 6")
all states at various times ◆ □ ■

8. **RUBICON NARROW** 1029mm (3' 4½")
Rubicon Forest, Vic ◆ □

9. METRE NARROW 1000mm (3' 3⅜")
Hartley Vale, near Zig Zag Railway, NSW ◆ □ ■

16. APPLETON NARROW 700mm (2' 3⅜")
Port Melbourne, Vic ■

10. KOOLOOLA LOG GAUGE 991mm (3' 3")
east of Gympie, Qld ◆ □

17. GOLD NARROW 686mm (2' 3")
Woods Point, Vic ◆ □

11. LORNE LOG NARROW 940mm (3' 1")
Lorne Pier to mill, Vic ◆ □

18. CAPRICORNIA NARROW 661mm (2' 2")
Mount Morgan, Qld ◆ □

12. AMERICAS NARROW 914mm (3' 0")
industrial, including Newcastle, Portland, NSW;
Yarra Valley, Vic □ ■

19. CANE NARROW 610mm (2' 0")
Qld, Tas ◆ □ ■

13. MONASH NARROW 900mm (2' 11⅜")
La Trobe interconnecting, Vic □

20. SONS OF GWALIA 508mm (1' 8")
near Kalgoorlie, WA ◆ □

14. LECONFIELD NARROW 838mm (2' 9")
Greta, NSW ◆ □

21. SEMAPHORE NARROW 457mm (1' 6")
Port Adelaide, SA □ ■

15. SUEZ WALHALLA 762mm (2' 6")
Puffing Billy/Walhalla, Vic ◆ □ ■

22. BEACH NARROW 381mm (1' 3")
Bronte, NSW and beyond ◆ □ ■

LEGEND: ◆ In use 19th century   □ In use 20th century   ■ In use 21st century

Measurements are from inside rail to inside rail on railways operating a distance of
1.6 kilometres (1 mile) or more in Australia since 1831, when Australian Agricultural
Company built Australia's first railway in Newcastle, New South Wales, to transport coal.
In 2010 only Anglo Cape narrow operates in all states. Stephenson standard operates in
all mainland states and from Adelaide to Darwin for FreightLink and the Ghan.

Tim Fischer's
GREAT WORLD RAILWAY GAUGES

1. **BRUNEL BROAD** — 2140mm (7' ¼")
UK, previously Great Western Railway, now at Didcot, UK

2. **IMPERIAL BROAD** — 1676mm (5' 6")
including Argentina, Chile, India, Pakistan & USA

3. **IBERIAN BROAD** — 1668mm (5' 5⅔")
Portugal & Spain

4. **IRISH BROAD** — 1600mm (5' 3")
Australia, Brazil and Ireland

5. **CZAR BROAD** — 1524mm (5' 0")
including Russia & the Commonwealth of Independent States, Estonia, Latvia & Lithuania

7. **STEPHENSON STANDARD** — 1435mm (4' 8½")
worldwide, including Argentina, Australia, Iran, Malaysia, Peru, UK & USA

6. **SCOTTISH** — 1372mm (4' 6")
Japan and previously Scotland

8. **ANGLO CAPE NARROW** — 1067mm (3' 6")
worldwide, including Australia, Indonesia & Japan

9. **LAWRENCE MIDEAST NARROW** — 1050mm (3' 5⅜")
Jordan, previously Beirut to Damascus to Medina

10. **SUPREME METRIC NARROW** — 1000mm (3' 3⅜")
worldwide, including Algeria, Bangladesh, Bolivia, Malaysia & Thailand

11. **ITALIAN NARROW** — 950mm (3' 1½")
including Eritrea & Sicily, Italy

12. **AMERICAS NARROW** — 915mm (3' 0")
including Columbia, Peru, Isle of Man & USA

13. **SUEZ WALHALLA** — 762mm (2' 6")
worldwide, including Australia, China, India, UK & USA

14. **BOSNIAN** — 760mm (2' 5⅞")
including Austria, Bolivia, Bosnia, Bulgaria & Hungary

15. **PATAGONIAN NARROW** — 750mm (2' 5½")
including Argentina, Indonesia, Russia, Spain & Uruguay

16. **CANE NARROW** — 610mm (2' 0")
worldwide, including Australia, Brunei, Japan, South Korea & UK

17. **DECAUVILLE PORTABLE NARROW** — 600mm (1' 11⅝")
including Eritrea & France

18. **BEACH NARROW** — 381mm (1' 3")
worldwide, including Tasmania

These key gauges have been selected on criteria including uniqueness and current usage. The table has involved research in 60 countries, with verification against Jane's comprehensive 44th *World Railways* edition and help from many individuals, including Dimitry Zinoviev, John Birchmeier, Alex Grunbach, Owen Johnstone-Donnet, Dr Rob Lee, Scott Martin and Gerry Willis.

LOCOMOTIVE MATTERS

Tiny *Rocket* to mighty Big Boy

Much has already been said about George Stephenson and matters of gauge but as the father of modern railway he is at the centre of locomotives as well. George was born at Wylam next to Newcastle-upon-Tyne in 1781, and was still illiterate in 1799. He only learned to read and write at night school in the early 1800s, but by 1830 he had built the railway that was to become the exemplar to the world.

George was just 22 when son, Robert, was born on 16 October 1803. Robert's mother died when he was just two, so it was the huge commitment that George made to the education of his son which made for the basis of a truly great partnership. Perhaps George felt especially obliged because education was something he had missed out on. Perhaps George also thought it made up for the long periods he had to be away as Robert grew up. Robert was effectively raised by his aunt, George's spinster sister, Eleanor Stephenson, and was a keen student.

In George and Robert, the world had not one but two brilliant, practical inventors and together they stuck to their belief that mobile locomotives were better than cable-hauled trains powered by stationary fixed locomotives at key intervals along a track.

Richard Trevithick cranked up the first steam locomotive ever in 1804 and ran it along a plateway, with another taken up to London for exhibition running around a circle. It was called 'Catch me who can', and it led to a few more locomotives being built by Trevithick. As Hamilton Ellis says in his *Pictorial Encyclopedia of Railways*, a railway bible not to be missed, George Stephenson sighted the rudimentary Trevithick locomotive *Black Billy* and no doubt it had a big impact on his young mind. It presumably helped George Stephenson hit upon the essentials of a good steam locomotive very early on. One of his design breakthroughs was to use not one but two pistons and cylinders geared to different parts of the revolution, thereby ensuring both pistons and cranks would not be exactly at the level halfway mark at the same time with the danger of jamming.

The use of tubes and smoke stacks to draw the firebox-generated heat through was another practical addition, as he and son, Robert, perfected the early steam locomotive designs. Many attribute this design aspect to a French engineer, Marc Seguin, who may have just beaten the Stephensons to it, but perhaps it was a line ball thing.

The big opportunity for the Stephensons to demonstrate their superior engine came in 1829 with the Rainhill trials, and £500 prize money offered by the Liverpool & Manchester Railway for the fastest locomotive run between Liverpool and Manchester before the track was officially opened.

George, who had been working as an engineer on the track, and Robert got very busy and commenced building the trailblazing *Rocket*, the engine that changed the world. It weighed just over 4 tonnes; had a boiler with brass tubes through it to expand the area of heated surface and greatly boost water conversion to steam; and it had a very fashionable tall chimney, once again to create draught, especially when burning poor-quality coal.

Hunter Davies, in his biography of George Stephenson, points to the considerable correspondence between George beavering away on completing the Liverpool–Manchester line and Robert at the locomotive foundry and workshops at Newcastle-upon-Tyne during the design and construction phase of the *Rocket*. Once completed, as the biography details, the *Rocket* undertook a three-part journey from Newcastle to Liverpool, any stage of which could have proved disastrous. Initially and with some indignity, the locomotive had to be broken down into small pieces and loaded on horse-hauled carts for the first leg from Newcastle, west to Carlisle; the second leg was by canal barge from Carlisle to Bowness; and the final leg was by coastal ship from Bowness to Liverpool.

In the end the *Rocket* made it through in every way, performing with great stamina at the Rainhill trials and reaching speeds of 24 kph (15 mph) while hauling three times its weight. Yes, there were faster efforts on the first day from favoured rival the *Novelty*, which produced a dash at 45 kph (28 mph) — a huge effort but one that apparently did enough internal damage to the *Novelty* to destroy any chance of winning the decision from the three judges, especially when they took reliability into account.

Why was the *Rocket* the locomotive that changed the world? It demonstrated it could haul with some speed along flat sections of track and go uphill along lengthy grades; in short, it exceeded horsepower massively and beat fixed-engine cable haulage hands down. It was a shining model to the world and its key features are replicated today in steam locomotives, large and small.

MAGICAL BRASS BOX INJECTORS

Many argue that it was boiler tubes that provided an early breakthrough in locomotive improvements; others that it was the safety valves designed to let off surplus steam and stop boilers exploding that were a vital practical feature; still others claim the fact that weights were put into the wheels at exactly the right place to ensure smooth revolutions was the important factor.

To my way of thinking it is the water injectors that are the most important of all the components, because if the water cannot be placed in the boiler efficiently then trouble will brew quickly on many fronts and can result in an explosion. Further, the injectors must be designed to be one-way, letting water in but not letting steam out and therefore losing steam pressure in a useless way. Initially a pump mechanism was used on the *Rocket* and other early locomotives, but then along came the brilliant French engineer Henri Giffard. Born in 1825, Giffard, in a brave move around 1852, took to the air in a hydrogen balloon powered by a small steam engine slung on ropes below the balloon and above his basket, driving a propeller. Giffard survived the inaugural flight of over 24 kilometres (15 miles), however, his best was yet to come, with his water injector invention par excellence.

Giffard devised a set of cones that allowed steam to pass through the injector, creating a vacuum, which in turn allowed the collection of water

Giffard's Water Injector: 'Black magic' momentum creator!

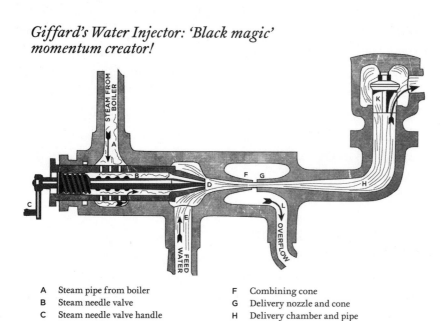

A	Steam pipe from boiler	**F**	Combining cone
B	Steam needle valve	**G**	Delivery nozzle and cone
C	Steam needle valve handle	**H**	Delivery chamber and pipe
D	Steam and water combine here	**K**	Check valve
E	Water feed pipe		*(modified from Wikimedia Commons)*

on the pass-through and most importantly, enough pressure for the combined stream to open the 'clack valves' and enter the boiler, topping up the boiler water in the process.

This set-of-cones approach was resisted at first, with suggestions that it constituted a form of black magic, but Giffard's system had one certain advantage: it required no moving part other than the taps and valves to let the water and steam into the cones, mixing area and the clack valve, and allowed the combined stream into the boiler but nothing out of it. The momentum of the steam created a vacuum that picked up the cold water and hurled it back into the boiler. In 1858 Giffard patented his idea and the 'no-moving-part water injector' has dominated ever since.

Sadly Henri Giffard took his own life in 1882, because of his fading vision. He was a loss to the world but his name is enshrined on the Eiffel Tower, deservedly so, and his water injector lifted the performance of steam locomotives as 19th-century railways rapidly expanded.

The vital role of injectors was underlined in the 1950s when the *Flying Scotsman* came close to a boiler explosion on a regular run from Leicester to London because both water injectors failed. Andrew Roden in his great book on the *4472* engine on the *Scotsman* details how the crew used every bit of experience to deal with the failure and nurse the big machine into London. A detailed inspection revealed something fishy, indeed fish feeding on algae in the tender and blocking the water feed to the injectors. The fish had entered the *4472* tender because of a failure with the filters back at the depot at Leicester, where the water had been loaded.

PORTA DOUBLE ADVANTAGE

If George and Robert Stephenson were the 'Fathers of Steam Locomotion' then to Livio Dante Porta must go the title of 'Godfather of Modern Steam Locomotion'. Porta played an enormous role in vastly improving steam-locomotive energy efficiency and overall performance.

Yet there is a sadness in the tale relating to this proud and innovative Argentinean — a case of so near and yet so far, as the bad luck of timing in political and economic cycles meant the design work of Dante Porta and that of his friend and mentor, the brilliant French SNCF steam locomotive designer André Chapelon, was never fully realised. Still, the spirit of Dante Porta is alive and well all around the South American railways of today, complete with the odd inferno in the fireboxes of a scattering of steam locomotives still operating.

What were the huge and practical changes that Dante Porta made? There were two seminal revamps to time-honoured designs that no one had bothered to upend for something better, indeed a whole lot better.

To be uncouth, the first one was to help steam locomotives break wind, or fart, efficiently — yes — to improve the emission of steam and gases and with huge fuel savings and performance improvements.

If a steam locomotive cannot breath properly, its performance drops off at an alarming rate. Over the years people have gazed at steam locomotives in full throttle climbing a grade or bank, such as the deadly Cowan Bank up to Hornsby on the Newcastle–Sydney main line. The noise can be deafening and the flume of smoke on a still, cold winter's day can stretch back for miles. What is not generally realised is that there are two ingredients to this flume: the low pressure steam emitted from the pistons, having done the pushing work, and of course the gases from the burning coal. In some cases the firebox might be burning oil or wood only, nevertheless it must emit its gases and with a suck-through drawing power to ensure the fire remains on the go.

It is here that the magnificence of Dante Porta's work can be seen. He first created the Kylpor ejector as an upgrade on the Kylchap ejector that André Chapelon had previously devised. But near enough was not good enough and so Dante Porta continued tinkering. The result of his work was the brilliant Lempor ejector, consisting of a Kordina, blast pipe, four-lobe exhaust manifold, mixing chamber and diffuser, all designed to maximise the vacuum after each chug, in turn creating the essential pull-through draught.

Simple in shape and design, involving four nozzles, it can be modified in size for heritage narrow-gauge steam locomotives, such as the 6A on the renowned Puffing Billy railway through the Dandenongs just to the east of Melbourne, allowing them to maintain the overall shape of the smoke stack or chimney on the locomotive, and thus the heritage vista, but boosting efficiency by a minimum of 10 per cent.

Dante Porta's second improvement was to develop the Porta Water Treatment system that greatly improved boiler maintenance and safety, as well as boosting steam production by degrees. Dante Porta devised a cunning mixture that greatly cuts down scales that form in boiler tubes. The PT system, as it's known, ensures much less build-up of any kind in the boiler, thus less requirement for back flushing and heavy maintenance, as well as conferring greater safety against dangerous internal boiler blockages.

STEAM-TURBINE-ELECTRIC

Sitting alongside these gains is another potential deal-maker for bringing back steam locomotion in certain situations; however, I accept certainly not for underground operations or lengthy tunnel operations. I refer of course to the generic 10 to 20 per cent gain in power and fuel efficiency by switching the drive mechanism from reciprocal steam-driven pistons to steam-turbine-electric. This is still a locomotive with basic firebox and firetube boiler, but the steam spins a turbine or several turbines, which in turn generates electricity that drives electric traction motors, usually mounted directly on the axles.

Radical, you say; unheard of, you might think. No to both of these, as it was back in 1897 that the first steam-electric locomotive burst forth — the Heilmann locomotive, generating DC power that drove the axles. The Heilmann locomotive had two bogies of two axles at each end of the long locomotive — another first for the French and the engineer J. J. Heilmann. One of the underlying advantages of this arrangement is the fact there is balance and no reciprocating action, although there is some loss of power as steam is converted first to electricity and then that electricity is used to drive the actual axle-aligned motors.

In 1938 in the USA General Electric produced a greatly advanced steam-turbine-electric locomotive, in fact fired by oil and with 5000 horsepower, so not to be lightly dismissed. After World War II, in 1947, the Chesapeake and Ohio Railroad developed three prototype coal-fired steam-turbine-electric locomotives that performed well, and in 1954 Norfolk and Southern went to Baldwins, now Baldwin Lima Hamilton, to build a new-generation prototype steam-turbine-electric. After testing, Norfolk and Southern wanted many more, but the dieselisation wave was sweeping all before it. Baldwins collapsed and most railways moved quickly out of steam of any kind.

Porta was not put off by the dieselisation trend; he acknowledged and learned from it, but still worked away on a range of rail engineering fronts until his death in 2003.

Today those who follow in Dante Porta's footsteps know that to achieve the greatest efficiency with steam, it must be by adopting steam-turbine-electric locomotives, which provide a smoother delivery system of power to the driving wheels.

Both Dante Porta and colleague Shaun McMahon had interactions with the US firm T. W. Blasingame, headquartered in Idaho state. It had commenced joint work in designing the ultimate steam-turbine-electric locomotive, initially for Stephenson standard gauge main-line operation in the USA and later with a subset for narrow gauge in Argentina.

At last the constellations were lining up to bring about this counterintuitive breakthrough: the 'better than diesel' steam locomotive in terms of cost benefit. The design work was done without great difficulty and all was set to go down the path of manufacture. Alas, the plunge in oil prices in two particular periods of the last part of the 20th century not only misled the world greatly, but it destroyed any rationale for staying with or developing a new genre of modern steam locomotives.

Still the plans sit there ready to go, and the huge US Powder River Basin coal project must be one likely contender, especially if millions of tonnes of coal have to head to the west coast for export across the Pacific Ocean. It makes sense for the huge trains heading west to be powered by the coal they are hauling, so they can replenish on completion of each cycle of basin-port-basin.

Likewise Rio Turbio coal mine in Argentina is in limbo at present, but if a revamp is ordered and the funds obtained, then look out for the first set of steam-turbine-electric locomotives burning Rio Turbio coal and operating on the very narrow practical gauge of 750 mm (2 feet 5½ inches). The distance is some 284 kilometres (178 miles) from the mine eastward and downhill to the port on the Atlantic Ocean.

Locomotive Safety

With all locomotives large and small, safety features are built in to cause automatic power shutdown in the event of zero driver response, although this feature is rarely installed on locomotive trolleys, only the larger versions. Sadly in Sydney with one class of suburban commuter trains in 2003, sticks were often put in place to jam the response and bypass the 90-second sequence dead man's handle — or automatic shutdown. All of this emerged in a Royal Commission investigating a dreadful railway derailment with seven fatalities near Waterfall south of Sydney in 2003. Although the driver involved in the Waterfall crash was in no way artificially or deliberately blocking the dead man's handle, unacceptable and irresponsible driver conduct of this kind was pursued by far too many, for far too many years, until fully exposed.

Today modern locomotives have improved dead man's handles; also most main-line locomotives worldwide have a form of black box to allow complete monitoring in detail of all aspects of driver use of the throttle and other controls, and in some cases in real time.

In terms of 'trains unlimited' there is little doubt this century will see the need for the steam electric locomotive. Indeed it is far too early to write off steam locomotion in general. As we will see, in the case of heritage and tourism rail operations, steam trains remain as popular as ever. In addition, steam locomotives remain in harness for freight roles in one or two parts of the world, operating commercially in places like Argentina and Bosnia to this day. Indeed, in Dresden commuters can enjoy steam-hauled trains on two feeder lines daily. The plea that Dante Porta would make, along with André Chapelon and even George and Robert Stephenson, is that if returning to steam locomotion then do it properly. Use the newest and best designs from Lempor ejector to modern water injector, to maximise efficiency and minimise carbon footprint.

Curiously enough, there are some features from the early days common to all kinds of line locomotives, including the new environmentally friendly modern locomotive. I refer to the humble sandbox and sandpipe, allowing the driver to direct a small stream of dry sand onto the track just ahead of the driving wheels to improve grip on steep grades.

The steam locomotive of every kind has come a long way since Stephenson's trailblazing *Rocket* in 1829. The heaviest locomotives were made during and after World War II and included the Union Pacific Big Boy class, which sported four sets of pistons, rods and driving wheels, and weighed in at around 550 tonnes. In its heyday its main role was on long mountainous hauls across the Union Pacific network — particularly heavy-duty freight haulage over Sherman Hill between Cheyenne and Laramine, Wyoming. Just 25 Big Boys were built and sadly none are operational today. They must have been a grand sight hauling 4000 tonne trains up grades through the Rockies, without any other locomotive assisting.

Canada should not be overlooked in the need to conquer long distances — the Rockies to boot — with steam locomotives. Nicely stored in Ottawa and in the revamped rail museum south of the river in Montreal are huge examples of big steam from the golden days of Canadian Pacific (CP) and Canadian National (CN). On the run from Montreal to Ottawa in the 1950s there were sections where the CP and CN tracks ran alongside each other and led to informal racing between the two giants, until the station terminals loomed up quickly. On occasions this necessitated huge braking efforts and too often a touch-and-go outcome, but it seems accidents were avoided.

DIESEL

The steam locomotive may have come a long way in its 200-year existence but it has now been all but replaced by the diesel-electric and all-electric locomotive giants of the 21st century.

It was Rudolf Diesel, born in Paris of German parents and raised in the UK and Germany, who invented the diesel engine with compression chamber and piston. He was a true early pan-European-type inventor and businessman, who in 1893 laid down his paper on the diesel engine and started building rudimentary engines, initially run on peanut oil. Ironically this fate might just await modern diesels again if 'post peak oil' conditions take hold and fossil fuel becomes largely unobtainable.

There are many who played key roles in all-electric rail locomotive development. The Italian Allessandro Volta invented the battery around 1800, and shortly later built a line to carry electric current from his beloved Lake Como to Milan. This was a precursor to the work of Thomas Davenport in the USA, Werner von Siemens in Germany, and many others. They developed early versions of electric locomotives running off a third middle rail and later off overhead electric wiring.

Rail electrification and the locomotives it requires developed quickly towards the end of the nineteenth century. They were found to be especially useful in underground metro lines in London and elsewhere. In a sense, anything was better than smoke-generating steam locomotives in tunnels, causing people to choke on unhealthy fumes in confined spaces, and massive soot build-up as well.

However, the biggest change since the introduction of diesel-electric and all-electric after World War II has been the leap forward in power/

weight ratios, with smaller and lighter engines delivering more horsepower and using less fuel.

While further increases in efficiency may bump against certain limitations, one aspect that remains unlimited is the number of smart locomotives that can be turned out to meet huge increases in rail freight and passenger demand in all six railway realms of the world. A consequence of the global financial crisis is that locomotive and rolling stock construction companies have caught up on a big backlog of orders from the rail boom times around the start of the 21st century. Just 45 years ago not one Bullet train or HSR train had been built or operated in the world. Today there are no less than 3474 HSR locomotives, or 1737 train sets, operating in

In tandem steam

For a large part of 1988, the Australian bicentennial year, the sight of the *Flying Scotsman 4472* alongside or ahead of the mighty *3801* was something to behold. Indeed, in some places in Australia that year two and even three steam trains ran side by side, in an extravaganza of steam never likely to be repeated.

Huge crowds lined vantage points along the Melbourne–Albury main line one late winter's Sunday to see an Irish broad gauge 707 special-charter steam train chase down the *4472* and the *3801* running parallel on the Stephenson standard gauge track alongside. The flume of smoke was a photographer's delight, the hammer of the pistons a charm to the ear, as this blast from the past swept through Chiltern and Barnawartha, heading north-by-northeast.

At one stage a big key part had to be repaired on the *4472*, which was done in Perth, but not without some graffiti being etched into the steel acknowledging Perth's rescue role. The question is: will this etching from the antipodes survive the big revamp to the *4472* currently under the auspices of the new owner, the National Railway Museum (NRM), York, UK? We shall see, but somehow I doubt it.

Europe, Japan, South Korea, Russia, Spain and Taiwan, with many more countries lining up with HSR projects, including Argentina, Turkey (part built) and even the USA. This aspect of locomotive matters — the ability to expand with the number of sets operating to meet demand with minimal impact on the environment — makes the future of rail exciting.

CLASSIFYING LOCOMOTIVES

For some obscure reason, the names of oceans, on which no railway locomotive can ever run, dominate the key descriptor phrases of steam locomotives and their wheel arrangements. I know there is the odd railway or train ferry boat, such as between Sicily and the mainland of Italy, but once the train has been shunted on board, the locomotive is shut down or taken back to shore, with its duties done.

Yet terms applying to steam locomotives, such as the Pacific Class and the Atlantic Class, not to mention the Baltic Class, are all well known to railway buffs. Usage and national pride were probably factors in the choices made and gradually a common scheme emerged. This is well laid out by Brian Reed in his book *Locomotives*, in which he explains the approach devised by an American engineer named Frederick Whyte.

Frederick Whyte (of Dutch extraction) worked for the famous New York Central Railroad, with its hub for many decades being New York Grand Central Station. It was a natural extension of his duties working for one of the railroad companies for him to create a definitive table of locomotive categories, often enough labelled by ocean names.

The key classifying factor was the most identifiable one: the wheel layout, which was and is easily sighted and counted. Thus, a certain class is denoted according to the number of front wheels, the number of big driving wheels connected to the steam pistons, and the number of support wheels behind these.

In fact, there are two overall locomotive category tables derived from the wheel arrangements: one, as exists for steam locomotives; and two, as exists for all other locomotives, most notably diesel, turbo, diesel-electric, all-electric and battery.

I am indebted to Brian Reed for the best illustrations of these categories, which I now summarise, starting with the ubiquitous steam locomotive.

The best steam locomotive to start with is the ever-popular Pacific type — the famous 4-6-2 — of which the *4472* (named the *Flying Scotsman*) is the best known locomotive still operating today, housed at the National Railway Museum (NRM) York. As a locomotive it frequently hauled the express train service that departed King's Cross at 1000, also called the '*Flying Scotsman*', bound for Waverly Station, Edinburgh. The numbers '*4472*' must be the most recognised set of four numbers in the world, excluding years. The engine was built way back in 1923 by the great Sir Nigel Gresley, with four small front wheels, six large driving wheels and two support wheels (4-6-2), with a following tender loaded with coal and water in matching colour. In 1928 the *4472* led the *Flying Scotsman* train out of King's Cross at exactly 1000 for a non-stop run to Edinburgh, done in eight hours and picking up water from a long trough between the tracks en route.

In its near 90 years of steaming, the *4472* has even visited the USA for some celebrity runs and conquered the east–west transcontinental route across Australia in 1988 and 1989, including the longest straight section of rail in the world — 478 kilometres (297 miles) across the Nullarbor Desert near the South Australia–West Australian border on the route to Perth.

Some of the world's most durable main-line locomotives were in this Pacific category; for example, the NSW Government Railways (NSWGR) pride of the fleet to this day, the 38 Class and *3801* in particular, a strong well-designed workhorse of 4-6-2 Pacific category configuration which has steamed to and through every state in Australia and to Alice Springs. It is still operating around Sydney from time to time today, at least when not out of service for boiler repair.

The Atlantic type of 4-4-2, utilised on both sides of the Atlantic Ocean, had just four, not six, big driving wheels. These locomotives were best used on level terrain.

The Christmas beer trolley disaster

Back in the golden days of the 1960s, the last hurrah for many country passenger services in Australia, a crisis developed on Christmas Eve with a runaway trolley on the old Echuca-to-Balranald interstate branch line of Irish broad gauge.

A ganger, or fettler, let us call him Fred, had gone down the line from Caldwell to Wakool on his trolley to buy a large load of Christmas beer for his mates, and this he did at the local pub. He also had a beer or two himself before loading the bottles onto the rail trolley, then attempting to start the 'brute'. Of course, it failed to start, so one trick employed was to put the trolley in gear and push hard with the ignition on and hope the engine would spring into life.

The trick worked; alas, it worked too well on the first hard push and the trolley took off back towards Caldwell and Echuca without fettler Fred on board, but with all the beer. Meanwhile, the passenger train from Melbourne, heavily loaded, as it was the last train before Christmas, was making its way northwards from Echuca through Moama and Barnes and along the single-track branch line towards Caldwell and Wakool.

So there was the unmanned trolley loaded with beer hurtling south directly into the path of the northbound passenger train, and due to the long working sections on this isolated single-track branch line, there were no signals or capacity to warn the driver of the passenger train. Local common sense came to the fore. The Wakool publican alerted by the fettler, Fred, rang John Vagg, who was a farmer living down the track near Bunnaloo, and explained the dilemma.

John Vagg sprang into action and set up some old sleepers across the track to derail the trolley. Just in time, the trap was laid, the trolley derailed and the passenger train spared, but, alas, the beer bottles were smashed into a million pieces. Our fettler Fred was assigned to the dog house by his colleagues for that Christmas.

The Adriatic type of 2-6-4 curiously came out of Austria, and for a period the Austro-Hungarian Empire did have some coastline down to the Adriatic Sea, near Trieste, Zadar and Split, but not for long. As names go the 'Adriatic' was not widely used, but, as Brian Reed points out, most tank steam engines, with their coal and water on the one frame and no trailing tender wagon, use this configuration.

Finally, continuing the oceanic flavour, came the Baltic type 4-6-4, known as this in Europe, but in the USA mostly called the Hudson type, because it roared along the Hudson River between New York and Albany, past the Hyde Park mansion of the Roosevelt family, to name one trackside resident. While broadly there was considerable harmony in rail terminology worldwide, local culture and descriptors crept in with this type of 4-6-4 locomotive.

Other types of steam locomotives include the 4-8-2 Mountain, the 2-10-0 Decapod, the 2-10-2 Santa Fe, the 4-10-0 Mastodon, and from Indonesia the incredible 2-12-2 Javanic type. More than six driving wheels generally meant the locomotives were designed for mountain runs, with steep grades requiring more wheels for grip. See the associated table for complete wheel arrangement listings.

Before turning to diesel and electric, I should mention the tiny locomotive trolley used by railway gangers. Often the larger trolley would have a 2-A-0 layout (see below) with just two driving wheels, be they manually operated or by small petrol or diesel engine. At times the trolley with the engine had a hood to provide some limited protection from the elements for the crew and it would pull a lighter wagon, with sleepers loaded on board along with some equipment.

The second group of descriptors, for the diesel, diesel-electric, turbo and all-electric, tend to be split up on an amended representation of wheel and axle layout from the Whyte steam locomotive descriptors.

In shorthand form, A equals one axle, B equals two axles, C equals three axles, and so forth but with a small 'o' added if the axle has its own drive or electric engine. This means in many railway realms the simply expressed

Locomotive Wheel Arrangements

This table highlights key category names, especially in relation to oceans. It was devised by Whyte and assisted by Brian Reed's definitive book *Locomotives* and reflects Whyte's Americas flavour. Large, bold wheels indicate a wheel and axle that are powered directly.

STEAM

CLASS	WHEEL ARRANGEMENT
Adriatic	o **OOO** oo
Atlantic	oo **OO** o
Baltic	oo **OOO** oo
Columbia	o **OO** o
Decapod	o **OOOOO**
Javanic	o **OOOOOO** o
Mikado	o **OOOO** o
Mogul	o **OOO**
Mountain	oo **OOOO** o
Pacific	oo **OOO** o
Prairie	o **OOO** o
Santa Fe	o **OOOOO** o

DIESEL/DIESEL-ELECTRIC/ELECTRIC SUMMATION

DESCRIPTOR	LAYOUT
Co Co	**OOO OOO**
Bo Bo	**OO OO**
A A	**O O**
A1A A1A	**OOO OOO** (Middle axle not powered)

Almost all diesel–electric locomotives built in the 21st century to date are Co Co.

Co Co dominates — three axle bogies with each axle having an electric motor attached — and of course two such bogies under the locomotive, be it diesel or diesel electric.

Many rail motors are in fact Bo Bo, that is with two bogies of two axles each, and power from the engine connected to each axle. Again see the table for details — and remember the little 'o' is applied only if all axles are powered, and the upper case lettering is only used on powered axles as well. So, as Brian Reed highlights in a teasing conclusion on wheel layout, a triple rail-motor with a middle carriage without any power, and with two power carriages or locomotives at each end complete with two axle bogies but only the inner axle power driven, would be given the descriptor 1A-A1+2-2+1A-A1. You are forgiven if you do not 'get it' first time around!

It is like variations on a theme and principle — not perfect but if all else fails then simply bend over a safe distance from the track and count the axles as well as the axles with a power source or electric engine attached. You will soon become an expert in this field. All of this is far more important than just writing train locomotive numbers down, as British train spotters are inclined to do.

In the contrarian way that some hold small is beautiful, meet *Yvonne* — at less than one-hundredth of the weight of a Big Boy and arguably the smallest standard-guage steam locomotive in the world. *Yvonne* can be found at Maldegem, Belgium, with the dynamic Stoomtrein group, where she is undergoing reconstruction for relaunch in mid-2012. No doubt *Yvonne* will seduce all and sundry when she starts running again in that area.

STATION MATTERS

The twelve greatest stations worldwide

S t Pancras is a stunning and superb makeover of an old workhorse. What used to be a near-deserted grime-filled second-best station of the 20th century, servicing the London–Midland system, is now sparkling in the 21st century. The revamp is so remarkable that a media report commented it was hard to believe Britain could carry this out.

In the following carefully chosen listing of the twelve greatest stations in the world at the start of the second decade of the 21st century, I effectively update a chapter from a previous book to take into account the great deal that has changed in the last decade in the major league of stations worldwide — and St Pancras International leads the field. I dare to say it is currently the greatest railway terminus in the world — beautiful, practical and brilliantly combining the old with the new, and with good tucker as a bonus.

Yes, it is not without some flaws, but the criticisms of those such as the formidable judges Christian Wolmar and Matthew Engel, both great

British rail authors of renown, seem almost light of touch. It is as if they, like most others, are in awe of the new St Pancras, and the fact that finally a big chunk of rail in Britain has been got right.

Now, you might ask, by what criteria has St Pancras been put at the top of a list of the best twelve in the world? How has this list been devised? In summary, it is those twelve stations that have 'a certain grandeur', the twelve great railway cathedrals of the world, albeit allowing that one or two are in need of a good scrub and revamp.

This certain grandeur is created by the design, the delivery of services to the public, the diversity of rail on offer, critical mass as a hub terminus, and the overall gravitas on offer. Unfair as it may seem, on these criteria no metro underground stations can make it onto the list, although some on the Moscow Metro go close, with their chandeliers and grand corridors. Sadly, twice this century so far, major bomb attacks by suicide bombers have been carried out on the Moscow Metro, killing many people.

There is also the nicely modern new all-underground Britomart station in Auckland, New Zealand. This is a great addition to Auckland public transport assets but, alas, is a dead-end terminus station, crying out for both quadruplication in and twin-track out under the CBD and across the bay.

So, why turn away from the all-underground stations, you ask. Because no major metro underground station in the world has the giant atriums, the splendour and diversity that above-ground stations or, for that matter, even above-ground concourses and atriums with tiers of below-ground platforms can produce. The soaring lines are there to behold, as uplifting punctuation marks in the strain and turmoil of the travel story today.

① In the case of St Pancras, the first thing to soak up is the revamped Barlow train shed, or central hall, a huge arch that has been stripped back to its original colour, a superb powder blue. William Henry Barlow completed the design and construction of this train shed in 1868 — a 240-feet (70-metre) wide roofed area without intermediate support, and a world record at the time. Barlow was no slouch and with his son, Crawford Barlow, teamed up to engineer the replacement Tay Bridge in Scotland,

The southern end of St Pancras, London. (Tim Fischer)

after the first bridge collapsed in a gale in late 1879. Sadly, this was just as the northbound mail train was crossing, a tragedy leading to the deaths of 78 people. The Barlow Tay Bridge has proved very durable and points to yet another successful father-and-son team.

There are now fifteen platforms in all at St Pancras, three groups at near-ground level (in fact at elevated level vis-à-vis Euston Road at the front), and then the two Thames Link underground platforms A and B for a fast north–south trip across London and through to towns in Kent, as well as Brighton and Wimbledon. Eurostar services to Europe operate from the central bank of platforms; Olympic trains and fast commuter trains to the east and southeast of London will operate during the games from the eastern side of St Pancras; and there are four platforms on the western side or (new) British Library side, allocated to trains bound for the Midlands and such places as Derby and Loughborough, where one can change to the heritage Great Central Railway through to Quorn and Leicester North.

In October 2009 I met Lord Richard Faulkner — who for several years was chair of the committee responsible for overseeing such icons as the heavy keys for clearance along single tracks, old station lanterns, signs and benches, and historic archives and records of the railways in Britain, now that they have been privatised — at St Pancras for a look around. Alas, the champagne bar of epic proportions was not then open, but the clever, modern design, combining the renovated old Barlow train shed with the new huge glass-and-steel construction, is something to behold when you get the chance.

It is to former deputy PM of the UK, John Prescott, that I give credit for leading the way with the bold decision to revamp St Pancras, with its expanded role as a Eurostar terminal and much more.

The St Pancras undercroft area, used over the decades to store and keep cool heavy brews from the Midlands has been made into a series of pleasant walkways, shopping malls and the like, with plenty of light permeating through the window panes, a long way up above.

Do not order Bombe Alaska, tasty as it is

I recommend the Bombe Alaska pudding, as good as I have enjoyed anywhere, at the Betjeman Arms, but do not order loudly or you might trigger a security scare. In fact, the item on the menu has been described as 'Alaskan xyz', perhaps because of the post 9/11 and post 7/7 tragedies, the latter being the dreadful tube and bus bombings in London in July 2005 that killed many.

As for the xyz, you will have to go along to find out the term used and how good the dish is. Further, you can consume your order at tables on the concourse proper and watch the Eurostars glide in and out, while debating with friends all aspects of modern rail.

When the British get it together in design and construction, they do it really well: from Christopher Wren's St Paul's Cathedral, arising in the seventeenth century, to the Royal Albert Hall of the nineteenth century, and now the retro modern St Pancras. In a rare gesture these days, the 20th-century campaigner and poet Sir John Betjeman, who saved St Pancras from demolition, has been honoured with a statue cast in bronze. Better still, he has been honoured decently in the naming of the Betjeman Arms pub on the southeast corner of the big concourse, with cold beer on tap and good cuisine.

St Pancras International deserves top billing; it is more than a railway terminal, because of the bonus of a grand hotel and elegant apartments to come at the front. At the time of writing they are still being refurbished, including the ornate facade and tower.

St Pancras has wisely been rebuilt with surplus capacity for the future, and just as well with the prospect of 'no change' high-speed train services between London and Rome, London and Berlin, and London and Madrid, on top of those already offered, plus perhaps one day just possibly London and Glasgow.

Who was St Pancras? Well, actually, there were two, both Roman saints who were martyred, one by stoning and one by beheading, more than 1500 years ago. Fortunately St Pancras International is now here to stay as a great beacon of excellence and doing much to promote modern rail by way of its exemplar role.

(2) A few years ago when I compiled my first list of top stations worldwide there were none from Germany, but this has now changed, with the glistening new Berlin Hauptbahnhof (Hbf) on the list. This station has now opened for business near the Reichstag and ten minutes' walk from the famous Brandenburg Gate.

The new Berlin Hbf opened in 2007. It is a huge multi-level master station of soaring glass and steel, with platforms and tracks at two levels — six tracks on high and eight tracks down below. One suspects its capacity will be tested in the future; it is already handling 1800 trains daily and over 350,000 passengers.

Colour employment bar challenged at Euston

I confess I have dropped one station from the list by the narrowest of margins, namely Bristol Temple Meads, as the original GWR Brunel train shed is no longer part of the station. Further, the current through station of curved platforms has Platforms 1 to 15, but for some obscure reason no actual Platform 14. So if they have no 14 then I have no space on my list of the twelve greatest stations — but, yes, it would be fourteen on a list of the fourteen greatest.

In researching the good, the bad and ugly among large railway stations and terminals, nothing ceases to amaze. The adjusted layout of Bristol Temple Meads, with its curved platforms, almost matches the original layout of Union Station Worcester, Massachusetts, USA. The latter happens to have been revamped and reopened in 2000, after years of non-use and neglect, at its location near Temple Street, Worcester.

Only one or two stations, such as Grand Central, New York, were developed with 180-degree curved tracks at their stub end to allow turnaround of trains from platforms on one side, right around to platforms on the other side of the platform layout. In essence, southbound terminating trains with electric locomotives could be quickly turned around, ready for northbound departure, without any locomotive uncoupling from carriages.

However, it is Euston Station in London that takes the prize for the ugliest, with an ordinary building revamp last century, and in employment practice: a ban on employing coloured or non-white people. It was not until as late as 1966 that a de facto ban on British Rail employing coloured personnel at that station was lifted. UK Transport Minister at the time, the formidable Barbara Castle, formalised the ending of this ban in mid-1966. It had been exposed by a West Indian by the colourful name of Asquith Xavier, who finally secured the job for which he was qualified, up front at Euston Station.

The station's first incarnation was as the terminus for the inaugural line from Hanover to Berlin, built in a classic overarch train-shed design. Then it was called Lehrter Bahnhof, and opened for business in 1871. The location had a troubled history through World War II, with much Allied bombing in the area, and then with the imposition of the Berlin Wall dividing the precinct from 1961 to 1989. It was the reunification of Germany that opened up possibilities of starting afresh on a grand scale and also completing some north–south linkage, not just the restored east–west linkages.

The result is an all-new 21st-century station with no makeover component in the sense that the previous buildings were all demolished and the rail tracks realigned. Starting from scratch has resulted in a good set of outcomes, perhaps not stellar, but certainly above average for the users. This includes the vital, conveniently located service for the storage of luggage.

If you come in on a train from, say, Hamburg or Frankfurt and have a two-hour layover before a connection, the trick is to dump luggage and walk the short distance to the Brandenburg Gate — it takes about fifteen minutes. After soaking up where U2 performed in a free concert in November 2009 as part of the 20th anniversary of the Berlin Wall coming down, a location where so much other history has unfolded, you can walk briskly on into the old East Berlin.

About three blocks further east and two blocks south you will come to the plaza, with two small matching church buildings, and the large Schauspielhaus concert hall, where Leonard Bernstein conducted the Berlin East and Berlin West orchestras playing together for the first time, on Christmas Day 1989. In a memorable concert, they played Beethoven's Ninth Symphony but with one change: instead of the 'Ode to Joy' it became the 'Ode to Freedom' for the choral fourth movement. The hope for peace and prosperity for the world for ever more with the Wall coming down and Eastern Europe opening up, sadly, was not to be.

The point of all of this: if St Pancras can have a bronze statue of Betjeman, then the forecourt of Berlin Hbf could or should have statues of Bernstein and Brandt. Willy Brandt was the famous mayor of Berlin when the Wall went up and also a former chancellor of West Germany. In short, statues of those who mattered to Berlin over the decades could emphasise the fact that in many ways Berlin was the ground zero of 20th-century world history.

(3) Third on the list is the giant Milano Centrale Station, Italy, a product of the between-the-wars Mussolini era of big buildings, also undergoing a major clean-up and revamp. Often enough, when changing trains at Milano Centrale, at least through 2009, the same said 'Ode to Joy' or 'Ode to Freedom' of Beethoven could be heard blasting out from the public speaker system. Perhaps this is a salute to the new European national, or, in fact, international anthem based on the fourth movement of Beethoven's Ninth. More likely it is a hurry-up to keep the big crowds moving.

The Milan train shed is in fact three train sheds joined: three huge arches of canopy straddling the 24-plus platforms that are all on the same level, except for the metro out the front. The architect, Ulisse Stacchini,

Milano Centrale.

All change Milan

Twice in recent months I have made connections as tight as less than five minutes from arrival until sitting on a train departing generally right on time. This happens easily enough because there are big signs clearly showing platforms, and also because at Termini Rome, Florence and Milan, the Red Arrow HSR long-distance trains are almost always allocated central platforms.

Clearly this makes sense as many people connect to or from these Red Arrow trains; further, if arriving on the Tirano regional or Domodossola regional, you know exactly which direction to head and can do so quickly, if need be. Such a commonsense approach does go missing too often in other railway realms.

One trick of the trade is to book an express Red Arrow non-stop Milan to Rome, allowing over an hour to change, but if in fact you arrive on a regional train and find a Red Arrow about to depart express for Rome do not hesitate. If it still has empty seats just two minutes before departing, jump on board and gain an hour. Queues prevent you formally adjusting your ticket, but the ticket inspector in due course will notice your switch forward and you pay on the spot some eight euros, but less than ten, for the advantage.

borrowed from the design of the mammoth Union Station Washington, so it is a case of the New World giving something back to the Old World in style and with style.

Walking through the main entrance, it is almost as if it is too big a building to comprehend and be comfortable in. In no way can it be said to be subtle or delicate in style; rather it is a giant testimony to a previous period of Italian excess. Nevertheless, the station works and works well in its fundamental role, and is designed to last a very long time. Again there is an efficient staffed luggage depository for short- and long-term stay — very helpful to those with layovers.

Milan deserves to be upgraded as a tourist destination, quite apart from its key business role. While it may well be better known as the business and industrial capital of northern Italy, the Duomo (cathedral) is a delight; La Scala Opera House is smaller than the Colon in Buenos Aires but also a delight, with a jewel of a museum open by day; and the Galleria is just unbelievable as a retail concourse framed in the beautiful style of a previous era. However, be prepared to pay big even for simple things like a cup of coffee.

The two greatest stations of Paris come next, namely Gare du Nord and Gare de Lyon, and in that order. After all, Gare du Nord is the busiest station in Europe, with over 180 million passengers a year. Originally laid out in 1861, it has had many revamps and expansions, and now caters for international high speed, especially Eurostar to London, regional and local, as well as the RER (Reseaux Express Regionale) Paris underground, lines B and D.

James Mayer de Rothschild was President of the Chemin de Fer du Nord railway company and he appointed Jacques Hittorff as architect around 1860 for the railway's premier Paris terminal. Again great foresight was displayed in the original size and standard of the structure, which allows it, albeit with some major revamps, to handle the population of Australia or Holland more than eight times over each year.

Over the decades many famous people, from Picasso to Piaf — or from the Anglo side of things, Churchill and Curzon — as well as agents provocateurs Lawrence of Arabia and even Ho Chi Minh, have arrived or departed or just loitered at Gare du Nord. Like most of the top twelve stations, Gare du Nord has featured in Hollywood films, and is set for a huge future as high-speed train networks and their usage continue to expand.

It is a great gateway to Paris, and with its hub role and diversity it is set for a grand future. When originally built in the middle of the nineteenth century this location was around the edge of the then city of Paris, but today it is inner city, as Paris has grown and grown. Gare du Nord is not too far from the famous Moulin Rouge, with its windmill and dancing girls, and in sight of the all-white Sacré Coeur church on the hill. So the choice in heading out from Gare du Nord is up the hill to the magnificent Sacré Coeur or down the street to the nightlife and various red-light zones — or both.

Nearby, but not in the top twelve is Gare de l'Est, recently given a big clean-up and bright enough. It has a concourse that marks a dreadful place in World War II — the departure point of 70,000 Parisian Jews, including hundreds of children, sent by the Vichy Government and Nazis to death camps during the Holocaust. A memorial plaque says it all in a dignified way.

Gare de Lyon is in the southeast corner of Paris, as it was when railways developed and expanded throughout the nineteenth century. It opened for business in 1900, with the hugely popular and enduring Train Bleu restaurant on the first level opening in 1901 and operating ever since. The murals on the restaurant walls are many and relate to train destinations right across regional France.

This is where the now taken-for-granted TGV started in 1981, serving a public only too willing to switch from short air flights between Paris and Lyon or even Geneva. The original orange-coloured TGV train sets have dominated the vista under the grand train shed as they loaded up for the swift journey to Dijon and places further south and east. Such named trains as Le Mistral, with a sumptuous dining car, leaving around noon for the run down to Nice, are long gone from the picture.

Gare de Lyon now has an expanded sister station, Gare de Bercy, about 1 kilometre down the track towards Dijon (and Rome), and this handles the more awkward trains, such as the remnant overnight train operating between Paris and Rome, and other overnighters from Paris to Italy and elsewhere in Europe. This Paris–Rome blast from the past comprises a locomotive and mainly SNCF (Société Nationale des Chemins de Fer) rolling stock, including sleepers. The carriages have bunk compartments of two or four or six, and allow passengers to arrive refreshed, at least by degrees, in Paris or Rome — ready for a day of business or whatever. The straight-through toilets down to the tracks are a curiosity in the 21st century.

In one sense there were always seven great stations in Paris for long-distance trains, including Gare d'Orsay, which was long ago converted to a brilliant gallery and museum. Meanwhile, the add-on Gare de Bercy has arrived as a poor cousin, so the number remains the same, with Gare du Nord and Gare de Lyon way out in front. The other three are Austerlitz, Saint-Lazare and Montparnasse (the seventh being Gare de l'Est).

The best planned national capital city of the world, namely Paris, is well supported in its effortless arrogance as a city at the top of the ladder in so many ways, including its set of seven well-placed great railway stations. Montparnasse, the huge terminus for the southwest, built post World War II, is the one exception. As part of that redevelopment, former President Pompidou allegedly did a deal to allow the one ugly glass skyscraper in the CBD to be built alongside it. The Montparnasse concourse is adequate, and a giant platform-allocation screen dominates, but in no way does Montparnasse have the subtle brilliance of Nord or Lyons.

Smart Eurostar and TGV travellers from London never change in Paris if they are going further south. The computers will not tell you this but it is much smarter to change on the near-empty platforms of Lille, picking up the TGV services that sweep around Paris and head on to places like Le Mans and Bordeaux. This avoids the mad crowds of Paris, full stop (even though journey times can be a bit longer).

6   So far the grand stations on the list have all been on standard-gauge rail systems. Atocha, Madrid, is the first grand station entering the 21st century with two gauges operating and comprehensive security checks for the HSR platforms. The introduction of high-speed trains from Madrid to Seville resulted in the need to introduce standard-gauge platforms on a new level and separate from the Iberian broad gauge platforms and local suburban platforms. As a makeover and complete renovation, the Atocha Station, Madrid, takes the prize second only to St Pancras. The old renovated train-shed area has been converted to a huge public concourse, complete with restaurant and rainforest, framed by a sweeping glass roof, in a brilliant display of extravagance but, it has to be said, mouth-watering architectural

Atocha Madrid.

Station hangover cure

I vaguely recall going to Atocha one morning for a pick-me-up cup of coffee, as I had a big hangover after a long dinner the night before dealing with prickly trade issues, including olive oil and fortified wine designations such as port and sherry. Yes, the Europeans wanted to stop the New World using these descriptors and, damn it, they succeeded by degrees.

As part of their attack they ensured the visiting Trade Minister had plenty to drink at the official working dinner. The next morning the slightly humid atmosphere, the strong coffee and the relaxing ambience of the vista, with large fully grown palm trees inside the station atrium, soon resulted in zero hangover and renewed energy for the particular busy program that lay ahead.

ambition. In late 2003 the King and Queen of Spain returned to Atocha to ride the new high-speed line to the east of Madrid, unveiling plaques as they went. In 2010 the new AVE line from Madrid to Valencia opened.

To Madrid must go the prize for the best multi-gauge modern station makeover, utilising the old with the new in a superb combination, but slightly let down, dare I say, by the cheapest white plastic chairs that you would ever encounter in the atrium.

As if to tear down this progress and success, in March 2004 terrorists attacked the Madrid rush-hour trains in ten separate bombings. Two hundred people were killed and many injured, a corner of the Atocha concourse was turned into a temporary emergency hospital and another into a temporary morgue. The people of Spain stood their ground and demonstrated in their thousands against the attacks. The Atocha Station was back in business the very next day, and from that day on it has stood tall and proud as one of the unbowed responses to terrorism.

(7) Grand Central (or GCT), New York, comes in at seventh position in the Top Twelve. At its zenith Grand Central had two levels with a total of 67 tracks serving some 44 platforms. In fact, this is the current situation but a new zenith is approaching because in the next decade, under the East Side Access project, at even deeper levels another eight tracks will be added with four platforms.

This means Grand Central Terminal will service an amazing 75 tracks and 48 platforms, but in reality 56 platforms because the newest East Side Access group will better connect the Long Island Rail Road, a very long way underneath the current lower level near Park Avenue and 42nd Street.

There has, however, been a cardinal and one or two others objecting to the placement of the dreaded necessary air vents for the East Side Access project. Air vents are required for the deep tunnels, the latest versions of catacombs in the New World. The location of one such large vent is near the New York Roman Catholic cathedral. I suspect the now-retired cardinal will lose out and the project will be delivered, but several years late, with completion only towards the end of the second decade of the

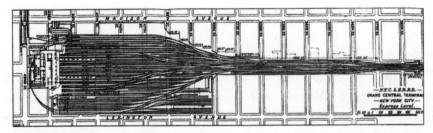

The layout for just one of the complex levels of NY Grand Central, circa 1908. (Wikimedia Commons)

21st century. This will guarantee Grand Central Terminal the record of the greatest number of tracks and platforms as part of one station complex anywhere in the world.

Sadly, the long-distance trains to Albany, Chicago and Canada no longer leave from the GCT, but from the underground and underwhelming Penn Central, a few blocks southwest of Park Avenue and 42nd Street. So the very best station in New York and much of the world, namely the GCT, is not the station for long-distance trains but it is the station for regional commuter trains on a grand scale — about 175,000 passengers served daily. Further, as previously mentioned, it boasts a set of 180-degree turning loops, built years ago and allowing trains from the north to turn back northwards without actually having the train reverse direction and drivers having to switch cabins from one end to another; very time consuming in a busy terminus.

The GCT started out as the Grand Central Depot in 1871, operating until around the turn of the century, then it became the Grand Central Station and, finally, after the depot was demolished and the great atrium and cathedral-sized windows were introduced, the Grand Central Terminal, opening in 1913. Since 1913 and the second major revamp, there has been a stunning Oyster Bar on the lower level. More particularly, the soaring lines and sweeping staircases of the main atrium are built to last, and built to remind us that America and New York has had its agonies but it is here to stay and in a way that matters.

This picture shows excavations for the magnificent NY Grand Central, circa 1908.
(http://hdl.loc.gov/loc.pnp/det.4a22981)

GCT has been a choice location for the making of many films, including *North by Northwest*, starring Cary Grant, and also starring the 20th Century Limited in its heyday. This train departed from GCT with a red carpet laid out for VIPs, and operated from 1901 to 1967, before air travel brought about its demise. For over six decades the 20th Century Limited plied the so-called water-level route, taking about fifteen hours to travel from New York to Chicago via Albany and the Hudson River Valley. It was one of the very best named trains of the USA, a practice discarded on many corridors as timetable planners have preferred the intercity model of regular departures at ten past the hour (or whatever) with no names attaching to the train — as in 'I will take the 1015 to Brighton'.

The 'knock it down again' brigade was to the fore in the 1960s when train travel was at a particularly low ebb in the USA, and especially as Penn

Central headed towards bankruptcy in 1970. Step forward one very brave lady, Jacqueline Kennedy Onassis, a New Yorker of renown with the odd gig elsewhere but always coming back to that city. She argued powerfully and persuasively that dismantling had happened too often in the USA, and the legal case pursued by developers wanting to bulldoze Grand Central, as happened with Penn Central, went all the way to the US Supreme Court.

In an enlightened decision, the Supreme Court ruled in favour of the preservation of Grand Central. It now holds the highest preservation order available in the USA and is set for a burst of enhanced activity as more and more people swing back to travel by rail in the land of the free. This phenomenon has been highlighted by the American Association of Railroads, with passenger increases noted over almost all train corridors, commuter to long distance.

So the spirits of the railway baron Cornelius Vanderbilt, founder of the New York Grand Central system, and former first lady Jacqueline Kennedy Onassis are conjoined in yet another expansion of the GCT now under construction to cater for the East Side and Long Island commuters.

Moynihan Central maybe

One of New York State's great senators of yesteryear was Daniel Patrick Moynihan, whose rough-and-tough approach at times was loved by New Yorkers. He made the proposal to recreate the Penn Central ground-level atrium and shopping mall by revamping the huge General Post Office building with a grand façade alongside the entrances to the current underground Penn Central.

His proposal is still in the pipeline, but it is a great example of lateral thinking that will reverse by degrees the tear-it-down mentality of 50 years ago. However, progress on getting the job done will depend on the political will and bean counters matching the grandness of Moynihan's thinking and superb proposal.

(8)

Just three hours away from New York by Acela Amtrak train, or to be precise as it is currently scheduled, two hours 47 minutes on a good express run, you arrive at Washington Union Station. By the way, to do this you must go into the crowded underground cauldron of Penn Central, denoted by Amtrak as 'NYP', and catch the Acela train NYP to WAS. Penn Central is jam-packed most of each day with both trains and commuters. There are not enough tracks, and corridors are not wide enough for the crowds. The bonus is the contrast when you arrive at spacious Union Station Washington in all its glory. Union Station and its grand concourse and atriums are a short walk from the Congressional building and are in keeping with the monumental style of the buildings on the Washington Mall.

Decades ago the Washington Mall had a clutter of railway tracks and yards dominating, but everything was redesigned and shifted underground

Union Station Washington.

....

Big stations can be uplifting

The huge atriums of Union Station Washington are uplifting in a way airport terminals can rarely be. Further, today many grand terminals offer many services, including a movie complex down below. In Washington's case, I once took my family to see a forgettable film in the modern cinema complex, leaving behind my son's favourite drinker, which caused a major ruckus. The between-session cleaners were no help and so we had a screaming match down below in Union Station which actually had nothing to do with rail service or lack thereof, but did raise transit-police eyebrows.

On another occasion, I was so fed up with my schedule as visiting Trade or Commerce Minister that I asked to leave the ambassador's car near Union Station and said I would find my own way back to the embassy for a media conference.

I then spent 20 minutes looking for a train bookshop long since gone and arrived at the embassy refreshed all the same by a few minutes of freedom before my schedule cut in again. In other words, a stroll through the magisterial atriums of stations like Union Station Washington and the similar-looking Milan Central Station can be uplifting for mind and soul, and encourage adventure and fresh thought.

....

as well as consolidated in the huge two-level Union Station complex. Today there are sixteen tracks, or more particularly, platforms, on the upper level, mainly handling northern services to and from. Down below are another eight tracks, or platforms, handling both through rail traffic and southbound services. With the metro station alongside, it has an overall total of around 26 platforms.

It is another example of the phenomenon of great railway cathedrals having multimillion-dollar makeovers and often just in time before they are bulldozed in favour of high-rise steel and glass. Current US Vice

President, Joe Biden, was for decades a regular commuter using Union Station, travelling daily up or down from Wilmington Station, Delaware, to attend the US Senate. Just before the big 2009 inauguration, President Barack Obama and Vice President Joe Biden travelled from Wilmington to Washington by train, as a form of ceremonial arrival.

Officially opening for business in 1908, Union Station Washington reopened on a grand new scale after an overhaul in 1988, and I suspect is good enough for another 80 years, at least, by which time the Obama–Biden administration will be but a distant memory. I say Obama *and* Biden because it is Joe Biden who has driven forward stimulus funding for rail in the USA, including designating eleven high-speed rail corridor projects.

Many big cities across the USA have a 'Union Station' I gather because they had multiple users but also as a post-Civil War branding exercise in unity and cohesion.

It is unlikely that Congress will turn its back on rail completely, as it has threatened to do before, and so Union Station Washington will remain a showcase of what is mostly good about rail in the USA, but also what could be much better and faster, as we will discuss in chapter six.

The railway realm of South America boasts many gauges and many large stations. One that is bigger than most and with a grand colonnade is the Retiro Station complex in downtown Buenos Aires, Argentina. To stroll along the concourse in the early evening is to leap back into another era, perhaps to even glimpse an Evita or a Juan darting here and there before heading to a night at the opera in the giant and acoustically superb Colon opera house, a few blocks away.

The Retiro complex comprises the large Belgrano and Mitre stations, and next to these the smaller San Martin Station. The imperial broad gauge and the supreme metric gauge are still in use at the complex. In days of old, the Tukeman mail train would power out of the Mitre Station heading broadly west then northwest. Even earlier, there was a narrow-gauge carriage service that would come all the way from Antofagasta on the Pacific Coast in Chile, via Salta to Buenos Aires. On a good run the very same coach would make it all the way through on this four-to-five-day international run. For the brave passengers involved, after days on board and crossing part of the challenging Atacama Desert, the bright lights of Buenos Aires and the Retiro complex must have been a dream come true.

There is a mixture of British and Spanish architecture in this part of bustling Buenos Aires; sadly also a degree of decay and dilapidation in so many of the wonderful buildings from a wealthy era, around 100 years ago, when the big railway stations were built. Even sadder is the monument close to Retiro to the fallen from the 1982 Malvinas (or Falklands) War, just another flurry by a dictator needing a big distraction.

The Retiro Station was designed by British architects Eustace and Roger Conder and Sydney Follet, and the engineer was Reginald Reynolds. The steel work was fabricated in England, and put together in kit form in Liverpool, just like a large Meccano set. It was then disassembled and shipped out to Argentina in bits. Eventually opened in 1915, the Retiro was considered to be the most important example of structural engineering in South America.

Large chunks of the rail networks in Southern America have gone missing, falling into disuse and becoming quickly overgrown or even turned into roadways. However, I am confident the Retiro complex will not be bulldozed, at least not the façade, and perhaps one day, high-speed trains to Rosario might depart from there.

(10) On balance the Retiro complex makes it onto this Top Twelve list but with a yellow signal for caution; in other words watch this space. In some ways the sprawling Victoria Station at Bombay, now Mumbai, India, is in the same category.

There is no doubt Victoria Station, Mumbai, is built along classical colonial lines and is very much deserving of being selected for the Top Twelve. A recent book completed by Charles Sheppard titled *Railway Stations: Masterpieces of Architecture* points out how extraordinary some of the Gothic lines dominating the exterior of Victoria Station are, but inside it is something altogether different, with a superb central dome as the key feature.

Victoria/Chhatrapati Shivaji Terminal, Mumbai.

Like so many buildings of its era, Victoria Station requires a good spring-clean to bring out the best in its ornate décor. I recall being ushered upstairs into the stationmaster's office on one visit, where the pecking order of bureaucracy in India was very much to the fore. There were people everywhere, most of them station staff, but all of them aware of the various ranks of same, with the stationmaster commanding absolute respect and even salutes as we made our way along the various corridors to his office.

For colour, action and movement, there is nothing to compare with a big Indian railway station, and in particular Victoria Terminus. Here, in the course of one hour, the people ebb and flow, in some cases bringing what seems to be almost all of their belongings. In other cases, the traveller is obviously a very important Indian with his own retinue of servants and luggage bearers behind.

Mumbai is now the starting point for the world's newest imperial broad gauge main line, from nearby Churchgate Station direct along the coast to Goa. This station is smaller than Victoria but very colourful, and helps service the very crowded and historic downtown area of Mumbai. Sadly, in 2008 there was a terrorist attack on Mumbai, involving gunmen shooting randomly at the crowds in Victoria Station, with many killed. The trains were soon running again, with one of the terrorists caught alive; he is under arrest and awaiting trial at the time of writing.

I should clarify that, in the mad way names get changed these days, Victoria Station is now officially called Chhatrapati Shivaji Terminal, or CHT for short, but the golden statue of an angel remains on top of the grand structure. Clearly, it is not one of Queen Victoria or it would have been dealt with in the campaign for Indian independence, a campaign opposed by Churchill to the bitter end. Perhaps it was his memories of the trains in India he rode as a young subaltern, complete with a bathtub in the portage, that caused him to want to retain British rule till as late as 1947.

Kolkata and New Delhi also have interesting stations but nothing quite like the 115-year-old Victoria Station.

⑪ Two to go, and the modern Kuala Lumpur Sentral Station makes the cut, with its diversity in so many ways and its dominance of steel and glass. It is the new main station for the national capital of Malaysia and scores well on maximum convenience for passengers, with plenty of capacity put in place at inception, a couple of years ago. Its diversity comes in catering for local suburban trains, as well as for the metre-gauge system from Singapore through KL to Ipoh, Georgetown and on to the Thai border and beyond.

In addition, KL Sentral has a standard-gauge connection for the 160 kph trains to KL International Airport. This service is tailor-made for international passengers with heavy baggage; it is clean and comfortable, swift and spacious. Furthermore, the signage is such as to be easily utilised by people arriving in Malaysia for the first time. Baggage can be actually booked in at the downtown Sentral Station and not seen again until arrival at the ultimate destination; at least that is what the system is designed to deliver and it has worked for me at least twice.

Critics might say this station is too modern to be added to the list of Top Twelve stations of the world, but it certainly has dimension and diversity. No doubt it will develop a degree of dignity and gravitas, and it points the way for when the hard decisions have to be made to replace beautiful but overcrowded original central stations. The old main terminus in Kuala Lumpur looks deserted these days but is a superb all-white colonial structure serving as a suburban station.

The Malaysian railway system is leading the world in metre-gauge railway systems in many ways. It remains government owned yet enjoys a good priority of capital allocations to allow upgrading, at least until the global financial crisis hit in 2008.

(12) Last but not least is the grand old dame on my home hunting ground, namely Sydney's Central Station, a construction of local sandstone, the largest station in the southern hemisphere, and in its centenary phase.

Central Station has its own set of secrets deep underground, including the mystery ghost platforms Number 26 and Number 27, accessible through an unmarked door past some building debris. These platforms are perfectly constructed but have never been visited by trains of any kind, as the tracks have not yet been laid or electric overhead wiring installed. The theory goes that they stand ready to service Sydney–Canberra–Melbourne high-speed trains but, given the surplus capacity in the main section of Sydney Central Platforms 1 to 10, this is unlikely.

Nevertheless, I suppose it is useful to have some surplus capacity for possible future usage. In the meantime, the other 25 platforms give sterling service day in and day out for every kind of passenger train. This includes the Indian Pacific to Perth, the XPT services to Brisbane, Dubbo and Melbourne, and a range of regional commuter and local suburban services.

On special occasions, the Sydney Central grand concourse has been used as a ballroom and even as special exhibition space. Today it is much cleaner than it has ever been, and from the main concourse there is now access to the light-rail, or tramways, service to Darling Harbour and the inner suburbs beyond.

The clock tower at Central Station, Sydney.

It is not generally realised that the original terminus of the NSW Government Railways (NSWGR) was built on a temporary basis, but went on to serve for 20 years. It became known as Redfern Station but was in fact Sydney Station (the first), southwest of Devonshire Street, and so the likes of the Temora Mail, the Melbourne Express (conveying Mark Twain) and many others, all departed from Redfern.

Sydney Station (the second) was right alongside and on the southwest side but abutting Devonshire Street, broadly south of the separate and

Sydney Central as colourful hub for fans

One Saturday evening in winter my family and I visited Sydney during school holidays and then caught the train back from Central Station to Mascot from Sydney Central, after a walk around Darling Harbour. The place had a real buzz about it even though it was the middle of a weekend. This was due to the fact that there was a big rugby test on at Olympic Park, Homebush, and the Sydney Swans were playing at the Sydney Cricket Ground, so there was hustle, bustle and flashes of colour everywhere as supporters wore their team stripes proudly. In the case of the Swans, bright red and white dominated, showing a commitment to the Australian rules football team in a city otherwise known for various rugby codes and soccer, while clashing colours emanated from the different rugby and rugby league supporters.

All of this was topped off by a special vintage train operated by the *3801* Group, but on this occasion diesel-hauled, which swept along the through platforms of Central and on into the underground system to gain access to the Sydney Harbour Bridge and the northern suburbs line to Hornsby.

There is much to behold at Sydney Central, helped greatly by the fact it was built at the turn of the nineteenth century into the 20th century, and was able to take advantage of improved design and construction capability and extra space through the resumption of an old cemetery on the location.

The Mortuary platform that used to handle funeral trains to Rookwood Cemetery still stands, but perhaps mainly ghosts use it now, along with the odd special charter train and special event.

magnificent Sydney Mortuary Station. Ultimately it grew to have a dozen or so platforms during its 30 years of activity. A huge hay shed formed part of the railway yards and all platforms were terminating, but with some provision for extension.

In a display of real vision, the decision was made to build Sydney Station (the third) closer to the city proper, with a capacity to handle both terminating country and interstate trains, as well as through electric suburban trains. Ramps and bridges were also included to bring electric trains up to the concourse level. Sydney Central, as it became known, opened officially in 1906 and is not only the biggest station in the southern hemisphere, whichever way you look at it, but has platforms on four different levels.

With its cleverly designed flyover junctions (more often called flying junctions) for suburban trains, and its switchover junctions for all non-suburban inter-urban and regional/long-distance trains, it is well set for its next 100 years. The light railway, or tram, level was also a bonus, but remains to be further developed with a modern network. Located under a giant awning, this part was well designed decades ago and, after a break of 30 years, is back in use with modern trams. A bonus for Central Station is the recent overall upgrade, including lifts for all suburban platforms and extra access, along with a big clean-up. We can thank the Sydney 2000 Olympic Games for this.

The time on the grand clock has been frozen at ten minutes to two to allow a complete overhaul and clean of the famous Sydney Central Station clock tower, as you may have heard on the *Great Train Show*. It is a long climb to the top of this tower but worth doing in every way.

So there it is: the Top Twelve railway stations of the world in this phase of the 21st century, all of them but one with relatively recent revamps and handling larger and larger volumes of traffic, as the world returns to rail with a vengeance.

I acknowledge the list is Tim Fischer's chosen stations on a raft of subjective criteria. The good news is that, with fine tuning, these stations are

Top Twelve Railway Stations

1 St Pancras, London

2 Berlin Hauptbahnhof (Hbf)

3 Milano Centrale (Milan)

4 Gare du Nord, Paris

5 Gare de Lyon, Paris

6 Atocha, Madrid

7 Grand Central, New York

8 Union Station Washington

9 Retiro complex, Buenos Aires

10 Victoria/Chhatrapati Shivaji
    Terminal, Mumbai

11 Sentral Station, Kuala Lumpur

12 Central Station, Sydney

able to handle almost unlimited expansion away from peak hour, and even some expansion during peak hour. The twelve also have a level of comfort and efficiency that even the best airport terminal in the world cannot match.

Further, wonderful but grime-creating steam locomotives rarely visit the twelve today. Likewise, human beings that smoke are severely restricted, so the ambience and cleanliness stay brighter longer in all twelve. Most continue to look spick and span, even late on Friday afternoon in the middle of the longest peak period of the week.

For many of the solitary single dwellers in modern society, the large station is also a good interface with fellow mankind, as, once on board the commuter train (as opposed to long-distance trains), the worldwide unwritten rule of no eye contact and no conversation takes over. Interface zones are highly desirable, and I think we need more oyster bars and long champagne bars to enhance this dimension, and provide easy meeting places, as the twelve grand stations impress into the 21st century.

Further, I hope they will all have quality bookshops that stock a certain book. More particularly I hope they keep updating and revamping to cater for increasing millions of travellers but never by destruction of their overall original facades or grand core structure.

STATION DESIGN PRIORITIES

In considering all aspects of what makes railway stations, or terminals, work best, one cardinal rule pertains: the priorities of the passenger ought to be paramount. This rule applies to everything from good signage to clean washrooms and toilets; above all else, they need platforms of adequate width for safety and comprehensive protection from the weather.

At Sofia Central Station, in the capital of Bulgaria, the roof above Platform 1 is so high as to be useless. At about 40 metres above platform level (somewhere towards the clouds) wind and rain are certainly able to reach all passengers standing on the platform. It is an example of monumental Stalinesque Bulgarian architecture, and the good news is that it is about to be demolished.

In recent years some signs designating 'Meeting Place' have been put up at airport terminals and railway station concourses, but begging the question of whether said meeting place is one of several in the locality. I leave you with one final thought about helping passengers around the world: all 'Meeting Places' should have one letter of the alphabet added, for example 'Meeting Place A', 'Meeting Place B', and so forth. Even when there is only one, it should still be denoted as 'Meeting Place A', as it helps bring clarity to meeting-up instructions.

Too often you hear the phrase: 'You cannot miss it.' Often I say meet at the end of Platform 10 (generally at ten past the hour to reinforce) but, alas, this can come unstuck. The mighty and haughty Gare de Lyon has a crazy platform numbering system and, by the way, no clear end of Platform 10. Best to meet on the grand staircase into Le Train Bleu, I think, then proceed inside for a long lunch.

THE IMPACT OF RAIL AND HIGH-SPEED RAIL

France is different, the French are different and of course 'Vive la différence', and so the French Revolution imposed the decimal approach to time with a ten-hour day. Around the bloody year of 1793 they adopted 100 minutes in each hour — ten hours in each day! Just over ten years later, in 1805, the great Napoleon ordered a return to a 24-hour day and 60 minutes in each hour. (Interestingly, Napoleon was actually born in Italy and the Italian unifier Garibaldi was technically born in France, albeit in an area that swapped around over the centuries.)

Later in the nineteenth century the French had another go at being different, trying to establish Paris Mean Time (PMT) based on the longitude through Paris, which lies just over two degrees or a little more than nine minutes east of the longitude anchored firmly on the Greenwich Observatory (and now the Millennium Dome), the basis for the long-established Greenwich Mean Time (GMT).

The 1884 conference in the USA on the matter of world time voted in favour of GMT over PMT. I guess we were lucky it was not CMT — Chicago Mean Time — as the Yanks knew how to grab key positions. Guess which country is '1' for international phone dial? The USA of course.

Notwithstanding Napoleon's intervention, most cities and towns went with their own time at the start of the nineteenth century, loosely tied to solar time. This was the case in every large country in the world. Even in Great Britain there was a ten-minute time difference between London and Bristol as Isambard Kingdom Brunel rolled out his Great

Right side, left side

There was another dynamic flowing from the French Revolution, which created a real impact on rail and is often overlooked among all the brutal glory of the overworked guillotine.

This particular twist affected the world and really was a most curious one; it arose from the need for aristocrats and others at risk to fit into the mob. This resulted in everyone scrambling to pass on horse or horse and buggy on the right side of oncoming traffic so they could avoid being noticed and picked out for the guillotine. Until then, worldwide perhaps, but certainly in sword-bearing Britain and Italy, one passed on the left side of oncoming traffic, to leave the right sword arm well positioned for any eventuality.

Today this phenomenon dominates a majority of the countries in the world, with Sweden the last big country to switch in 1967 to French-side driving. Western Samoa switched to British side in 2009, and curiously the French SNCF massive railway system operates this side. From inception and even with the TGV double track, the SNCF passes on the left (or British) side of oncoming trains. Likewise Belgium and Italy, but I vividly recall whenever crossing into Germany, trains swiftly switch sides. Of course this situation could not be tolerated with the Paris Metro, which operates its double track on the French side.

Western Railway to connect the two places. May I acknowledge here the writings of Clive Cookson in the *Financial Times* for reminding me of the above; he has highlighted the confusion this created in the early days of rail.

So once upon a time the measurement of time was very different to now. Not only did each town and city have its own scale allowing a close relationship to solar time, in part driven by the need to maximise the use of daylight hours, many Protestant countries also avoided the Gregorian calendar, originally devised by Pope Gregory XIII in 1582.

It was the advent of the railway that brought about standardisation of the measurement of time worldwide. As rail networks grew rapidly in the lead-up to the middle of the nineteenth century, railway operators found it impossible to devise timetables and templates, when different towns along the route had variations of ten minutes here and 25 minutes there.

The British led the way, in 1856 adopting a common time zone across Scotland, Wales and the Home Counties, with the Greenwich Observatory longitude being used as 'time zero' and hence the term 'Greenwich Mean Time' or 'GMT' arising. Westminster formally locked this into law in 1880, just ahead of crucial meetings in the USA.

In the USA, the various rail companies had collided with the same problem, and by the 1880s they had had enough, especially as the confusion could lead to deadly train collisions when using time-controlled working on single tracks. In a bold move for those times, in 1883 the USA adopted just four time zones across the country.

Meanwhile, the east–west giant of a country, namely Russia, for a period went to 'Moscow time only' right across the huge expanse. Later this part-European and part-Asian country eventually adopted eleven time zones.

The conference of officials from 25 countries met in the USA in 1884 and formally adopted the concept of measuring according to GMT, along with the concept of north–south time zones. One of the convenors of this timely conference was Sir Stanford Fleming, at the time the Chief

Engineer of the Canadian Pacific Railway. He is credited with first drawing up the map proposing 24 time zones and thus laid the foundation for the successful enduring outcome of the conference.

Along the International Date Line, stretching in theory from the North Pole to the South Pole, you meet the one day difference on the globe. The zones allow for some bends in this key longitudinal line; for example, it changes course through the Bering Strait to ensure all of Alaska is on one side and all of Russia on the other. It was probably just as well the USA purchased Alaska from a near-broke Russia in 1867 for $7.2 million in the real-estate deal of the century, if not the millennium, placing Russia entirely on one side of the Date Line and the USA on the other. The Date Line is not set in concrete; indeed in 2011 Samoa switched to the Australasian side, abolishing 30 December 2011 in the process.

The advent of rail thus had its first impact, rendering a huge change to the measurement of daily time worldwide. It is a pity that every year since railways sorted out the issue of time, they have struggled to adhere to it as printed in their timetables, with only a few exceptions such as in Japan and Switzerland. To avoid fines for late running, these days companies often expand the definition of 'on time running' from within two minutes to within ten minutes or more. This is not true in — you guessed it — Japan and Switzerland, but it is in many other railway realms.

The second huge impact of rail was the mobility it conferred on people and goods when suddenly a two-day coach trip was reduced to five hours or less by train. London–Manchester came down from around 20 hours by horse and coach — generally over two days of nine to ten hours' travel, total journey time being 35 to 36 hours — to just five hours by train in 1852. By 1914 this was further reduced to three hours 30 minutes. Furthermore, the early-period train trips usually cost less than the coach fares, so much so that soon enough long-distance coaches were wiped out.

Suddenly it was possible to make day trips to London from the Midlands, albeit long days with early starts and late-evening returns. It was physically upending of the status quo and went hand in hand with the introduction of the telegram system. Telegrams and telegraphic systems had commenced operating around 1845, spurred along by the advent of the railway and the need to manage rail traffic.

Later on, in 1872, the telegraphic system started operating between London and Sydney. Again suddenly news which took around twelve weeks to travel this corridor could do so in less than twelve hours (one sector in the Northern Territory initially was by courier), and in theory in less than twelve minutes, a huge revolution in communications. In Australia the need to build an overland telegraph line from Adelaide to Darwin led to the discovery of Heavitree Gap, which cuts north–south through the MacDonnell Ranges, near where bustling Alice Springs is these days. This was a very helpful route over the mountains and in turn this gap has been used by rail for over 80 years, initially using narrow gauge and now by the world's newest transcontinental, the Adelaide–Darwin Stephenson standard gauge modern railway.

While the invention of rail conferred mobility, this was not all positive, as, for example, outbreaks of infectious diseases were facilitated by it. Conversely outbreaks of that phenomenon known as the 'Great Exhibition' took off through many railway realms at capital-city hubs. London launched a huge exhibition in 1851 and Sydney a few years later, after the rail links were put in place. Many country people suddenly had the opportunity to make their first-ever trips to the big capital city, often nicknamed Down Under as the 'big smoke'.

Landed gentry were greatly nervous that this phenomenon would encourage revolution and disturb the order of things, in particular the maintenance of the style and luxury to which they had become accustomed.

In most countries, railway did the opposite, and in fact helped unify countries and provide cohesion, with the exception of Russia. German unification was driven along by the various early rail links between the key states, helping to build domestic trade and military links. Soon Germany was at war, in 1870 against France, then in 1914 and 1939 against the world.

Belgium and Italy used early rail development to help build national unity and identity. Both Australia and Canada had to promise transcontinental railways to their west coasts before their western-side people would come on board to support federation.

RAIL IMPACTS THE GREAT WAR

Rail was used in the American Civil War as the Unionists drove south, converting the southern broad gauge to the northern Stephenson standard gauge, as referred to earlier. But its impact in World World I was immense

In the 1914–1918 Great War or 'War to End All Wars', Germany opened up two fronts but took decisive action to end hostilities on the eastern front against Russia by the curious use of rail. As Christian Wolmar details in his comprehensive book *Blood, Iron and Gold*, Lenin was invited to board a sealed train for a safe run from Switzerland, where he was in exile, across Germany and onto a Baltic Sea steamer, to ensure his return to Russia.

Upon his arrival at St Petersburg, Lenin gave a speech and soon the Bolshevik Revolution was under way, and the Czar overthrown, banished and later murdered. In power in Moscow, Lenin quickly ended hostilities with Germany in late 1917. Rail was then used to quickly shift 42 divisions of the German Army from Russia and the eastern front to positions in France on the western front, ready for the big breakout. This last big attack on the Allies unfolded in March and April 1918.

This German 'Operation Michael' did not reckon on the do-or-die fight-back mentality of the Allied forces and, in particular, the holistic planning of giant leaders in the field, such as the Canadian Arthur Currie and the Australian John Monash. Both factored rail into their planning, especially for resupply and strategic positioning. On 4 July 1918 Monash conducted the Battle of Hamel using 1000 American soldiers from the Prairie Division out of Illinois, who had been brought forward by rail. To this he added 6000 Australians, plus a masterful set of battle orders devised, written out and explained by Monash personally to all senior levels. The result was victory with few casualties in just 93 minutes, and at last a battle plan showing others how to do it.

To this day a break of gauge exists between Germany and Poland but not the Ukraine and Russia. This was a key break of gauge that impacted on the vital resupply efforts of Germany on the eastern front in both World War I and World War II. The need to transport all freight and munitions from one gauge train to the other caused bottlenecks and delays.

Josef Stalin used rail constantly to mix and match, or more accurately 'unmatch', the population, ordering thousands of European Russians to move east to build Moscow's hold in the Siberian wastelands, with, as time would tell, mixed outcomes. Harbin in China was developed in Czar broad gauge by Communist Russia as a major rail centre, and as a shortcut to the Pacific and Vladivostok, instead of the more northerly route on completely Russian soil via Khabarovsk. Later Harbin was captured by the Japanese and the gauge standardised, then it went back to Russia for eight years after World War II, before returning to its original country, namely China.

A mobility of large armies that a Duke of Wellington or a Napoleon could only dream about was conferred by the advent of the railways.

COMMUTING

Around the world, cities large and small have developed massive rail commuter systems over the last 175 years or so; in 1836 the London and Greenwich Railway opened as arguably the world's first commuter railway. It was in 1863 that the first underground railway in the world was opened. The line of the Metropolitan Railway linked Paddington and Farringdon Streets in the City of London, and by 1884 that had been extended to create the Circle Line, with one rail company having the right to operate clockwise and another anti-clockwise, resulting in various points of acute congestion where other tracks and trains used part of the Circle. Eventually mergers and other moves prevailed to get the operation sorted.

It was not long before the phenomenon of commuting daily by rail took off around the larger metropolitan cities, initially in a haphazard way, but soon enough by underground and elevated railways, with Paris leading the way — and to this day, with its metro and RER mixture of modern services. The RER was introduced into congested Paris in the 1960s and now has five lines operating. It is generally at a lower level than the Metro and allows an express-type approach, dashing from point A to point B with no stops, whereas the Metro, closer to the surface, might have five stops on the same corridor section.

People in big cities no longer had to live on top of each other or in factory areas, where smoke belched forth from foundries and smelters. Likewise livestock markets and abattoir areas could be avoided or moved out of the city, as often became the case.

For regular commuters, the initial radius from the centre of the CBD, often best denoted by the location of the General Post Office (GPO), was some 8 to 16 kilometres (5 to 10 miles). Today many people think nothing of commuting daily from distant suburbs up to 80 to 100 kilometres (50 to 60 miles) from the GPO by fast or reasonably fast double-decker 'heavy rail' electric trains.

Initially around the world the steam tank engine was the workhorse of suburban networks, but as many networks were built partly underground, even in the early years, the switch was on to electricity-powered propulsion as quickly as possible. And in some places towns and cities began to twin and supply residential suburbs or jobs for each other. Of course, the story of passenger and freight rail began with the twinning (linking with direct rail) of Liverpool and Manchester, which rapidly proved to be to the benefit of both. Glasgow and Edinburgh are another example of twinning but sadly for years with an average train service lacking real modernity; however, recent years have seen some improvements in frequency and also now in change of routes.

Much smaller than Johannesburg, Pretoria is a perfect commute distance of 50 kilometres north of the big Chicago-type South African hub.

For decades Pretoria, the national capital of South Africa, was a dormitory centre for the big metropolis just to the south, although in more recent years this has switched around by degrees, with commuters travelling in both directions in peak hours, the dream of every rail operator. The Anglo Cape gauge line between the two is very busy, with everything from commuter trains to large freight trains and even the right royal luxurious Blue Train.

Bombing Pretoria Station

Once, when visiting Pretoria as Australian Deputy Prime Minister and Trade Minister, I asked then Vice President Thabo Mbeki when he last visited Pretoria Railway Station, as I had been for a jog past it that morning. Mbeki paused and smiled and replied that I should not ask this question as it was about 20 years ago and he (Mbeki) was trying to blow the place up, in a manner of speaking. No doubt he was having a lend of me but, chastened, I quickly turned to the trade-policy topics set down for discussion.

In the 21st century Pretoria and Johannesburg now have a new fast commuter train service, the Gautrain, operating at speeds of up to 160 kph on standard-gauge track. Significantly, rather than graft a new service onto the old narrow-gauge system, a whole new generation of high-speed tracks in Stephenson standard are being provided for the Gautrain, complete with the direct cross-link to the Johannesburg International Airport. The race was on to have the airport line operating for the World Cup in South Africa in the middle of 2010, and Gautrain won that race. The Gautrain represents visionary thinking in 'deepest, distant Africa', and well ahead of many other southern-hemisphere countries.

While rail quickly galvanised mobility for people over short, medium and long distances, this has not been the case everywhere. The true potential of rail was not realised in places where political leadership over the decades did not understand this mode of transport and the need to develop and deliver holistic transport strategies. In short, where they 'got rail' the big cities have enjoyed huge advantages and better quality of life, compared with the 'all motor car' cities of which there were too many in the 20th century, particularly in developed countries such as the USA.

It is emerging that cities going for holistic approaches to public transport including a mix of modern light rail, heavy rail, bus and trolley bus, along with hubbing and seamless intermodal junctions, are jumping ahead. This is especially so where there is a progressive government that can plan and facilitate delivery.

An example of 21st-century enlightenment is Phoenix in the USA, which opened a modern light rail in late 2008. Soon all usage projections were exceeded by 15 per cent and large extensions are now planned. One-third of passengers were new to public transport; better still, around 40 per cent use the network for non-work trips, as detailed in an excellent article by John Diers in *Trains* magazine. He notes accurately, the success has been by having good hub destinations served by the network, such as sporting arenas, an airport and a university campus.

Phoenix can be very hot. It is a typical 'sunrise' modern desert city previously wedded to the motor car, but give commuters a reasonably priced, reasonable service and watch how usage changes. Lessons for all transport planners abound from this — and from the busy Trinity Express that operates between Dallas and Fort Worth. In fifteen years since inception it has established huge patronage, helped by adding an airport connection.

Edmonton in Canada gained a lasting benefit from staging the Commonwealth Games in 1978, with the successful installation of light rail; likewise Calgary with its system expanded for the Winter Olympics in 1988.

Artificial national capital cities such as Brasilia and Canberra should have been the catalysts for superb rail links to the nearest large coastal port cities but curiously this was not the case, at least to date. Both cities owe their existence to balancing two giant rival cities, San Paulo and Rio de

Janeiro in the case of Brazil, and Sydney and Melbourne in the case of Australia. The problem was one of timing: if these two new capitals had been developed in the nineteenth century, before the advent of the motor car and modern truck or lorry, I venture to suggest rail would have played a bigger role.

DECENTRALISATION

Off the back of the mobility provided by rail came decentralisation, as both a catchcry for regional- and rural-based parliamentarians and congressmen and a public-policy priority for various governments. Many mistakes were made with the implementation of decentralisation, as we will see. Nevertheless, the concept of rail driving decentralisation was broadly the right way to go and at times this has involved national security concerns; at other times it has been a forlorn attempt to relieve the big cities of their overcrowding.

Decentralisation came to the fore worldwide after World War II and during the Cold War, with nuclear threats abounding. Many national governments wanted to decentralise away from the big coastal port cities; others were driven by postwar international boundary alignments, so Bonn sprang up or greatly expanded as the national capital of West Germany, until the Berlin Wall came down and reunification occurred in 1990, and the capital reverted to Berlin.

Milton Keynes north of London was a much-vaunted 'new town' built on a good set of rail connections but never seemed to quite get things sorted. In my view, from a couple of visits — albeit last century — Milton Keynes seems to lack a timeless British mixture of old, or at least retro, and new character; rather the buildings and layout seemed almost too contrived and without diversity and dignity.

The NSW State Government was one of the few in the southern hemisphere that made a serious attempt at decentralisation, especially between 1965 and 1976 when Sir John Fuller was the inaugural Minister for Decentralisation. While he was in the style of a smooth Tory grandee in the antipodes, he was also both a good strategic thinker and as sharp as a tack; further, his word was his bond.

This was an era of 'new town' approaches and so the NSW cabinet chose Bathurst–Orange, an area about 160 kilometres west of Sydney, over the Blue Mountains, as its first growth centre.

Choosing an inland national capital

On the day a group of parliamentarians came to inspect the potential of Albury–Wodonga for the location of the national capital of Australia (which had been operating temporarily in Melbourne, from 1901 to 1927), a huge red dust storm blew in from the Riverina in the west and shrouded Albury–Wodonga in choking dust and semi darkness.

So thick was the dust that the delegates were greatly deterred by the otherwise attractive and convenient location. Albury–Wodonga was effectively eliminated from contention then and there. Ultimately, Canberra, further north on the Monaro Plains and on the Molonglo and Murrumbidgee Rivers, was selected.

One of the first departmental units to be moved from Sydney to Bathurst was the Central Mapping Authority, and so a special train was hired to give the public servants and their families involved a free daytrip to Bathurst. All went well until the train arrived at Bathurst around 11.00am on a clear, sunny day. Alas, there were 2 inches of frost and ice on the platform from an overnight freeze. To top it off, late in the afternoon as the train was loading for the return journey to Sydney, there was a snap deluge. Despite these portents, the move went ahead, as well as the move of the NSW Department of Agriculture HQ to Orange, and both relocations to this day are adjudged as being successful.

Under the John Fuller policy approach, factories were encouraged to up stakes in crowded Sydney and move to the inland of New South Wales or up and down the somewhat empty coastline. Akubra Hats, of worldwide fame, moved to Kempsey, along the mid-north coast of New South Wales, and has never looked back.

The NSW Government also joined with the Federal and Victorian State Governments to produce the Albury–Wodonga Development Corporation and the Albury–Wodonga National Growth Centre project. These twin towns are located on either side of the Murray River on the NSW–Victoria border, about halfway between Sydney and Melbourne.

However, the missing link, or links, in the approach was the failure to build fast rail connections to these growth centres and along key coastal corridors, especially as Shinkansen and later TGV technology was developing and readily available. One suspects if all the subsidies for development and growth at Bathurst–Orange and Albury–Wodonga had been channelled into offering one-hour TGV or HSR train services back to the coast, then solid population growth would have really taken off.

In Italy a policy of 'scatter the factories', in part using European Union (EU) subsidies, has been followed in recent decades, in the main alongside Red Arrow and other improved rail corridors. The area around Chiusi Centrale, halfway between Rome and Florence, is dotted with large new factories, or relatively new factories.

Way up north in the Valtellina region of Italy at Sondrio and Grosotto there are EU regional subsidies at work and a further scattering of factories just short of the Swiss border but near good regional rail connections.

If the last 50 years could be turned back and if the USA, Australia, Argentina, Canada and South Africa, along with most other large countries, had switched to fast passenger rail with an eye to boosting decentralisation, then coastal city population congestion would undoubtedly have been eased, by some degrees.

HIGH-SPEED RAIL (HSR)

The most revolutionary revamp of rail unfolded in the last half of the 20th century: it was the operation of trains at a sustained speed of over 240 kph (150 mph), which has now carried rail forward into the 21st century. The advent of fast and super fast high-speed rail rescued rail as a mighty mode of passenger transport from collapse and oblivion. The French with the TGV and the Japanese with the Shinkansen lead the world in fast trains, upending transport patterns and greatly boosting efficiency as well as better environmental aspects of transport. These systems, and later the ICE in Germany, Thalys through to Belgium and Holland, plus the Eurostar through the Chunnel, underpinned a worldwide swing back to rail and rail revitalisation. The AVE network in Spain has a route mileage of HSR longer than any other country in the world, until the huge developments in China.

The impact of this new genre of rail can be summarised fourfold.

(1) Firstly, the treasuries of the governments committed to high-speed rail projects had to get used to some big funding asks. Private enterprise could not launch these systemic projects without considerable government seed funding and beyond.

The state-dominant culture of Japan and France greatly helped massage this through these two democracies, along with the help of early success. High-speed rail took off virtually from inception, with huge passenger increases and resultant closure of some domestic air routes.

If George Stephenson was the father of modern rail, then Shinji Sogo was the trailblazing father of high-speed rail. As president of Japanese National Railways (JNR) he knew the costly switch from narrow gauge to standard, if not broad gauge, had to be made.

However, to get the first big project from Tokyo to Osaka going, Sogo had to deceive the Japanese Diet (parliament). As he told a senior offsider, he could not directly ask for the full 300 billion yen or the opportunity would be lost forever; it was simply too big an amount for the Diet to swallow first up. I quote 'Old Man Thunder', as was Sogo's nickname:

What you must understand is that not only would the Diet reject an appropriation for 300 billion yen, but those short-sighted politicians would demand that we go back to the less expensive plan to simply improve the narrow-gauge system. The standard-gauge project would be dead, perhaps forever, and our country would be denied an opportunity of a lifetime. You and I must not let that happen.

We now know the world's first high-speed train project of moment was massaged through the Diet on a cost estimate that was deceptively halved for the exercise of getting the project up. An untidy if not illegal approach, but it led to possibly the best decision ever made by the long-reigning Liberal Democrat (LDP) Government in Japan, and the Bullet train, or Shinkansen, soon became an exemplar to the world.

The big impact in a financial sense was on the treasuries and taxpayers, not only in France and Japan, but soon enough Germany as well, with its fast ICE train system.

The second big impact of fast rail was that train travel became popular again. It was seen as cool and climate-friendly, and above all else it was practical and punctual. In France, the separate high-standard tracks that had to be built ensured local passenger traffic and freight traffic was never allowed near the TGV pathways, so there were few delays due to mixed-speed traffic. Occasionally delays might occur on entry into the large rail yards of, say Gare de Lyon or Gare du Nord, especially if there is a delay in platform allocations, but this happens rarely.

Millions flocked to fast rail for their travel needs. In fact over the 45 years the Shinkansen has operated (since 1964), some 4000 million passengers have been carried without injury to any of them, and in Europe fast rail has enjoyed 10 per cent annual growth rates over the last decade, as highlighted by the International Union of Railways (UIC) from its HQ in Paris. Business meetings are being held on ICE trains, and on the Eurostar in special conference-room cabins there is full internet connectivity on most routes. And you can eat reasonable-quality meals — but, alas, nothing to match Le Mistral dining car of yesteryear.

③ The third impact is an inflow of the best research engineers and other experts, drawn by an industry seen to be going places. Careers in the rail industry are fashionable again, including for business leaders. One example is the Italian syndicate planning to use EU liberalisation to start competing into and out of Paris on routes through to Milan and beyond.

Many European business leaders are behind the initiatives and routes to and through the key hub of Milan have been selected first up for the new service.

Cabin crew and other positions associated with fast rail engender pride and professionalism, albeit with the odd exception among staff, especially

Washroom availability

In and around Rome there is a longstanding policy of providing almost zero convenient conveniences. I am told it is to force the public to visit restaurants and coffee bars, where they will then feel obliged to buy something. Only in St Peters Square are large-scale public toilet and washroom facilities provided.

The Trevi Fountain area, the Pantheon plaza and Termini have almost zero toilet accessibility, but in breaking news, after decades a set of semi-public toilets have actually arrived on the ground-floor main concourse level at Termini. They are, of course, in the new Eurostar passenger lounge and you have to have a first-class ticket or lounge membership or enough bluff in a business suit to be allowed to go in. It does beat the alternatives: a 500-metre walk downstairs and around the corner in one direction to a pay-to-go. The Romans of yesteryear built big sewerage pipelines to the Tiber; the skill set is clearly needed again.

when blizzards bring on breakdowns and long delays, as happened with Eurostar in the lead-up to Christmas 2009. Nevertheless, a fast-train passenger requires a lot less attention than an aeroplane passenger — no seatbelts for starters — and the setting and ambience are more relaxing than the cabin of a crowded airbus or jumbo. The pride in the high-speed rail workforce is both a good thing and an under-appreciated one. It is a phenomenon at all levels of the HSR workforce.

(4) The fourth big impact relates to the huge revamps and improvements at key terminals such as St Pancras and Gare du Nord, and even a modest upgrade at Roma Termini driven by Eurostar and the Red Arrow services. There is no way the millions would have been found for these upgrades short of the introduction of a new genre of rail.

There are smart railway lounges aimed at the upmarket and business traveller at Berlin, Dresden, Frankfurt, Munich and many other places in Germany, but also Austria, Italy and Spain. All have opened railway-station lounges to cater for premium customers of fast rail — a far cry from the hard benches and bare bricks of freezing waiting rooms that once dominated at railway stations the world over, large and small.

The previous chapter dealt in more detail with this, but revamped old stations and new fast-rail ones, sometimes a mixture of both, have resulted in some stunning architecture and buildings that will last for centuries to come.

DEATH AND RAILWAYS

Railways in the early construction years racked up huge death tolls due to accidents, especially with tunnelling. When forced labour, such as prisoners of war, are used to build railways, the death toll can be so bad as to earn the railway a name in perpetuity — such as the Burma Death Railway. The Japanese ordered this railway built by whatever method to connect Bangkok with Rangoon, a distance of 415 kilometres (258 miles) over rough jungle terrain.

More than 90,000 Asians forced to work on this project at the height of World War II in 1942 and 1943 died of starvation, disease and overwork or were killed by cruel guards; 16,000 Allied prisoners of war also died of the same treatment. Parts of the Thai end of the railway are in use this day, but the key Konyu Cutting, or Hellfire Pass, is now a superb memorial. To walk through Konyu Cutting even on a hot day leads to eerie feelings that are sad to the core.

Trains have another strong association with death. Millions of Jews were transported by Nazi-organised trains from Paris, Rome and many other European cities to Auschwitz and other concentration camps, where they were despatched to their deaths in another brutal chapter of World War II.

The rail tracks leading in through the main gate of Auschwitz have been deliberately preserved and add to the chilling atmosphere. They are a sharp reminder of this deadly misuse of rail transport. Through chance we know Hugo Lowy was one of the transported Jews who bravely resisted brutality and was bashed to death. His family helped restore an A2 four-wheel rail wagon, which now stands in isolation on the outer loop at Auschwitz Camp 11, in salute of the thousands of Hungarian Jews and others killed there. Hugo's youngest son, Frank Lowy of Sydney, with others helped dedicate it in 2010. The two small plaques attached say it all.

The plaque at Gare de l'Est in Paris recording the fact that 70,000 Jewish French citizens were despatched to concentrations camps from this station in World War II is worth not only noting again, but if visiting the main concourse, pausing in front of in order to take in the enormity of this movement of men, women and children. Then there was the famous Kasztner Train, which in 1944 conveyed Jews by agreement and payment to the Nazis from Hungary to Switzerland. More recently, on a brighter note, railways have saved lives, as was the case with what I would dub as the 'Sarajevo Life In Death Express (SLIDE)' or, if you like, the 'Great Slide Railway'. From 1992 until the end of 1995, beautiful Sarajevo was under siege and faced daily shelling and bombing; thousands were killed in the city. This railway allowed thousands of people to slide into

17/06/2010

On the 'SLIDE railway' underneath Sarajevo Airport. (Tim Fischer)

a famous narrow tunnel near Sarajevo Airport and, once underground, pass in relative safety along a full 700-metres of 80-centimetre-gauge underground track, many people pushing rail wagons laden with vital food and medical supplies. In fact it was two-way traffic, allowing people in and out of surrounded Sarajevo, as well as vital supplies into Sarajevo from the Mostar area and the coast.

The tunnel and mini railway were built mainly by the Bosnian army, and they became the only reasonably regular way in and out of Sarajevo for people and goods, including those injured and needing evacuation. The real problem was getting to and from the tunnel; most of this movement took place during the night to avoid snipers, rocket grenade, mortar and artillery shelling mounted by the Serbian forces.

One family maybe more than any other contributed to this brave endeavour: the Kolar family, who gave up their house to the project so it could be used as a disguised point of entry and exit, with air ventilation pumps housed there. They then physically manned the operation for long periods. After this modern-day siege was finally over, with the signing of the Dayton Accords, the Kolar family moved quickly to preserve the key entry point and part of the tunnel, creating a raw and meaningful museum.

Edis Kolar is rightly proud of the family's endeavours. The 'Sarajevo Life In Death Express', he told me, at its peak had 24 railway wagons built and designed for human push–pull operation, but of the 24 normally four were out of service for maintenance and repair.

Today the section opened to the public has a quiet dignity about it with its beautiful raw timbers continuing to bear up, and the narrow-gauge track in good shape. This tunnel that turned the tide, allowing Bosnia to stop Serb annexation of Sarajevo by a narrow margin, is absolutely worth preserving so that future mankind can learn from it and hopefully avoid creating the need for this type of temporary railway again in this new century or ever.

The threads that hold an uneasy peace together in the cauldron of the Balkans are few enough: inter-faith dialogue is one key ingredient; expanding tourism and an accurate portrayal of history are also vital. In this, the related role of railways large and small should never be ignored. While you cannot ride the 'Sarajevo Life In Death Express', you can do the next best thing — slide into and walk the underground track and tunnel through which many thousands of different faiths passed, to an uncertain situation at their destination. After observing the conditions, you might like to make a donation in salute of some very brave people.

Of course it was at Sarajevo that the starting gun for World War I was fired with the assassination of Archduke Ferdinand and his wife on the afternoon of 28 June 1914. Millions were to die in the Great War, and Germany only completed paying World War I reparations in October 2010, but it was French General Joseph Joffre who said it all at the start of this so-called War to End All Wars: 'This is a railway war. If we win this war it will be largely due to the railways.' Again the role of the railway was to the fore.

PART TWO

CONTINENT BY CONTINENT IN THE 21ST CENTURY

EUROPE LEADS

with AVE, ICE and TGV speed

There is one outstanding element flowing from the European realm of railways: it is speed — not the drug but the record-breaking speed of trains. While not the first to offer high-speed rail, clearly Europe has led at almost every stage of rail development, with the fastest trains and now the fastest systems of HSR, such as the new French TGV Est line east of Paris. Let us take a few revealing snapshots of rail and speed, most notably of passenger trains, and the progress with speed over 200 years.

BURSTS OF SPEED

Since 1830, railway networks across Europe have initially expanded, then contracted (most notably the third quarter of the 20th century) but now are expanding again. During all of this, most categories of trains have enjoyed faster and faster schedules.

Kippers for British Rail breakfast

There has always been a Colonel Blimp aspect of the absurd about UK railways, all perfectly reasonable (as surely the birthplace of rail is allowed a little nonsense). Yes, there are the station improvements being commenced on the very day the branch line to the station is being permanently closed. Likewise, key junction lines such as those of the Great Central Railway closed in 1967, just when their superb alignment, large loading gauge and corridor location would have been near perfect for the huge expansion in rail traffic and population growth in the area over the next three decades.

As if to prove Chair of British Railways Board Richard Beeching and his massive cuts to rail routes doubly wrong, the Great Central Railway operates as a superb and profitable tourist steam operation over a short section through Quorn today. It is one of the greatest tourist-train operations in the world and the only one that can boast a length of double track, allowing working steam locomotives to regularly pass one another on most weekends.

Letters in the UK *Daily Telegraph* often lament this particular closure, but there have been other closures that have brought censure and it is a letter to the London *Times* of yesteryear that takes the cake. A retired Army colonel wrote about his objection to British Rail removing kippers from the breakfast menu on his morning train to London. He stated: 'Not because I ever ordered them for my on-board breakfast but because I want the comfort of knowing I can order them if ever I wanted to.' Yet, as Matthew Engel observes in his sad but hilarious and excellent book *Eleven Minutes Late*, against the odds it was rail that came good and propelled colonels and thousands of others around the UK to successfully contribute much to winning both world wars in the 20th century.

In the nineteenth-century, rail speed was the direct outcome of the locomotive, sometimes helped by a downhill grade or even a tailwind, at least until the arrival of self-propelled train sets with electric and diesel engines on or near axles in the underneath of carriages. The rail motor or set of railcars developed between the wars in the 20th century.

Much has been written about the first steam locomotive trials involving speed and reliability — the famous Rainhill trials conducted on the partly completed Liverpool–Manchester double track in 1829. Above all else, the performance of the Stephensons' *Rocket* in the race set the standard for speed and reliability for years to come. Now move forward a few decades to a British summer when all hell broke loose on the south–north rail corridors, when competing railway companies commenced to race each other the length of Britain with both their overnight and daylight expresses, in part to provide gentlemen with ready and fast access for the short grouse-shooting season in Scotland.

But it was in 1888 and again in 1895 that the big overnight express trains from London to Scotland really accelerated. What happened in 1888, as O. S. Nock has laid out brilliantly in his book *150 Years of Mainline Rail,* was a secretive decision by the west-coast rail operators to steal a march on competitors by accelerating express trains from Euston to Edinburgh by one hour. In fact, in the summer of 1888 by means of better tracks, stronger locomotives and better signalling, they ended up slashing the journey time from nine and a half hours to just seven hours and 38 minutes.

The east-coast route operators were not to be beaten, especially as their route from King's Cross through Doncaster and York to Edinburgh was 11 kilometres (or about 7 miles) shorter. They succeeded in bringing down travel time to seven hours and 27 minutes. Both routes at that time involved stops, especially as the long water troughs that allowed steam locomotives to pick up water at speed had not yet been devised.

Then in 1895 came the other burst of speed, with the average times on many of the London–Scotland trains smashing through the 96 kph

(60 mph) speed barrier, including on the through services further north of Edinburgh and Glasgow to Aberdeen and Inverness. It is interesting to note that in the antipodes on the standard gauge between the two big Australian cities of Melbourne and Sydney, not even on a good day in the first decade of the 21st century does the only through express train, namely the XPT, reach this average speed.

British rail product was leading the world with speed and, to some extent, comfort in the golden years of steam, but it was slow to switch to new technology, including diesel and electric as well as diesel-electric locomotives. Enter the Continental Europeans, led by the Italians who had already given the world voltage through the electrical-engineer pioneer Alessandro Volta, and also radio through the great work of Marconi.

Between the world wars, Il Duce Mussolini put a big effort into the Italian railways, including building some very big central hub stations, most notably Milan, as mentioned previously. With companies such as Fiat investing in leading-edge automobile production as well as leading-edge rail rolling stock and motors, Italy was able to claim the world speed-record for a period.

It was Italy that provided the bridge between the two big bursts of speed that came towards the end of both the nineteenth and 20th centuries, when on 6 December 1937 the Italian ETR 200 (ElettroTreno 200) three-carriage train set burst through the 200 kph (125 mph) barrier to clock in at 201 kph between Rome and Naples, not far from the famous Monte Cassino Benedictine Monastery. The monks looking down from above across the valley would have been impressed by this glistening fast train racing along where chariots once dominated centuries ago. However, they would not have sighted from that distance one of the secrets of why the ETR 200 was so fast: it had merely four bogies rather than the normal six bogies, thus reducing weight. In other words, the three carriages were articulated with one bogie on each of the joins between carriages, a trick of the trade replicated on some but not all very fast train sets to this day.

1939 and the Italian job

As recorded by Chief Rabbi Zollo of Rome, who in 1945 converted to Catholicism, Mussolini stated around that time: 'Scratch a German and you get a barbarian.' Churchill was recorded as being fascinated by the Italian boost to train speeds but when told that Mussolini had decided to lock in on the Axis side in 1940, he remarked: 'We had them on our side last time, they [the Germans] are welcome to them this time.' All of this is a little unfair on both the Germans and the Italians, who invented so much and, it should be said, often enough sing so greatly. It is particularly unfair on the generations post World War II that lifted both Germany and Italy to new economic highs.

Germany has the ICE surging ahead and Italy has streaked away with its Red Arrow rail, providing fast speeds down the spine of Italy following some new tunnelling between Bologna and Florence, in particular — today it's just two hours, 59 minutes Milan to Rome at a mere 300 kph maximum speed.

Then on 20 July 1939, in that period just ahead of World War II when Mussolini wavered between supporting the Allies and the Axis powers, the ETR 200 reached 203 kph and so set a fractionally higher world rail-speed record.

Many ETR 200 sets were destroyed in Allied bombing during the war, but one set went to the USA for an exhibition of the best on offer from Europe. It was even faster than the renowned Burlington Zephyr, which operated between Chicago and Denver. The Zephyr introduced the combination of streamlined design with lighter stainless-steel material and stronger diesel locomotives.

Two world wars were a dampener on gains in speed due to the railways being mostly in survival mode. In the UK it was a case of coping with bomb attacks while handling extra troop movements and massive extra freight, but dieselisation, with the coming of all-diesel or diesel-electric locomotives, led to a big increase in average speeds for long-haul trains, as the diesel used almost zero water and required little running maintenance compared with the always-thirsty steam locomotive. In other words, the advent of dieselisation knocked out steam on all counts, not the least of which was abolishing the need for costly technical stops for servicing and loading of coal and water.

Well after World War II a number of key trunk lines or corridors in Europe began to reach saturation point for both freight and passenger services, especially the long double-track main lines, with their mixture of commuter, national and international passenger trains plus freight trains. The unusual three-track, or triple track, main line heading from Gare du Nord to the northeast of Paris through Chantilly could cope better than the long sections of double-track main line in France. The rare sections of four track (quadruple track) coped better again, and overall modest maximum speeds applied, but a mixture of passenger and freight traffic operating at different speeds added to greater congestion.

THE TGV GENERATION ARRIVES

It was in the 1970s that planners in France began thinking about a serious big change for the future involving completely new high-standard tracks and new very fast train sets. In short, enter the Trains à Grand Vitesse, or TGV. The French had a lead to follow, namely the Shinkansen, approved by the Japanese cabinet on 19 December 1958 and operational between Tokyo and Osaka, with the first so-called Bullet train departing Tokyo on 1 October 1964.

TGV 001 was in fact a turbo gas-powered train that emerged from Alsthom (now called Alstom), the big French railway locomotive and carriage construction company. It was built as a prototype to point the way and remove gremlins, such as with the complex area of high-speed braking. It exposed many problems — not only braking at high speeds but reducing wind resistance, ensuring stability and that the pantograph connecting to the overhead electricity cables could cope. Jack Cooper, who was born in Britain but who crossed the English Channel to work on the TGV design from the start, was a busy man as he helped eliminate many of these problems. The TGV is distinct enough to say it is not a copycat of the Shinkansen, especially the nose of the early TGV units. Two of these trains were nicknamed *Sophie* and *Patrick* and they took the testing of the electric-powered phase to a new high standard to ensure both pantographs on the roof of the TGV train sets and cantilevers trackside did not melt at the proposed high speeds.

On 8 December 1972, TGV 001 smashed through the 300 kph speed barrier to reach 318 kph (or 198 mph — as good as 200 mph) and nothing derailed, but much was learned by all involved. The test led to fine-tuning of the design and weight distribution, going into commercial production, and the TGV entered regular service in 1981, once the TGV track had been completed from Paris' Gare de Lyon to the hub city of Lyon.

I can vividly recall a working lunch with some British rail officials back in the 1980s. These executives were snorting at the prospects of the TGV, saying their British Advanced Passenger Tilt (APT) trains were the way to go. They highlighted a minor derailment by a prototype TGV in a rail yard at slow speed as pointing to how dangerous the TGV system was. But by then it was clear the TGV was going to be a great success, with its dedicated-tracks conceptual approach, and of course the APT on one famous VIP run tilted over for a big curve near Carlisle but refused to tilt back again.

The APT in Britain was right in principle but not in application and suffered an early withdrawal. Conversely the Milan–Geneva mountain corridor has had tilt trains operating successfully for years, and the Pendolino train sets also worked well in the UK, when eventually introduced.

Le Train Bleu

There is one railway-station restaurant above all others: as mentioned the fabulous Train Bleu restaurant upstairs at Gare de Lyon and now approaching its 110th birthday. With its velvet curtains and heritage mosaics, it is the most glamorous railway-station restaurant of all and was a perfect place to have a very good lunch with plenty to drink before boarding a TGV for a run to Lyon in the driver's cabin.

When travelling as a motivated member of parliament, at least very motivated to learning more about all matters relating to rail transport in the world, I rode on two occasions — once to Lyon and once to Nantes, which is high speed as far as Le Mans. More recently I rode in a Red Arrow driver's cabin for half the journey between Rome and Florence, observing the greatly expanded computerisation of these single-driver trains.

On these trips I learned much about the in-cabin signalling system, the superb trajectory of grade and curve of these special tracks, and of course the superb standard of engineering of the railway switches, or points, for example where the Bordeaux line takes off from the Nantes line with the TGV Atlantique. These included a much longer turn-out so that the angle of change for a train leaving to cross from one track to another was much more gradual than traditional slow speed points.

On my trip to Lyon, not wishing to miss anything and not really thinking I should ask whether there was a loo near the driver's cabin (in fact there is), I was forced to hold on until the end of the ride. Upon arrival at our destination my farewell to the driver was very rapid indeed as I made a beeline for a toilette, or as the British would say 'rest room'. When travelling, clearly it is wise to go often and whenever opportunity presents, even on the very fast trains of the world.

It is worth laying out how generic high-speed rail (HSR) has been boosted by TGV speed improvement as it has unfolded over its first 30 years of operation or thereabouts:

- 26 February 1981 — a world record of 380 kph (236 mph)
- 18 May 1990 — TGV Atlantique sets a new TGV record of 515 kph (320 mph)
- 3 April 2007— TGV Est sets another record-smashing effort of 574.8 kph (357 mph)

These increases have not been effortless, and many aspects of the train have required fine-tuning. Indeed, the proud French are the first to admit the effort on 3 April 2007 to reach 574.8 kph was using a number of special features not in regular service. However, there is no doubt the average TGV train speed will close the gap on this maximum, and so 400 kph start-to-stop as the norm not the exception awaits later this century.

By the way, a TGV running at regular speed would cover the distance travelled by the Stephensons' *Rocket* from Liverpool to Manchester in about ten minutes today, versus up to six hours back in 1830.

The French TGV has been way ahead of rivals such as the German ICE and the Japanese Shinkansen, at least in the speed stakes up until 2010. Likewise the Alstom-related product, the Thalys train on the Paris–Brussels–Rotterdam–Amsterdam services, along with the Eurostar Paris and Brussels to and from London are right up there in the speed stakes.

The German ICE is made by Siemens and is distinctly heavier per passenger than the TGV, but is closing in on rivals, especially with the distributed power approach. It also has the unique design feature of offering a group of passengers at the front and back end of the more modern train sets direct-track views, the same as the train driver's.

Frankfurt Airport is well serviced by ICE and everything else, with many commuter train connections, including shuttle trains into Frankfurt Main or the CBD. It is a short journey by ICE from Frankfurt Airport Station to historic Cologne, although one sad fact is that the high-speed tracks depart the Rhine for this by a more direct route, with plenty of tunnels and no sweeping curves hugging the banks of the majestic river.

The great vista of the busy Rhine River full of barges and boats of various description, complimented by castles and vineyards and everything else as a backdrop, is still available on the regular train to Bonn. So it is necessary to carefully examine railway maps if wanting the views that were so readily available from daylight train services of the last century. However, if it is the fastest service point to point desired, be ready to go underground for long periods.

The choice is yours, along with price variations to take account of the speed of service being offered — which is fair enough given the extra energy costs in lifting from a 160 kph service to 240 kph, then towards, and ultimately beyond, a 300-kph average speed. And, as mentioned, the fact you never leave the ground and do not face the typical airport hassle and various in-flight restrictions on cabin movement is a priceless bonus.

Spain is now well down the path of HSR networking, with key routes, such as Madrid to Seville, proving very popular. Likewise AVE (Alta Velocidad Espanola) Madrid to Barcelona has quickly captured a majority of the previous air traffic. The first Paris HSR service right through to Madrid by a TGV-type train is expected around 2012. It will replace the long-serving Talgo, with its automatic wheel adjustment for change of gauge conducted near the Franco–Spanish border.

Overall in Europe at the start of the second decade of the 21st century rail transport splits broadly two ways: the rich advanced rail countries and the rest. In the former category you have five of the original six countries who were all members of the Treaty of Rome (establishing the European Economic Community) from 1957, and who have moved quickly down the pathway of HSR in an enlightened way. They have built the special tracks, often against strong local opposition, and provided greatly improved train services on those that existed in the immediate post-World War II period.

In this grouping of HSR rail leaders there are the notable pioneers of France and Germany. Later on came Belgium, the Netherlands, Spain, and Italy. Portugal is next cab off the rank, with tenders finalised for the new HSR double-track corridor from Lisbon to Madrid. Switzerland and Austria are moving down this pathway, with some short sections of HSR double track constructed or being planned, all of course in Stephenson standard gauge.

Within these countries, the question arises as to whether the TGV and ICE implementation has reached the point where it is starting to bump up against a demand ceiling and a lack of regions still needing HSR services.

A quick look at any rail map of Europe reveals this is not the case, not even in France, although in much of France the task in terms of the main network of HSR or TGV is certainly well advanced. Thanks to the double-decker arrangement of many TGV units and closer density of operation with trains only minutes apart on the same track, capacity exists to still further increase the passenger volumes on key corridors in peak times, even on the original TGV line from Paris to Lyon.

From the junction of Macon, just north of Lyon, along the international rail corridor to Geneva more needs to be done, and a shortcut route has now been introduced. Debate rages about a new low-level high-speed 50-kilometre-long super tunnel from Lyon itself through the Mount Cenis 280-kilometre corridor to Turin. This would greatly shorten the rail link from Lyon into the grand northern Italian city, the original 'House of Savoy' capital of 'uniting Italy' in the mid-nineteenth century.

Spain, with its comfortable AVE system, is aiming to have 90 per cent of its population within 50 kilometres of an AVE station by 2020 — an extraordinary set of objectives. This all flows from previous Prime Minister Felipe Gonzales, who launched Spain down this pathway for the Seville Expo in 1992, and bravely, and correctly, took the big decision to switch to Stephenson standard gauge, as mentioned, for the new network.

Alas, the global financial crisis of 2008 and 2009, the 'Great Recession', as many describe it, has had its impact on passenger numbers for rail and a mixed impact on infrastructure projects. In some countries there has been less to spend on capital works and transport infrastructure; in others rail has been boosted with specific extra allocations for upgrades via government stimulus packages.

In the rest of Europe furious debate continues over the onward expansion of HSR. In 2010 Sweden, to nominate one country is in a 'boil over' debate about the real advantages of a northern HSR. The Balkan states, emerging from a bitter war that dominated the last decade of the 20th century, have a great deal of catching up to do with existing regular services before HSR can be contemplated. Many Balkan trains operate at speeds that make most Australian train timetables almost respectable by comparison

NEW HIGH-SPEED CORRIDORS

Thinking carefully about all of this, it emerges that the obvious international European routes awaiting a TGV, ICE or Red Arrow are fourfold.

First is Hamburg to Copenhagen and on to Stockholm, although perhaps Oslo could stake a claim as a destination, given that it is the first OECD capital city in the world where a majority of households are single person, presumably with a mobility greater than most. The dynamic of the Scandinavian countries might just bring about a full HSR network in the first half of this 21st century. In 2000 the mighty Oresund Bridge opened between Denmark and Sweden with double rail tracks and — damnation! — a four lane roadway. By degrees this sparked a rail usage revival in Scandanavia, and with reasonably strong economies and general prosperity, even with the GFC, greenhouse fixation and good governance prevailing, there is every chance that rail will get a greater priority. However, the powers that be in Sweden are still debating the so-called north route for HSR.

The second possible high-speed corridor is from the mighty hub of Berlin, as the city looks economically more to the East, least as far as Warsaw, capital of Poland. In fact Poland is now moving down the HSR pathway, with the city pair of Warsaw–Krakow being further investigated.

Red on standard gauge; blue on broad gauge. On 27 January 1974 these two rail motors — CPH 27 from New South Wales (left) and 22 RM from Victoria — met for the last time at Oaklands in the NSW Riverina, before the Oaklands-to-Urana and later to Boree Creek, New South Wales, section was closed. Ironically, the Victorian line from Benalla to Oaklands was converted in 2010 to standard gauge. (Courtesy ARHS)

The ultimate railway tease in 2011, this carriage sits in splendid isolation on a disconnected bridge but visible from the castels of San Marino. It was part of a narrow-gauge railway from Rimini to the tiny country of San Marino. The electrified train line operated for about 30 years last century. San Marino has existed as a republic for 1710 years — the oldest continuing small republic in the world. (Courtesy David J. Ritchie)

A lone stallion stands serenely in the middle of a paddock of rusting wheels and bogies at Werris Creek in the New England Tablelands of New South Wales. In contrast to the rusting bogies, Werris Creek is today a busy rail junction for coal and grain trains, plus it has a vibrant rail museum and memorial. (Courtesy Andrew Downing)

A high-speed Thalys train running alongside trucks in France.

ICE trains at Cologne, Germany.

A Eurostar train at St Pancras Station, London, after engine problems due to extremely cold weather in France in winter 2008–2009.

A Shinkansen Bullet train in Tokyo, Japan.

The Wodonga rail bypass was completed in 2010, allowing the removal of the rail line and more than ten level crossings from the Albury–Wodonga area of Victoria, Australia. This shows the first freight train to use the new bypass over the Lincoln Causeway. (Courtesy *Border Mail*)

The little freight train of Artouste, the highest railway in Europe, at 2000 metres (6500 feet) is one of the most beautiful wanderings in the Pyrenees part of France.

A Union Pacific freight train travels east on CSXT tracks, 16 June 2008, in Berea, Ohio. The Union Pacific railroad uses CSX Transportation track via a trackage rights agreement.

Great luxury can still be experienced on the Danube Express, one of the newest train services in Europe. It has been operating from Budapest to Istanbul and other destinations since 2005. (Tim Fischer)

This photo was taken by Reverend John Flynn (Flynn of the Inland) in the early 1920s outside Marree in South Australia (often known as 'where the outback begins') – long before the Ghan offered direct travel between Adelaide and Darwin. (National Library of Australia)

The Ghan travelling over the Fergusson River Bridge. Built in 1918, the bridge is 128 metres (420 feet) in length, and the only bridge capable of being switched from narrow gauge to standard gauge. What foresight 100 years ago! (Tim Fischer)

The spectacular cane-gauge Avontuur in South Africa sweeps across its signature railway viaduct over the Kabeljous River. (John Browning)

The *Fire Fly* replica at Didcot Railway Centre, built for and operating on Brunel broad gauge in the 21st century. (Tim Fischer)

The Darjeeling Himalayan Railway, nicknamed the Toy Train, runs on a narrow cane-gauge railway (2 foot/610 mm) from Siliguri to Darjeeling.

Inside heritage-protected Grand
Central Station New York.

The famous Train Bleu
restaurant at Gare de Lyon
in Paris.

Garabit rail viaduct in central France,
built by Gustave Eiffel just before
building that tower in Paris for the
Exposition Universelle in 1889.
(Courtesy Jacques Bence)

Cambodia's Toll Royal Railway is making good progress with its quality metre-gauge track laying, ultimately to connect Bangkok, Thailand, to Phnom Penh, Cambodia, and on to Ho Chi Minh City, Vietnam. (Courtesy Toll)

Sugarcane trains, mainly on cane gauge of just 2 feet or 610 millimetres, pop up all over the world, such as in Indonesia. (Courtesy John Browning)

The Australian Friendship Bridge, the first ever bridge over the Mekong River between Thailand and Laos, was completed in 1994. It connects Nong Khai province and the city of Nong Khai in Thailand with the Vientiane prefecture in Laos and nearby Vientiane, capital of Laos. Road traffic on this key bridge has to cross sides on entering Laos, from British driving side to French! (Courtesy Michael Mann)

The Pichi Richi Railway offers a historic rail journey on the oldest remaining section of the narrow-gauge Ghan railway between Quorn and Port Augusta in South Australia.

At the platform in Albury, one of the longest platforms in the southern hemisphere. In the past, passengers from New South Wales and Victoria had to cross over from one side to the other to change trains, often in the middle of the night, due to break of gauge. (Courtesy Allison Jess)

The third corridor would be from Vienna, across the border to nearby Budapest, the twin-city capital of Hungary. I guess there would be an argument as to whether it would go to Buda or Pest on opposite sides of the Danube or perhaps both. Certainly there are some grand stately railway stations in Budapest capable of double-decking, with a level of platforms below or above the existing level but linked to the same concourse, in the main.

In fact some corridors are at an in-between stage, such as Budapest-to-Vienna, with a 200 kph (125 mph) Railjet service provided by OBB based in Austria and set to be accelerated further in 2013. The big international Vienna hub airport helps anchor this corridor.

Finally, the fourth corridor would be from Venice to the capital of Slovenia, namely Ljubljana, then to the capital of Croatia, beautiful Zagreb, with its grand hotel alongside Zagreb Station still there from the Orient Express days, but modernised and made for rail-travelling business people and conference delegates. This corridor could then continue through to Belgrade, capital of Serbia, but it would be a tall order to see it go beyond Belgrade — say, to Greece — at least in the next few decades.

However, at Belgrade, it could split back to Split (only half joking) and make a second split on to Athens and a third split on to Istanbul. Pigs might fly, you say, but the potential is there, especially if other forms of transport are taxed accurately on their contribution to greenhouse gas emissions and trains are given a fair and accurate treatment with taxation (see Chapter 12). As of mid-2011, all though-connecting passenger trains to Athens from Western Europe have ceased operating.

All four of these corridors connect the rich centre of developed Europe with the north, due east, southeast and south of Europe. All four make strategic sense, political sense and environmental sense, but the economics of the projects might have to wait a decade or two.

For those who like acronyms, these are the COSWBBIA international corridors of future fast trains: to Copenhagen, Oslo, Stockholm, Warsaw, Budapest, Belgrade, Istanbul and Athens. Now I hasten to add I am neutral about these priorities and accept it is a matter for the governments of Europe to sort out, along with Brussels in its overarching role as the capital of the EU; still COSWBBIA has a nice ring to it. I do not overlook Prague; I would merely suggest it should upgrade its regular rail links and also its river links, and above all else preserve its beauty, and it may not need a full-scale HSR set of linkages to do this.

Before proceeding further, I hear you say speed is not everything and there are examples to be found where other non-speed factors provide a magnificent rail product, including the combination of reliability, comfort and vista. Take, for example, the ever-punctual Swiss and one of their international expresses operating on narrow gauge through the Alps. Right on time the international Bernina Express glided out of Tirano Station in the Valtellina region of northern Italy, heading across the border to St Moritz in Switzerland. Along the way there was a spiral, where the track does a complete 360-degree circle to gain height and so

Bernina Express.

Station pickpockets

Diplomats in Europe are not exempt from the business of pickpocketing around railway stations, although they try to set an example by being vigilant. Alas, dedicated Australian Department of Foreign Affairs and Trade (DFAT) officer Mark Pierce fell victim at Cologne Station after shopping at the Christmas markets near the huge Cathedral of Cologne. His ticket and travel pass for his return back to Brussels had been nicked and he was in a flat panic, as he heard the departure announcement for his train.

He made a split-second decision and in a sweat jumped onto the train which quickly glided out of Cologne Station. He then went looking for the conductor to explain in halting German his predicament. The Deutshe Bahn (DB) conductor smiled and asked if his name was Mark Pierce. Absolutely stunned, Mark replied yes. The conductor then reached inside his coat and handed Mark his ticket and travel pass, saying the nicker had been nicked and the ticket and travel pass had been found in possession of the thief by police, who had promptly handed the stolen goods to the conductor of the train indicated on the ticket.

The conductor did not accept any reward but offered Mark a cool drink and all was well. The moral of the story is that when in doubt, it is usually best to jump on board and proceed!

---

cross over itself, along with many tunnels and double-backs woven into the Alps, when I checked this train out in mid-2009. Within minutes, the narrow streets and one roundabout in Tirano itself had been conquered, the international border crossed seamlessly and the serious ascent begun. Welcome to precision travel on a section of 1-metre narrow-gauge track, now listed as a UNESCO Heritage Site, and rightly so.

While not exactly a fast train, in many ways it is an exemplar of what can be done with rail, in this case metre-gauge rail, when combining both tourism and local commuter passenger traffic. Indeed, even business people from big cities can be found on the Bernina Express, enjoying a peaceful way to travel north–south from nearby Davos, without air flight delays and missed connections.

It is just one of the great mountain-railway experiences that can be obtained through various forms of easy ticketing available in Europe, but also in some other parts of the world. At both ends it connects to adequate Stephenson standard gauge heavy-duty rail passenger services.

It is difficult to see a huge expansion in the narrow-gauge Swiss railway system that has operated for over a century, if only because of the topography. However, elsewhere in Europe, as we have seen rail is benefiting from a huge expansion in high-speed rail (HSR), in ordinary, or regular, passenger rail (RPR), and in freight rail (FR), as we move through the second decade of the 21st century. Even new and expanded metros and light rail are unfolding in such medium-sized cities as Mulhouse, France, and Malaga, Spain.

TGV FOR SCOTLAND: BRAVEHEART

The question of whether Britain gets its north–south high-speed rail corridor with TGV-speed capability bubbles along. In the May 2010 UK general elections, thanks to some good footwork mainly by Lord Andrew Adonis, (the Brown Labour Government's Secretary of State for Transport), real progress was at last made re a policy for high-speed rail north of London through to Scotland.

There would be something very special about a modified TGV offering a direct service from Paris to Glasgow or Edinburgh, bypassing London, and there is one obvious name for such a service, Mary Queen of Scots, given the history of her beheading in the Tower of London. Alternatively, it could be just called the 'Braveheart', as funding same will involve a set of brave calls!

The many problems of such a service include selecting the route and overcoming local opposition. There is also the fundamental question of whether to go London then Heathrow, before turning north but this option is unlikely. The new Cameron–Clegg Government and new Transport Secretary, Philip Hammond, are starting to examine this question and many others, including as the overall cost–benefit and who actually pays for the project.

Had Lord Adonis become Transport Secretary in the early days of the Blair Government, then this huge, much-needed project might be nearing completion in 2011. The trouble was that Lord Adonis came along too late in the life of the Blair–Brown Government. Adonis was the son of a Greek Cypriot immigrant who worked as a waiter, and a mother who abandoned them both when Andrew Adonis was three. He was placed into care and brought up in a children's home, until he was sent away to boarding school. He leaped up the ladder of success, greatly helped by a very good education.

Along with one or two of his party colleagues, notably Lord Richard Faulkner, Adonis understood rail well and started to bring about big changes for the better, achieving a cross-party commitment to building a new high-speed railway from London to Scotland. His proposals on electrification of many key routes, including much of Brunel's Great Western Railway, were also on target.

EURO RAIL FREIGHT

On the matter of rail freight and the European railway realm, alas, the picture is bleak and the same huge effort that has boosted passenger rail has simply not been there to push rail freight forward into the 21st century. In one sense this is inexplicable, given that it is a part of the world that gets so much right on transport logistics generally.

The European Commission is meant to be the 'harmonising driver' of freight transport seamlessness, especially intermodal road and rail transport. The big growth in freight in Europe over the last two decades has caused this to become a vital task. The EC has come up with a new catchcry, although the concept has been around for a few decades — co-modality. This is a kind of bureaucratic transport porridge designed to help sort through that which is best transported on road, best on rail, best on canal barge, best on seagoing ship or even in the air.

So in Belgium there are modern, efficient intermodal freight hubs, allowing seamless movement between road, canal barge and of course rail, with some government subsidy applying, mainly to start-up costs. Given the size of the ports in this part of Europe, for example Antwerp and Rotterdam, all this cross-mode coordination makes sense, so much so a special rail freight corridor is being developed from Rotterdam into the heavy industrial areas of Germany.

Rail freight will be examined in more detail later through the prism of some of the other railway realms of the world; suffice it to say that Europe, which has led the world on so much of rail, has, despite the examples of Rotterdam and Antwerp, failed repeatedly on freight.

Continental Europe and Britain have had their fair share of closing and ripping up railway lines since World War II. In some cases these closures have been just a few years ahead of a huge regional freight expansion, with the arrival of a new factory in the area. In the absence of rail, all freight to and from the factory has to go by road, often on roads running alongside rusty old rail tracks.

The Italian electrified branch line from Spoleto to Norcia is probably one that would never be competitive for freight or passenger trains, but certainly would have been perfect if it had been switched to a steam tourist railway, instead of being closed abruptly 50 years ago. It was a case of the ultimate insult, as the land occupied by rail through the two narrow gorges that lead up to Norcia were needed for widening the road to two full lanes. It was just another example of the total domination of the cult of road post World War II.

There is great ugliness and much local complaint about new intermodal road–rail freight yards, with bitter opposition from groups who well know how to work the protest levers of modern Europe. The NIMBY (not in my back yard) phenomenon is matched often enough by the growing NIMBYANAA phenomenon of not in my back yard and not at all.

The huge breakthrough in rail freight of double-decking container traffic is yet to arrive in Europe, some 30 years after its introduction in the USA and Australia. Lowering the floor of tunnels to allow the passage of double-decker freight trains is a trick of the trade often used in the Rockies of the USA, but this can be very costly. The problem for Europe is that it is bridge after bridge and overhead wiring that makes the task challenging.

Railways of Europe have huge potential for freight expansion, if they could win new freight from new factories that should only get location go-ahead if connected directly to rail, and if they could win freight share back from road and even from air on certain HSR corridors. It will take time and enlightened effort from all the stakeholders involved but it will occur, driven by road congestion, environmental requirements generally, and the energy equation that makes rail the best transport future for Europe, not just with passengers but also with freight into the future.

As I observed a lonely small-sized Hoyer bulk-liquid railway wagon at Ostiense while I was en route by train to Rome Airport in the tenth year of this 21st century, I realised how far Europe freight rail has yet to go. It was part of a small through freight train that had obviously been shunted, as it had missed its pre-peak-hour slot; it did have modern connected air brakes but was without modern bogies — just a set that were clearly a blast from the past and most likely with a speed restriction applying as well.

The wagon was covered in a kind of transport grime, presumably accumulated on its long journey down from Germany but unlikely to be given a good clean anytime soon; no glistening fast-moving unit freight train here, and of course no double-stacking. Now if it was bulk wine on board, extra delay might help age the wine; if beer then I am not sure. It was probably some bulk chemical, I mused, at least using the safer mode of rail rather than road through the Alps between Germany, Switzerland and Italy.

Conversely, a few years ago I watched a unit train load (freight of one type of commodity) of agricultural machinery depart the Klaas factory in Germany for a hub in France and Spain, in turn for dispersal to distributors and farmers — an impressive sight and a window into one example at least of daily well-managed, efficient rail freight.

There is one bizarre exception to the drift in rail freight. The year 2009 saw a 50 per cent boost in rail freight and wagon storage in the tiny Vatican rail system. A third wagon was brought in from the Italian network, into the Vatican gardens and Vatican railway station in the dead of night. So suddenly where there were once two wagons, or louvre vans, there are now three. Alas, the last Papal train from the Vatican was in 2002 when Pope John Paul II travelled to Assisi. In May 2011, the Caritas Express operated successfully from the Pope's platform on a fundraising daytrip to Orvieto, and return to Rome: watch this space for more.

The Caritas Express *at Vatican Station in preparation for the arrival of the steam locomotive!*
(Courtesy Luigi Cantamessa)

NORTH AMERICA

BART to SMART and intermodal rail-freight excellence

If Europe has badly let things down re freight, the USA has been charging ahead, at least over the last 30 years. Throughout most of the 20th century in the USA, against the might of the motor car and trucking industry, the rail freight business simply staggered along. The huge and ever-popular interstate highway system, pioneered by President Ike Eisenhower in the middle of the 20th century, was almost the final straw for the rail freight business.

When nearly broken and busted, three major breakthroughs emerged that completely regenerated long-distance rail freight, to the point that in more recent times 'golden touch' investor par excellence Warren Buffet started buying railway stock in a big way. In 2009 he completed the outright purchase of the Class 1 (big interstate) US railroad of great might, the Burlington Northern Sante Fe, or BNSF.

This resurgence in rail has revealed further potential to expand, with momentum in the USA spreading into Canada and Mexico, and as luck would have it, all three are standard-gauge systems throughout, and all three belong to the North American Free Trade Agreement (NAFTA) communities, with economic ties growing between them.

What were the three breakthroughs that swept rail freight forward? In fact there were four if you count the gains from dieselisation replacing steam locomotives, but that is a little before our time frame. Dieselisation brought huge fuel savings and greenhouse gas emission reduction just after World War II. By 1960, diesel had completely replaced steam in the USA, with little use of electric for freight or passenger trains on any main lines.

CABOOSE ABOLITION AND LABOUR FLEXIBILITY

(1) The first breakthrough was simple enough, and logical. It was the abolition of the caboose, or, as it is called in some Anglo-Saxon countries, the guard's van. (By the way the biggest split in train terminology relates to the 'train driver', mostly the term used in Europe and Australasia, versus 'train engineer', the dominant term used in the North American railway realm.)

For decades the caboose at the end of the train had been the butt of many great Hollywood film jokes involving robberies, rescues of damsels in distress and just about everything else. However, its days were numbered. The caboose rapidly became superfluous, as radio and various electronics provided better rear-end-of-train monitoring than a guard or guards half asleep and bored brainless riding up the back.

Further, in shunting yards and at train assembly points, the caboose added to rail inefficiency because it had to be separated from the freight wagons on arrival at freight yard or port terminus and then stored somewhere until the very last movement of assembly of the new freight train. The caboose was then attached to the end by a shunter locomotive, its brakes checked, then clearance given, and finally the freight train would depart.

Today in the caboose-less train, the driver, or engineer, can tell by the dials and readouts the exact pressure in the critical brake line or air hose that runs the length of the train. Further, a device put on the last container carriage or ore wagon acts as a form of tail light, as the freight trains keep rolling through the day and night. This device also has electric pulse reporting back to the front locomotive, so if, for example, the last two carriages or wagons on the train broke away on a grade, the alarm in the driver's cabin would sound immediately.

The various rail unions worldwide were not keen to see the caboose or its equivalent abolished. Many jobs were at stake, given that some US railroads operated with a caboose crew of three even as late as the 1960s — greatly adding to cost. This meant that US rail companies had to both abolish the caboose and also introduce more flexible train crewing templates.

The Chicago–St Louis main-line corridor led the way after a tense meeting between union leaders and rail management way back in 1975. It was a do-or-die situation, as the trucking industry surged ahead with bigger and bigger rigs (and enjoying in some countries to this day huge, favourable tax treatment) and rail lost more and more freight share.

Bloomington, Illinois, was the location for the fateful meeting, as detailed by David DeBoer in his book *Piggyback and Containers*. The union leaders realised it was a case of big cultural change or the loss of all railway jobs, as company after company cut back freight-train operations. Indeed, in many cases, rail companies ceased operations completely.

The union representatives proved to be real leaders and struck a deal which essentially abolished the manned caboose forthwith and a switch to more flexible crewing, in this case a slingshot arrangement, which not only reduced crew members, it reduced the need for crews to have costly overnight stays away from home base, and companies' maintaining barracks and meal rooms in lonely crew-change locations. Today it is motel standard accommodation that is demanded with all the associated costs.

The template spread like wildfire across North America and beyond, even to government rail systems Down Under in Australia, such as the NSWGR, with its strong tradition of unionism. The legendary Sydney-based railway union leader Bernie Willingale could not stop this essential productivity boost. As a result of this change, if you knew where to look in the 1970s especially, you could find loops or sidings over networks worldwide filled with disused cabooses, or guard's vans, until rail management could sort out their demolition for scrap metal or conversion. In a few cases, it was conversion for other rail usages, such as

Shower with or without a friend

If ever you want a fair-dinkum shower on a train with plenty of room to spare and loads of hot water, then you ride in the crew car of the APT/FreightLink train between Adelaide and Darwin. These are purpose-built carriages, although sometimes former luxury sleeper carriages are used from discontinued trains such as the Southern Aurora that ran between Sydney and Melbourne.

You can shower as the freight train keeps rolling, and there is even room to shower with a friend — not that I have done so, I hasten to add. I doubt if there is a bigger bathroom or amenities room on rail anywhere in the world than those used on the world's newest transcontinental that cuts north–south right across Australia.

Conversely, some train sets of the various versions of the Orient Express in Europe have no showers or baths on board at all; however, the superb Danube Express of MÁV Nosztalgia Kft, operating out of Budapest, comes with showers. In some cases heritage rules prevent retro fitting of showers or large bathrooms, such as with the more famous of 'des Wagons lits' carriages, which also have no air-conditioning. At some risk, may I observe that this is clearly why the best perfumes come from Paris, being located along the famous Orient Express route from London to Istanbul!

storage of fog signal detonators or other items. Some were converted to crew cars for long distance freight trains, where the crews rotate at the end of a shift, the train stopping and the crew walking between the crew car and the locomotive to change over.

DOUBLE-STACKING CONTAINERS ON FREIGHT TRAINS

(2) With the caboose despatched and train crewing made more flexible, the next big breakthrough came from the railway design engineers, again as they looked to boost productivity and make rail more competitive.

The large loading gauge above track (that is the maximum height permissible above the top of the rails and the maximum width of carriages and wagons) allowed for radical lateral thinking by a cell of railway planners and engineers based with the Southern Pacific system in and around Los Angeles. They had the capacity to think big and they did so. Executive Mike Mohan was one of those who helped lead the way. A manager with determination to think and deliver laterally, combined with a thoughtful can-do sunny Californian attitude, he was one of the railroad leaders of the time who made a difference in the USA and later in Western Australia, especially boosting freight performance.

Intermodal container freight traffic was starting to expand, especially from the big container ports on the West Coast of the USA, across America to hubs such as Chicago, Detroit and Atlanta, handling containers of imported goods from China and Japan, which took off in the boom years when Ronald Reagan was president.

The rail freight problem was twofold: capacity heading east; and congestion around the huge ports at Long Beach in Los Angeles where container ships unloaded. It was 1977 when Southern Pacific developed better use of the improved containers of the era and their corner-locking devices. Senior people like Mike Mohan saw the capability of stacking one container on top of another to increase capacity for general merchandise handling, so long as track standards were maintained and line capacity was adequate, and all loading gauge aspects were covered off, especially through tunnels.

In some cases shallow trenching was developed with a roof then added to place rail track effectively out of sight and (relatively cheaply) underground; also, but costing a great deal more, rail tunnels were taken out completely and the relevant sections converted to open cutting. With better tamping track equipment to ensure accuracy, the exact placement and slope on the top of each rail, and the virtual elimination of sideways swaying by heavy freight trains, railway companies found double-stacking worked and worked well.

Those operators converting to double-stacking had a huge leap in their productivity and today it is the benchmark for efficient rail freight operation. Wind storms and train despatchers (or controllers) putting double-stacked freight trains onto loops with low clearances, as once happened in Adelaide, can lead to disasters, but both phenomena are rare enough around the world.

Alongside double-stacking has developed the art of designing the makeup of each long freight train with computers to maximise efficiency and safety. This is very complex but also maximises revenue and yield. Freight trains can be 2 to 6 or more kilometres long and locomotive placement is critical, along with the placement of heavily loaded — or equally any empty — sections of the freight train. The composition of these trains is simple enough: three or four locomotives followed by kilometres of double-stacked containers, including refrigerated containers, all generating heaps of revenue. Remotely controlled dispersed locomotives, 'distributed power' units, are placed at the rear or in the middle of the trains to improve their performance across difficult terrain. This is a far cry from years ago when I watched a steam-hauled eight-wagon freight train on the Boree Creek branch line, in the Riverina of Australia, which had managed to end up with guard's van and locomotive in the middle of the train. As it was a speed restricted branch line operation, this did not matter.

The bellwether Cajon Pass, the first big pass just east of Los Angeles, has been host to many derailments over the decades, including the middle of freight trains being pulled off the big long curve towards the summit of this historic pass, as well as freight trains running away down the big descents. It now boasts three tracks on an improved grade and layout. It remains a great desire of mine to drive up the Cajon to see the might of US Class 1 railroad trains heavily loaded with imported goods hammer through to the east, and return to the west with loads of US-made manufactures destined for export and the large Californian domestic markets.

It is, of course, where the best of intermodal freight rail can be seen in operation: long, modern double-stacked super freighters, along with the lonely LA-to-Chicago Amtrak passenger train, still operating along one of the great historic rail routes of the world, but often having to give way to freight trains.

STAGGERS ACT

(3) The third breakthrough in the US freight was the *Staggers Act* — legislation to deregulate US rail passed and signed into law in 1980. Perhaps it would have been better named the 'Removal of Rail Staggers Act', as this was its positive impact. The name, of course, comes from the sponsoring congressman, generally the chair of the relevant congressional committee, and this was the case with the *Staggers Act*.

Harley Orrin Staggers was elected after World War II from the Second District of West Virginia. He became the powerful head of the relevant transportation and commerce committee of Congress. In fact, Harley knew how to campaign on trains in the era when you stood on the back observation platform of the last carriage and gave warm-up speeches. This he did when President Harry S. Truman was coming through in the famous 1948 campaign, which saw Truman beat Thomas Dewey and the Democrats pick up strongly against the odds in both houses of Congress.

Truman's shock win was put down to many factors, not the least of which was the 31,000-mile presidential campaign train across America. While most pundits got that election result wrong, even after the polls closed on the east coast, more reflective analysis points to the campaign train as playing a huge role in turning the tide.

Staggers departed Congress in 1981 but, as is typical in that which constitutes a congressional career, it was in his very last term when seniority had dealt him powerful committee positions that he delivered for rail in a big way. His Democrat colleague one-term President Jimmy Carter signed the legislation into law before he was ousted by Ronald Reagan.

What did the *Staggers Act* do? Firstly, it effectively deregulated pricing for freight tonne-miles in an essentially modern way, to allow competition, especially giving shippers some traction in the complex equation and helping to create more flexible and competitive rate cards for consignments.

Secondly, the *Staggers Act* provided templates to allow or encourage so-called 'reciprocal switching' and also 'tracking rights'; in short, allowing flexibility across different rail tracks of competing rail companies. This removed, in particular, the suppression of trade-veto rights from any one company against another. So if you had the only bridge in an area or the only mountain pass rail route through the region where access was sought, you could not unfairly block it.

Thirdly, the *Staggers Act* encouraged railroad mergers, and this in turn allowed the creation of longer distance rail corridors with just the one combined rail operator and track owner, reducing the number of railroads a shipper or freight forwarder had to deal with and greatly boosting efficiency and effectiveness, especially on long east–west haulages.

So effective has the *Staggers Act* been that during the first decade of the 21st century there have been calls by the road and trucking lobby for the *Staggers Act* to be repealed or at least cut back. Yes, you might even describe it as an attempt to make the US railways stagger along again — sad pun intended.

Senator Jay Rockefeller, also a Democrat from West Virginia, has pushed forward legislation known as the Surface Transport Reauthorisation Bill, with some so-called regulatory reform aimed at breaking down remaining rail-monopoly price setting. However this repeal bill of the vital *Staggers Act* did not pass the Democrat-dominated 111th Congress, not even in the very busy lame-duck session. Meanwhile the railways keep rolling along right across the huge USA, on the freight score at least, with flow-ons to Canada in particular but also to Mexico.

From these factors — dieselisation, caboose abolition and labour flexibility, double-stacking and the *Staggers Act* — I turn to some observations made by rail analysts about the turnaround of rail in the USA. To the above list they add the 1971 creation of Amtrak (thereby extracting costly passenger operations from the big freight operations); creation of USRA (United States Railroad Administration) to sort and restructure,

US railway all at sea

There is one railway line that is absolutely no more today in the USA: the Florida Miami-to-Key West trestle line. It scampered from island to island over causeways and trestle bridges, in fact connecting 28 islands over its 250-kilometre (155-mile) route. After 22 years of operation, with mixed success, along came the most muscular hurricane the world had ever recorded till then, clocking in at 25.35 in Hg or a very low 892 hectopascals.

From this extremely low core, on 2 September 1935, horrific winds battered the area, sweeping trains into the sea, including a rescue train. Several hundred people were killed or drowned by the force of this ultra deep depression and super hurricane. The railway itself was smashed to pieces, bridges and causeways swept out to sea, never to be rebuilt as the car and truck were in the ascendancy in the USA by then. On this occasion nature and the sea soundly and sadly defeated the railway engineers.

mainly through merger, the bankrupt railroads in the northeast of the USA — and leading to the emergence of Conrail, a combination of several struggling railways including Penn Central; development on a large scale of the Powder River coal basin, necessitating use of rail to handle the huge tonnages of this valuable coal; rising oil prices impacting on road trucking especially; and huge technological advances in rail, particularly relating to fuel savings, which of course are still ongoing.

It is a great list — some of the initiatives emerging as much by accident as design. Sadly there was a period 50 years ago when, if put to a vote to develop rail or go road freight, there would have been an ugly decision to turn away from rail.

What of the future of rail in North America? Is it really a case of 'Trains Unlimited' for rail freight, as well as regular or conventional passenger rail, and in particular will the USA ever get serious about high-speed rail?

The European exemplars over the decades have shown that rail only leaps forward when there is positive intervention by government, including

The rebooting of US rail

1 Abolition of the caboose (guard's van) and related crewing flexibility and labour reforms.
2 Double-stacking containers on long distance freight rail.
3 *Staggers Act*, 1980.
4 Hiving off passenger services from freight railroads into Amtrak, 1971.
5 Forming USRA in the northeast of the USA to help sort the bankrupt Class 1 railroads.
6 Development on a large scale of the Powder River coal basin.
7 Rising oil prices and their impact on road trucking.
8 Technological advances, especially those delivering huge fuel savings, with more to come.

outright subsidisation of capital works and running costs. Economic drys should stay calm at this point and ponder the fact that since Roman times the state has provided huge subsidies to roads. In the best light, rail subsidies can be seen as catch-up and an issue of overdue practical justice.

While private enterprise was how rail started in many countries, it soon switched to government ownership, including full nationalisation at various times — often but not always during wartime.

Public sentiment against the role of government generally in the USA has waxed and waned over the years, but typically it has been totally opposed to involvement in big rail projects. Worse still, it has often delivered policy outcomes at both federal and state level that have been distinctly pro road and anti rail. Road has hidden subsidies for all users, especially road freighters, whereas rail has to provide capital for just about every kilometre of track and every dollar of its construction, maintenance and rare extension.

Indeed extension only takes place when rail-company cash-flow conditions and demand permit, with usually some top-up monies from government. Government bonds are one way to obtain funds and California has often voted for big rail projects such as BART in San Francisco. So wholesale upgrades are a rarity but do occur occasionally; for example the aforementioned Union Station revamp at Washington, DC, and the currently under-construction expansion at New York Grand Central eastern side. The CREATE project at Chicago, also already mentioned, is only limping along, but the brilliant Alameda corridor Project, between Long Beach and the rail centrum of Los Angeles, is an interesting exemplar.

ALAMEDA CORRIDOR

The Alameda corridor is an example of the can-do attitude of the USA at its best, showcasing holistic, strategic planning and good leadership, along with some key mergers and trackage rights that made it possible. The corridor, between downtown LA and the ports of Long Beach, is an unusual triple-track corridor some 32 kilometres (20 miles) in length, with, for the most part, the main tracks dropped into a cut-and-cover trench, thus avoiding all road traffic. Almost simultaneously with its opening in 2002 there was a huge upswing in container freight, mainly 'from' but also 'to' the two big ports in the locality.

On the personnel front, the essential key to the project getting up was a quiet, tall American railway planner and engineer who could size up landscape and railway opportunity whether in the Libyan Desert, the Great Salt Lake state of Utah or on the west coast of the USA. Enter once again John Rinard, who started the Chicago CREATE project and led the Alameda project. He took the first steps by securing the purchase of the corridor involved in 1994. By dint of his leadership, the project was completed by 2002 (pre GFC) with 60 trains or more rolling along tracks free of level crossings and train congestion, once cleared onto the corridor.

John Rinard argued that a service road to allow light service vehicles to pass alongside the tracks from time to time for maintenance reasons was not really required — better to build a third track within the corridor trench that was being dug out, thus conferring greater flexibility for maintenance and of course greater capacity overall. It was brilliant thinking for which Californians can be very grateful. More particularly the noisy, long super-freighter trains created less disturbance for suburban communities when operating in a shallow tunnel rather than at ground level.

The Alameda corridor involved bringing together railroad operators and port authorities and the state and local government, along with some helpful federal funding. It was a big task for John Rinard but one he relished, and as a result some great exemplars were created for transport in the USA relating to the removal of rail choke and road/rail congestion points.

Other big cities in addition to Chicago and LA began to examine rail–road level crossing elimination, and in some cases both double tracking and triple tracking.

Go BART

One energy crisis does not a railway boom make, but one earthquake, 6.9 on the Richter scale in 1989 throughout the San Francisco Bay area, does a commuter-railway boom make.

In 1962 the people of San Francisco voted to give the go-ahead to the Bay Area Rapid Transport system, or BART, which includes a line connecting the CBD of San Francisco across the big bay via tunnels to Oakland. Ten years later, on 11 September 1972, BART commenced operations on the unusually wide imperial broad gauge of 5 feet 6 inches, and after some minor mishaps it operated well.

Then, at 1704, on Tuesday, 17 October 1989, the massive 6.9 Richter-scale earthquake known as the Loma Prieta hit San Francisco hard, causing great damage in just fifteen seconds — but not to BART. In fact, after post-earthquake inspections BART was running the next morning, whereas many bridges and collapsed freeways were closed for months, including the key Bay Bridge to Oakland.

Patronage was immediately up 50 per cent and stayed up permanently on most routes — the luck of timing and happenstance, it could be said, but sadly more than 60 people were killed in this earthquake. Nevertheless, BART remains one of the best metro systems in the Americas, and indeed in the world.

More recently the people of California approved another rail bond issue, this one for high-speed rail between Los Angeles and San Francisco — a perfect distance for HSR. Extensions ultimately to Sacramento and San Diego are also planned. Montreal–Toronto and Portland–Vancouver are also attractive city pairs with HSR potential.

So even in the USA, with its 'hate big government intervention' mentality, boosted by the Tea Party movement and right-wing radio shock jocks, big commuter and other rail projects have been approved at referendums. On occasions this has involved the related approval of municipal bond raisings to help pay for the projects.

SUPER RAIL FREIGHT HUBS

Take Texas, for example, after all, home of big oil and several former presidents and powerful senators. Everything is bigger in Texas, it is often said; the Dallas–Fort Worth area is the Chicago of the south, the core of the sun belt and often contrasted with the so-called rust belt of the north of the USA.

In more recent times Texas, with its many 'sunrise' industries, for example computer manufacture, has become the super hub for some very big intermodal depots, or industrial parks. Initially they were laid out with much room for expansion, a very wise move. Indeed they were so large as to be deemed ahead of their time, but filling fast with manufacturers and freight forwarders. For size they are mostly big — very big.

On the outskirts of famous Dallas there are two big competing intermodal hubs: Dallas Logistics Hub, spread over 2400 hectares (6000 acres), and Texas Alliance Hub, complete with an airport and air freight component, spread over 7000 hectares (17,000 acres); and both near big interstate highway connections and of course good rail connections. More recently another hub has sprung up at San Antonio, 430 kilometres (270 miles) away, so far on a smaller scale, but clearly entrepreneurs and state planners 'get' intermodal rail in Texas and are switching more freight to rail.

These hubs are helped by the double-stacking capacity of trains using the east–west rail corridors through Texas, but also corridors northeast to Chicago. The provision of smooth, seamlessness transfer in modern facilities is a win–win for both trucking operators and railway companies, with the heavy lifting over the long distances being done by rail, allowing for more truck drivers to work shorter, more reasonable shifts and be home more often.

For the equivalent of an intermodal all-container super freighter with a crew of two, on average you need around 250 drivers and 250 trucking rigs taking those containers by road. The carbon footprint using rail is, of course, hugely reduced and fuel consumption as well — a win all around.

The question is: can the Texas intermodal hubbing model be matched in the other big states and provinces in the USA, Canada and Mexico?

The Canadian Pacific Railway Company (CP) in some ways points the way with its trackage rights and outright purchase of rail assets down from Canada through the central hub zones of the USA, but not yet directly through into Mexico. Today CP freight trains rumble along *to*, and on a good day *through*, the rail congestion of Chicago; likewise USA rolling stock can be found north and south of the US international borders.

Certainly modern intermodal hubbing — the pure essence of profitable rail freight in the 21st century — and expansion of rail capacity between super intermodal hubs still have huge potential to be fulfilled and broadly the will is there in North America. However, its full realisation will have to await the comprehensive doing-over of those who argue there is no role for government in transport or almost anything else. The win–win consequences might cause the commentariat to advocate for rail, but do not hold your breath.

NORTH-SOUTH AMERICAS CONNECTION

What could you do, what would you do, if there was abundant capital for infrastructure and you were starting afresh south of the NAFTA countries while harnessing the best from the existing rail assets of the NAFTA countries?

A Canada-to-Chile transcontinental comes to mind, featuring, say, the Vancouver-to-Valparaiso Express, a bit like the Cairo-to-Cape Town dream of Cecil Rhodes, and like that dream, certain to remain one in the 21st century and a long way beyond.

However, you cannot rule it out altogether, as peak oil has its impact, and as Brazil and other countries in the Americas hit their straps. Such a line should be Stephenson standard gauge, because that already exists from Vancouver and Halifax in Canada, through the USA and much of Mexico, but then the going gets tough.

It would need to pass through Guatemala, El Salvador, Honduras, Nicaragua and Cost Rica, just to make it as far as Panama. These countries have rundown remnant narrow-gauge rail systems in such a state of disrepair a clean start would be required. We will deal with South America in another chapter but, for the record, such a north–south transcontinental would then need to pass through Colombia, Ecuador, Brazil, Bolivia and possibly Peru to reach Chile.

Sections may yet be built due to local demand, and interestingly the Panama short-line transcontinental railway from the Atlantic to the Pacific is booming. This was actually converted to Stephenson standard gauge just a few years ago from, curiously enough, Czar broad gauge. Now, I would like to think this was in anticipation of the 'Great American North–South Spine Transcontinental', but not true — even though this cross-Panama line actually runs more north–south than in fact east–west. Go look very closely at a map of Panama and you will see what I mean.

The potential for expansion is greatest between Canada and the USA, with upgrade work commencing on the city pair Vancouver, Canada, to Seattle, USA, for both freight and passenger services helping to build linkages between these two cities.

Other big city pairs that should go ahead for TGV-type HSR are Montreal–New York and Toronto–Detroit–Chicago, the last one a city triplet. These are massive cities and if they existed in such proximity in Europe there would be rail connection at an average speed of 240 kph already, if not 300 kph. Historically the low priority for 'think big' international transport projects in the Americas will ensure these are unlikely to proceed immediately, but things may yet change as, for example, the Orlando–Tampa HSR, (to be discussed later) takes off.

On the passenger front, the reality is that rail development will take off in the next phase within each NAFTA country and even internationally, for example between Vancouver and Seattle. Currently Amtrak shows the fastest train service is still a long three hours 55 minutes on a good day between Vancouver and Seattle, a distance of 250 kilometres (or 100 miles) and, yes, with freight train congestion in the region. If the old-generation TGV speed applied, this time would drop to around one hour ten minutes, and for a nonstop service at modern TGV speed, a 50-minute service maximum could be offered on this expanding city pair, especially if all passport checking and border control could be carried out on the train en route. So a four-hour service could be reduced to 50 minutes and at that speed beat all competitors hands down.

That it is obtainable, as demonstrated in Japan and Europe every day of the week, does not mean that it will be quickly implemented, but the goal is there for all to behold. At least a small start has been made to improve

Cascades corridor

In July 2008 I took my family on the Coast Starlight from LA right through to Seattle. Throughout the journey I was terrified by reports that the train was often placed in loops for hours to give freight trains a fast-through priority run. Our luck was in; while there were some delays, most freighters sighted were in the loops, and Amtrak and its prized west-coast (almost luxury) train had a fast run. Towards the end, as we approached Seattle along the Cascades corridor, there was a great burst of speed ensuring our arrival on time.

Perhaps the drivers, or engineers, to use their American name, might have been stirred along by the sight of an old Concorde and an even older Air Force One in the Aviation Museum just south of Seattle if they had been there. Well worth a visit I might add. In any event it was a great train ride and the scenery was superb, but it is America, so do remember to tip early and often.

Canada–USA rail cooperation on the ticket front, with the 30-day North American railway pass now readily available to passengers keen to try the border region for a month of rail derring-do.

Usefully the corridor from Vancouver through Everett and Seattle to Portland and Eugene has been badged the 'Cascades corridor' and has attracted good patronage — more than any Amtrak corridor outside the northeast of the USA. In 2009 Amtrak increased by 100 per cent — that is, actually doubled — the number of train services between Seattle and Vancouver. I have to be honest and record it was an increase from one train daily in each direction to two trains daily in each direction, in part tied to the 2010 Whistler/Vancouver Winter Olympics, but still a small step in the right direction.

US BIDEN HSR

In 2008 the people elected Barack Obama president, but also elected one Joe Biden vice president. As mentioned previously, it is a case of enter Joe Biden again as the only US senator who regularly commuted by train to and from Washington. He is now a reasonably powerful Cabinet member as vice president of the Obama Democrat administration. He has pushed a number of key rail projects and has helped ensure that rail in the USA gets a fair share of the stimulus package funds announced in 2009, and in a more detailed way in 2010.

The first city pair and corridor to get the green light is Tampa to Orlando in busy, bustling Florida. This was a curious choice for the first true new tracks in the USA that will match HSR standards and provide speeds as in Europe. But it will be an exemplar to the rest of the country. About a dozen other projects have all been cleared with federal dollars attaching, but the new Governor of Ohio, elected in November 2010, shows how difficult progress will be. He announced straight after his win he would be refusing to accept $1.4 billion of federal rail-grant money. Further the big Northeast corridor from Boston to New York and Washington remains a half-baked plan.

Acela trains have, when operating, slashed travel times on this route, especially between New York Penn Central and Washington Union Station. The advantage of departing from and arriving in the middle of the city has helped make this run competitive with air, but nowhere near what third-generation TGV can and is offering in parts of France. Currently when in the mood and track permitting, the Acela runs along at up to 240 kph (150 mph); in France the TGV is now regularly doing speeds not much short of 400 kph (250 mph).

At one stage technical problems with the Acela trains forced their total withdrawal, but today the Acela product is getting there. Yet it still takes three and a half hours Boston to New York (300 kilometres or 190 miles), and two and three-quarter hours New York to Washington (360 kilometres or 225 miles). If TGV speeds applied, then the travel time on both sectors would be slashed by at least an hour each, and real competition would emerge against all comers.

The problem is that a band-aid approach has too often applied to the Northeast corridor rather than an attempt to go with long sections of totally dedicated high-speed track, complete with bypasses at some of the complex junctions and big city stations along the route. Patching here and revamping there does improve running times but falls well short of the trailblazing Paris–Lyon all-new TGV tracks of last century, not to mention the Tokyo–Osaka all-new Shinkansen tracks started mid last century, and now Rome–Florence with several rail bypasses in place, for example at Orvieto and Chiusi Centrale.

Even if all these problems could be overcome to tap into this huge potential for rail, I hear you say the Americans will never give up their car culture and the freight forwarders will never switch entirely to rail. This may in fact not be exactly true.

Regional commuter trains using normal or heavy rail, as well as light rail to and through CBDs of modern cities, both in Canada and the USA, are already enjoying explosive growth, as demonstrated when I travelled in 2005. Take the Northwest corridor out of Montreal, an old railway line that is back in play for commuters in the direction of Mont Tremblant, but sadly stopping well short of that ski resort, and for that matter only making it all the way downtown during peak hours. As I found in 2005, out of peak hour you have to detrain and walk to a nearby metro for the last leg into Montreal CBD.

SMART COMMUTING

In the Bay Area around San Francisco, it is a case of going forward from BART to SMART, a new project that is planned to feed in from the north to the busy Larkspur ferry terminal and thence by express ferry to San Francisco CBD. BART and other services remain, including the age-old colourful cable cars, with their strong-armed gripsters operating the levers that engage the clamps on the cable underneath. SMART is expected to commence operations modestly in 2014, running from Cloverdale along 112 kilometres (70 miles) of largely single track corridor into the Larkspur ferry terminal.

There are three notable aspects about this SMART project. Firstly it is one of many on the go in the USA and backed by state legislatures. Secondly, it does not offer seamless, direct CBD connection but involves a change to ferry, which is now adjudged acceptable if the ticketing is seamless and timings coordinated. Finally, it is at the lower end of the range of capital start-up costs for distance covered, at US$41 million, helped by the use of an existing rail corridor. I hasten to add it has been featured in the reliable *Trains* magazine (March 2010), and so clearly SMART has crossed a threshold. I happily acknowledge some but not all of the above information originates from this magazine.

SMART is a very good exemplar of how project planning is in full swing for expanded regional heavy rail and for light rail to cater for commuters up to around 160 kilometres (100 miles) from a hub CBD. The bigger the population of the city, generally the further the reach of regional commuter rail.

In some ways the good and not so old San Diego Trolley is where the rejuvenation started. It opened nearly 30 years ago in 1981 with a north–south line only, but a bright and breezy service that won hearts and minds and actual passengers. It could be said it was driven by an act of God when Hurricane Kathleen knocked out an underused Southern Pacific rail connection in far south California east of San Diego and freed up rail-corridor access. Today it has expanded to three large trolley lines, or light rail, with modern equipment including low-level carriages of the new 21st-century type. These allow passengers to negotiate a step of a few inches or centimeters, not three or four big steps. I have fond memories of an escapade to San Diego, mainly to sample both the then new San Diego Trolley and Tijuana — dare I say a cool, clean experience in one, and a hot, dusty, dirty experience in the other. You can guess which.

In the honour roll set out in Wikipedia of the 34 light rail systems in the USA, the San Diego Trolley comes in at sixth position on usage, and is first in the rebirth phase of light rail emerging over the last three decades.

You ain't seen nothing yet. In Phoenix, as mentioned, and Sacramento, it is go, go, go, with clever light rail. Many more large cities will climb on the bandwagon. Denver is trying but huge budget overruns and the GFC have stalled planned expansion there. While most other passenger rail modes in North America are depressing in terms of what might have been, light rail and regional commuter heavy rail, along with freight, are where the action is and will continue to be.

In Canada there are many projects in the pipeline, driven broadly by voter demand for alternatives to the car and heavy truck. As the Skeena train on the west coast of Canada heads inland from Prince Rupert through Prince George, to Jasper, it delivers the mailbag to the town of Penny in a very isolated section of the mighty Rockies in western Canada, the last town in Canada to rely on mail delivery by train.

So the continent where trains still deliver the mail, the continent that delivered the first man to the moon and delivered the key NAFTA treaty in the 20th century, but almost wrecked all forms of rail in the same century, must get rail right in the next century. It has the capacity to do so, and eventually the political leadership and resolve will be demanded by a majority of the people to see it happen.

Throughout the 20th century, for 65 years the famous 20th Century Limited luxury train conveyed the rich and the famous between New York and Chicago in about sixteen hours' travel time on its best days. It will be incredible, in fact despicable, if train speed between those two giant cities goes backwards in the 21st century and rail more broadly is allowed to stagger in the USA again. Not only can North America not afford the price of this but the world cannot afford the unnecessarily large carbon footprint this would entail.

The USA has 4.5 per cent of the world's population but consumes 25 per cent of the world's daily oil production. For its own sake and all our sakes rail must be further developed and allowed to shoulder more of the transport burden across the dynamic country.

The American investor Warren Buffet recently said it was all about rail and its benefit for the next generation: 'Rail just moves goods so much more efficiently than can be done over the roads. So, over time, I think you will see more and more tonne-miles moving on the railroads.' To this I say amen, shalom and salaam.

AUSTRALIA

World's best in bulk rail freight

It is a dubious record to hold but, in fact, Australia invented and developed more railway gauges than any other railway realm in the world — an amazing 22, as already noted. However, there is another record of substance from the early days of rail in Australia: it has the world's longest section of dead-straight track, in the centre of the Nullarbor Desert, about halfway between Perth and Adelaide.

This east–west transcontinental was vital for political reasons and vital as a great east–west connector, across the southern half of the huge continent of Australia. West Australian voters were reluctant to vote yes in the referendum forming the Federation of Australia, but the promise of an east–west railway was the commitment that did the trick.

So, after just sixteen years of federation, the mammoth project of the linking transcontinental railway across southern Australia was opened. It was built against considerable logistical odds and wisely in Stephenson standard gauge. This was a brave decision because Western Australia at the time and South Australia, the two states the line connected, had zero Stephenson standard gauge rail; this was to come much later. As part of the project, surveyors found the terrain easy for creating that very long straight section of single track.

The straight track in question clocks in at 478 kilometres (297 miles) and is for drivers and passengers deadly boring. It is almost level throughout, travelling through predominantly low scrub bush, at least in odd years of good rain, but of course it is a desert and there are no trees. In fact Nullarbor stands for just that in Latin and not the local Aboriginal language: it really is an expanse of 'no trees'.

The Tea and Sugar

Today the original Tea and Sugar can be found in the main pavilion of the National Rail Museum of Australia, located at Port Dock, Adelaide, the capital of South Australia. The butcher's meat wagon is done out as if still operational today, with a big cutting block and a carcass or two hanging realistically; a great display.

The Tea and Sugar was a mobile shop across the Nullarbor Desert and a good one; there was even a pay wagon attached for the railway workers' pays. Presumably the all-white outside walls and roof of each carriage were to help keep things cool.

I have always contended that the NRM Port Dock is the greatest multi-gauge railway museum in the world, with huge collections of glistening steam locomotives right through to splendid dining cars in each of Irish broad, Stephenson standard and Anglo Cape narrow gauge types. This is in the same way that York, UK, is the greatest Stephenson standard gauge museum in the world, but that gauge only. Both are well worth visiting and enjoying a cup of tea with sugar while there.

The towns across the Nullarbor were artificially created — all are rail towns to service the track, and at Tarcoola, the junction for the Alice Springs–Darwin south–north transcontinental, provide a crew rest house. For years a famous train called the Tea and Sugar serviced these lonely towns before centralised work gangs were established and the big towns at either end, namely Kalgoorlie in the west and Port Augusta in the east, became the main bases.

The culture of the state-based administration of railways in Australia, all different entities and often using different gauges, led to a degree of secrecy and conspiracy. At interstate borders and other locations where the railways met each other, even if there was no break of gauge, huge time-wasting barriers were created to stop any kind of seamlessness.

The secrecy reflected two motivations: to fool the Treasury for as long as possible and with that the politicians so things could drift along unexamined; and fool the public so they would accept second best. It was a misguided way of protecting fiefdoms state by state. Trade union leaders and parliamentary committees had to battle hard to obtain accurate and fair-dinkum information from the HQ of the state rail monopolies in a way that was reminiscent of the culture of British Rail over the decades. British Judge Joseph Dean once remarked, when doing battle over the route of HSR 1, the project to provide very high speed alignment connecting London to the Chunnel through Kent, that 'getting information out of British Rail is like trying to open an oyster with your fingers'. Likewise in the Australia of yesteryear, with its various state rail systems, such as the giant NSWGR, and even now with Queensland Rail (QR) now partly privatised.

Partly due to these secrecy aspects, it has been difficult to pinpoint cost shifting and exactly how well or badly many branch lines really have been operating in terms of freight revenue. Despite this it is possible to reach one overarching assumption that is dismaying to the core. In the sixth and seventh decades of the 20th century, the railways of Australia came to within a whisker of collapse and closure so far as intermodal interstate rail freight was concerned. Whole sections of various state-based networks were on the point of closure or actually closed; all the tricks of the trade that were used in the UK were used by the authorities to cut back the networks, especially the branch lines, mainly by stealth. There was little new capital investment in track, rolling stock and locomotive modernisation. Further, dieselisation and other key modernisation decisions were often too late and badly handled.

There was also hopeless overstaffing, not by hundreds, but by thousands, especially in HQs. Several decades ago, the Pope was asked how many worked in the Curia at the Vatican. His famous reply was 'About half,' and this adage applied especially to the big monopoly government-owned railways dominant in Australia after World War II. Yet in a crazy move, when cutbacks came, those who might win business for rail were the first to have their positions abolished — for example, freight managers and country stationmasters.

In 1997 Professor Philip Laird of Wollongong University, a tireless campaigner for rail as a mode of transport, recorded that Australia had the highest road freight usage per capita in the world: this for a country with an expansive but not modern set of railway networks, but too many of them often rusting away.

Then came change and again there were four factors driving it.

STANDARDISATION

(1) The first and biggest change was standardisation, not as previously recommended involving whole states in one expensive burst, but selective standardisation. In an unusual outbreak of lateral thinking, Sydney–Brisbane had been standardised between the wars. Then post World War II the key Melbourne–Sydney corridor was tackled, standardising the section between Melbourne and the border at Albury. This was achieved by laying a new single Stephenson standard gauge track east of the existing Irish broad gauge track, and completed and connected for operations in 1962.

There was just enough political will to drive this project forward, and one William Charles Wentworth, a dynamic MP who headed up a key

An MP who made a difference:

Who was William Charles Wentworth? A short, fiery, indeed colourful, character from a great Australian family of explorers and pioneers, who won election as the centre right Liberal (conservative) party candidate for a Sydney seat to the Federal Parliament in 1949, at the age of 42. This meant he was on Menzies' side but in fact was more of a thorn in it — that is, Robert Gordon Menzies, Australia's longest-serving prime minister.

In 1956 Wentworth chaired a Coalition Government committee that strongly recommended selective standardisation. He was backed up by powerful and effective criticism that dated back to one Field Marshal Herbert Horatio Kitchener, who had said ahead of World War I that the railways of Australia were designed to help the enemy invade, not help Australia defend. Kitchener got that right but much else wrong. He went on to mastermind, with Winston Churchill, the disastrous Dardanelles campaign of 1915, in which thousands of British, Australian, New Zealander, Indians and various Allied forces were killed at Gallipoli.

The Wentworth Report was so persuasive and practical, it was replicated and supported by the then opposition Australian Labor Party. By Australian political standards, the Wentworth Report's key recommendations were implemented rather quickly.

Alas, when the first official passenger train, the Southern Aurora, departed Sydney Central for Melbourne in 1962 during a parliamentary sitting day when the government had only a majority of one, Mr Wentworth, MP, was not on board. He could not get a voting pair arrangement from the parliamentary whip, but after the Federal House of Representatives adjourned for the night, he jumped in a car and raced from Canberra to Yass Junction to join this first train in the middle of the night as it paused on its historic roll straight through to Melbourne.

committee on standardisation, did a great deal to lay the foundations and urge action upon the federal and two state governments. Further, his committee urged other key standardisations and Sydney–Perth followed in 1970, standardising the non-conforming gauge sections. Later in 1994 Melbourne–Adelaide was standardised, thus connecting through to Perth on standard gauge. When the world's newest transcontinental opened for business in 2004, connecting Adelaide via Tarcoola and Alice Springs with Darwin, finally after 173 years of railway operations, Australia at last had all its mainland capitals connected by the same gauge of rail.

So the first big, bold brush that began to turn the tide was standardisation. But even this was not straightforward and for 48 years led to the most bizarre double-gauged railway corridor arrangement anywhere in the world — the 200-kilometre (125-mile) Seymour–Wodonga stretch (with many branch lines connected, although by the year 2000 this was down to one, namely Benalla to Oaklands in southern New South Wales). The Australian Rail Track Corporation (ARTC) operated a single track along this corridor as part of the national rail freight system, but with daily periods of congestion. Yet alongside lay the Irish broad gauge of V/Line, almost always vacant except for three lonely passenger trains on a good day and one or two weekly freight trains (other than at harvest time).

This used to make me wince whenever I happened to be travelling the corridor, observing from the window of a passenger train or from the adjacent Hume Highway. It then happened that the Victorian State ALP Government picked yours truly to chair the Victorian Rail Freight Network Review (RFNR) committee in 2007 and I, as an ex-Coalition federal minister (Federal Nationals Leader and former deputy PM) and ex MP, finally had a chance to make a contribution to rail policy sense, helped greatly by my outstanding fellow committee members.

Uppermost in my mind was the template that William Charles Wentworth had laid down over four decades before of a united committee delivering within the terms of reference. They produced a practical and achievable set of recommendations in a punchy but easy-to-read way, and without too much delay. In short, go for the possible and practical.

We had about six months to tour Victoria and southern New South Wales, collecting evidence and examining key witnesses, working out where the fiefdoms were and what was preventing efficient operations. Our first discovery was that there had never been a comprehensive attempt to categorise the large remnant multi-gauge Victorian network. With an eye to building understanding and momentum with our findings, we went for an easy-to-understand template.

I suggested a set of at least three categories: Gold for the more heavily used branch lines; Silver for the less heavily used but lines with some prospects; and Bronze for those that should be put on care and maintenance only. Bronze was better than recommending outright closure, always difficult for politicians to push through and not always wise due to changes in demography and freight patterns re-invigorating some previously disused branch lines, but the difference between closure and Bronze was minuscule in places. Traditionally in Australia, the sort of method of benign neglect plus the odd flood taking out key bridges has been the haphazard way many branch lines have ceased to operate and closed for good.

Deputy Chair Peter Wilson chimed in with Platinum for the existing trunk main lines and away we went. It was all very logical and the map produced with the lines so marked was mostly well received.

Interestingly now, within few years since our report was accepted, most key recommendations have been funded and implemented, against the odds. The Victorian State Government has broadly followed the template and recommended upgrading the Gold and Silver lines finding the millions of dollars required.

Regarding the ugly Seymour–Wodonga corridor, I was galvanised by remarks made by David Marchant, CEO of ARTC, that it would soon start putting in extra passing loops further to the east of its single Stephenson standard gauge track, the effect of which would have been to cement into place for another four decades the crazy dual-gauge nature of this corridor.

Instead we recommended that the almost freight-train disused Irish broad gauge be upgraded and converted to Stephenson standard over three years. Suddenly in 2010, after last-minute wrangling over which signalling system to use, the line was cut in — thus providing standard-gauge double track on this section of main line connecting Sydney and Melbourne, with maximum speeds of 130 kph (80 mph). Yes, in the 21st century this is adjudged as 'Australian slightly faster rail' speed. Still the cut-in was not trouble-free — many quagmires, or 'mud in ballast' places, have emerged, resulting in very slow speed restrictions and passenger-service suspension until rectified.

There is still one single-track section between the two biggest Australian cities, being the stretch between Albury and Junee, but long super-passing loops installed by ARTC have eased this burden. On a good day centralised traffic controllers allow trains to pass on these 7-kilometre loops at speed, saving considerably on the start–stop costs.

There have been many other wrinkles blocking effective seamlessness between the rail systems — an almost civil war at boundaries between the old Commonwealth Railways (known for a period as Australian National Railways — ANR) operating from Port Augusta to Kalgoorlie, and the West Australia Railways, or Westrail. All freight trains heading east or west would be required to spend a time in limbo there, waiting not only on crew changes but, for many years, locomotive changes as well and a good deal of planned stuffing around.

The ANR depot was in Parkeston and a short distance further west was Kalgoorlie and the Westrail depot. After 1970 it was fully operational standard gauge all the way, in fact from Sydney to Perth, but no train was ever allowed to run straight through. The same blockages existed for a period at Port Augusta and Port Pirie and, especially, at Broken Hill.

ARTC AND VERTICAL SEPARATION

(2) Enter the second big bold brush that made a difference: namely, the separation of the track assets on the east–west route and later elsewhere,

plus the privatisation of many of the rail freight units of operation (except in Queensland until the QR float and partial privatisation — 60 per cent — in November 2010) to create vertical separation. (In Queensland much is different and Anglo Cape narrow gauge continues to apply; ahead of the breakup and float of QR it was the last of the big gigantic rail conglomerates.)

Back in 1996 there had been a change of government at the federal level: the Labor government under Paul Keating lost office after thirteen years and John Howard and the conservative Coalition was swept into power. I had the privilege of leading the junior Coalition party at the time, namely the National Party, and became Deputy Prime Minister and Minister for Trade. I negotiated with John Howard about the key transport portfolio position and we agreed that this should go to John Sharp, a likeable and shrewd operator, both capable and with a natural confidence that I sometimes lacked. He had represented Goulburn, a big railway-junction town, since 1984, and had a good understanding at the macro level of what needed to be done to get rail revamped properly.

I acknowledge a good deal of formative work had commenced under previous governments of both sides, going as far back as Prime Minister Whitlam's days in 1975, with the establishment of Australian National Railways (ANR) out of the old Commonwealth Railways. Later, in the days of PM Fraser and Deputy PM Doug Anthony, the Alice Springs standardisation was completed as far as Alice Springs in 1982. Even PM Keating had funded part but not all of the standardisation of the Melbourne–Adelaide route in 1995. John Sharp moved quickly and cleverly to establish the Australian Rail Track Corporation (ARTC) in 1998 as the holder of the standard gauge rail track assets, initially Broken Hill through Port Augusta then to Kalgoorlie, and Melbourne to Adelaide through Port Augusta then to Alice Springs. By 2010 this had become all key interstate mainland freight routes and more — a total of 4430 route kilometres (2770 miles).

John Sharp massaged his legislation through cabinet and the parliament, including a hostile Senate and hived off the passenger side of the old ANR, including the costly Indian Pacific (which operates from

Sydney to Perth) to Great Southern Railway (GSR), part of the UK Serco empire. GSR immediately revamped the rolling stock and today is a good operator of the modernised Indian Pacific, the Ghan between Adelaide and Darwin, and the Overland daylight train from Melbourne to Adelaide.

Except for the company-owned iron ore lines in the Pilbara, Western Australia, broadly Australia has separated rail vertically. Typically this involves a sole government track owner, the ARTC, as 'below rail' owner and track maintainer; with old and new private-enterprise operators paying access fees to operate on the rail network or 'above rail'. Competition has at last been introduced in a meaningful way into the interstate railway freight market.

When freight company SCT (Specialised Container Transport) Logistics started a unique, modern computer-packed box-car operation in 1995 from Melbourne to Perth, it had to get track access permission and make payments to not one but three separate governmental entities. By 1998 this was reduced to just one — the efficient and effective ARTC. Furthermore, after 1995, SCT had become just one of several operators hauling freight across the Nullarbor, so things became more efficient and competitive.

The big question is: why has this template of vertical separation been successful in Australia and completely disastrous in the United Kingdom? It is a case of different horses for different courses. The ARTC network is almost entirely long-distance intermodal freight orientated, a very profitable modern mode of rail, and the network not hugely congested and rundown. In Britain, on some major commuter lines, for years there has been very rundown track and passenger rolling stock crowded to the brim, especially to and from London. Also, the ARTC strictly limits contractors further subcontracting out, so performance can be monitored, and keeps tight supervision and controls in place over the network. Sadly this was not the case in the UK.

For a more detailed examination of the factors in play, I commend the writings of Christian Wolmar and Matthew Engel, two British rail

Double-stacked freight train on the east–west transcontinental near Port Augusta. (Tim Fischer)

aficionados who do know their stuff. For my part, I also highlight that it was not Margaret Thatcher who 'did it' to rail in the UK, privatising in a way that has been a big leap backwards in many parts of the country, but PM John Major and one Chris Patten. They proceeded with a very clunky template for privatisation, necessitating tidying up attempts under the early years of PM Tony Blair.

UK transport ministers often changed in this period and/or went missing in action. The UK needed a Dick Crossman or an Alan Clark (former robust, can-do frontbenchers), or maybe an even bigger 'head-kicking bastard' like the mysterious Minister for War Information Brendan Bracken (who was not Churchill's illegitimate son as some claimed but a former sacked Australian farmhand), to stay the task and get the job done properly.

In Australia, federal transport ministers came and went. Between 1997 and 2007, after John Sharp there was Mark Vaile (two stints), John Anderson, Warren Truss and Anthony Albanese (with good departmental secretaries providing some continuity). It was in fact John Anderson who secured the participation of New South Wales against considerable odds, with the ARTC leasing key main lines and regional lines, even some branch lines, from the NSW State Government.

The basic core template adopted to carry rail into the 21st century is at last in place except in Queensland and has delivered much improvement on the freight front. As a result, rail freight has expanded massively, especially on the vital Perth corridor from Sydney and Parkes, as well as Melbourne and Adelaide. Around 90 per cent of freight east–west is carried by rail, versus coastal shipping and big rig road trains.

LABOUR REFORM

(3) The third big brush for change and makeover in Australia was delivered in part by the trade unions, and also by industrial relations legislative reform, so that one tiny dispute in Melbourne could no longer bring all freight trains in the nation to a halt. Above all else, days upon days of strikes over fiefdoms and territory, mainly inter-union disputes for coverage and maintenance of closed shops, with no contestable free flow of labour, have become accepted as ridiculous. Wildcat strikes involving sudden stoppages, often just before peak hour, have also declined. Smart union leaders have been putting effort into superannuation and productivity gains.

The ACTU was established as the big overarching union body in 1928 and almost immediately was confronted by the Great Depression, then shortly after this the upheaval of World War II. It had capable leaders in the main, including Bob Hawke, who went on to become prime minister and won four elections for the ALP.

Sometimes disputes got out of hand right under the nose of the

ACTU; this was the case with the tram strike in Melbourne in January 1990, right where the ACTU HQ was located. The big transport industrial issues were centered on single-person manned trains and trams and involved the proposed abolition of conductors on board. The tram strike lasted on and off for most of the month before a deal — or, as some unionists opined, a sellout — was agreed. The peak of this ugly period occurred when tram drivers in a related dispute parked trams in busy CBD streets and then welded the wheels to the rails so that they could not be moved. Nothing has matched this burst of craziness since, thank God.

As a result of reduced industrial action, transport and rail freight especially became more reliable, and with the bonus of lifting pride and productivity in the workforce, pilfering decreased. This was also thanks to containerisation and CT scanners, along with various other forms of tracking and surveillance.

The contribution of the union movement to the revamp of rail in Australia, the UK and the USA should not be underestimated. While there will be some slippages and breakouts from time to time, it is difficult to see large-scale destructive strike action arriving in the transport arena again, at least so far as the USA and Australia are concerned. The supreme irony is that the giant coal strike of 1949 in New South Wales and the pilots' strike of 1989 in Australia, plus that 1990 tram strike in Melbourne, were all done over by ruling Labor Party governments at the time. There are some who remain bitter about this to this day.

The other irony is that Melbourne and Sydney have failed miserably in getting seamless automatic ticketing for commuters up to speed, complex zone patterns that work elsewhere in the world proving to be too difficult for the system designers. Automatic ticketing led to the abolition of costly bus and tram conductors. In Rome the one ticket gives you 75 minutes on all bus and metro routes, fully interchangeable. Australia lags places like Rome on seamless automatic ticketing by a mile or even millennium perhaps.

Easter eggs go west by SCT rail

Specialised Container Transport (SCT) Ltd is based at Altona on the western side of Melbourne, beside rail yards that matter. Here since 1995 it has specialised in loading pallets into box cars and sending them west. Many cars are refrigerated to handle perishable goods, and the computers work overtime to spread weight loads and maximise freight revenue yield per wagon or box car. It is brilliant counterintuitive transport economics at work, all the more so when Lent starts each year.

This is, of course, 40 days out from Easter and so the time of the big seasonal movement of Easter eggs. In fact rich chocolate of all kinds travels by train from Altona to go to Perth, travelling across the hot Nullarbor in a cool box car monitored from HQ at Altona all the way to destination. Old rail could not have safely handled this, but new freight rail does it in a canter, with the train drivers barely knowing they have Easter eggs on board. It might be just as well, thus avoiding temptation.

BULK RAIL EFFICIENCY

(4) The final big brush forcing change in rail in Australia was the need to transport huge tonnages of bulk freight: iron ore in Western Australia; coal in New South Wales and Queensland; and when there is a good harvest, grain in most mainland states, especially New South Wales, Victoria, South Australia and Western Australia. This time it was private enterprise that led the way in a big way, especially in developing efficient long unit train operations with balloon-loop loading and unloading. This allows continuous steady train movement at mine and port, and has maximised efficiency.

In the 1960s the then federal minister for national development, David Fairbairn, DFC, lifted the ban on iron-ore exports, a ban that had existed for fear Australia would not have enough for its own protection. It had continued after World War II in a backlash against Japan, but in the 1960s Australia was moving on. Huge mines sprang up in the Pilbara in the north of Western Australia and that state's long-serving Premier and Minister for Development at the time Sir Charles Court made a critical and correct decision to insist on standard gauge for the new railways required. An old railway in the area ran from Port Hedland to Marble Bar in Anglo Cape narrow gauge, but this had closed and its gauge was ignored, again thank God.

To digress a little, about the same time the huge Bowen coal basin was opening up in central Queensland, QR operated a largely remnant system of Anglo Cape narrow gauge in the area through to existing ports such as at Gladstone, Hay Point and Mackay. Pity that the boldness of Sir Charles Court in the west was not matched by some who were directly involved in the new coal railway lines of Queensland, and pity that the decision was not made to use the larger capacity standard gauge from the new mines to the ports.

Gauge change was considered with the railway upgrade from Mt Isa to Townsville, again around the 1960s, but the decision was taken to stay with narrow gauge. In fact the Wentworth Report had highlighted that the massive Burdekin River Bridge between Charters Towers and Townsville, which had been built years before, had a design capability for standard gauge, but even this was not enough to sway decision-makers.

So the huge expansion in coal mining in the east was met with many new railway lines; in New South Wales all in standard gauge which it already used but in Queensland all in a restricting narrow gauge, reducing maximum loads to around 9000 tonnes per train versus around 10,000 tonnes in New South Wales with the capability to go higher in shifting the valuable black stuff. Coal is even more valuable, even more in demand, post the horrific March 2011 Japanese earthquake and related nuclear radiation saga. South Africa, on the same narrow gauge, has bulk trains operating around 30,000 tonnes due to very heavy duty rolling stock and very heavy rails.

In the west, the iron-ore railways were built at standard gauge and much heavier and longer trains operated from the start. The newest,

Fortescue Railway, operates at around the 30,000 tonnes mark, and BHP Billiton operates at around 42,000 tonnes of iron ore per train, today.

In a display of great might, in 2001 BHP, as it was then, operated a world-record iron-ore train of just over 99,000 gross tonnes, but kept it to a one-off operation. I think it was trying to see what might break with 86,262 tonnes of iron ore loaded on 682 wagons hauled by two locomotives up front, one at the back and the rest scattered right through. All in all, eight locomotives were used in this record-breaking effort from Mount Newman to Port Hedland. Nothing did bust but it was a one off — and yes, bigger, heavier and longer than anything in the USA.

The Pilbara area can be inundated with massive flooding caused by cyclones, and this happened when the race was on to complete the Hamersley Iron Railway. In April 1966 Cyclone Shirley dumped 175 millimetres of rain on the brand-new railway, causing line washouts at eighteen different locations. The engineer in chief just got on with the job — his name G.W. Hills — and a month later Hamersley Iron was delivering to port export-quality iron ore in large tonnages. The shipping program from Dampier and Port Hedland has not missed a month in the 40 years since.

Over the last four decades the two original iron-ore railways in Western Australia, Hammersley Iron and BHP, have expanded to new mines in the Pilbara region. They are regarded as the best exemplars of efficient bulk-rail operation in the world. They even rate ahead of the renowned Powder River Basin railway operations of the central west of the USA. The keys have been some great railway engineers in chief, and the culture of private enterprise, with governments broadly staying out of the way after setting the right parameters.

So four big brush strokes have swept the railways of Australia into the 21st century from a point of near collapse just 50 years or so before; firstly, selective standardisation; secondly, the introduction of competition above track through the setting up of ARTC and privatisation of much but not all rail Down Under; thirdly, industrial relations reform and improvements;

and finally, getting the bulk heavy freight from the big new mines right from inception, especially in Western Australia.

Overarching all this have been various helpful entities, notably the Commonwealth Railways, headquartered at Port Augusta and brilliantly led by Keith Smith from 1960 to 1981, and the Australian National Railways (ANR), which took over the Commonwealth Railways.

Professor Philip Laird has highlighted that in the last two decades some other outcomes have helped boost rail in Australia. Huge investment in the Queensland main lines, including major straightening and route shortening has boosted rail passenger and freight in that state. Secondly, the Victorian Regional Fast rail project has boosted V/Line passenger numbers between Melbourne and such places as the gold-rush cities of Ballarat and Bendigo. Thirdly, Perth's electrification and expansion of key suburban lines (often using freeway corridors) has worked miracles for commuters and hugely boosted patronage.

New Zealand rail: one government and just one gauge

Contrasting with Australia's development of rail is New Zealand, with a unitary system of government, and after a few early years' toying with multiple gauges, switching to just one gauge. This occurred under the brilliant leadership of Sir Julius Vogel, who became colonial treasurer in 1869 and NZ premier three years later. He sorted the railways into a national endeavour, operating entirely on Anglo Cape gauge.

In the 1990s the inevitable privatisation took place, but in a way that was more about asset stripping than providing a rail system for the 21st century. Today New Zealand can boast of some progress, as we will see in the penultimate chapter of this book. Despite the country's difficult terrain for fast trains, it is getting there with rail freight and slowly upgrading urban services, starting with its biggest city, Auckland.

What is Australia's further railway potential? Are there any large greenfield projects deserving implementation? The short answers are yes and yes. First is HSR from Melbourne through Canberra and Sydney to Newcastle, Coffs Harbour and Brisbane. Secondly, there is the inland freight railway project Melbourne direct to Toowomba for Brisbane and then through Queensland to Mt Isa. The link onwards from Mt Isa to Tennant Creek, thus connecting with the Adelaide–Darwin transcontinental, requires one or two big mining projects on the corridor and there is talk of these but nothing finalised. Yet in the 2010 federal election campaign in Australia, both the government and opposition announced their commitment to a feasibility study to build the Melbourne–Toowomba (for Brisbane) project to proceed.

In a more distant category, yet to be firmed up for construction, there is the third stand-alone project, a new–east west railway from the Pilbara iron-ore mines across Australia, passing just to the north of Alice Springs to the Bowen coal basin in Queensland. Many regard this project as a bridge too far in trying to take coal west and iron ore east to hopefully make steel somewhere near a gas field, perhaps near the Moonie or Bellara gas fields or on the coast of Western Australia, where the Rankin gas field pipeline comes ashore.

In one sense, all of Australia would benefit from these projects, albeit southeast Australia in a very direct way. Benefits would include a reduction of road freight and coach services along the busy corridors of the Hume and Pacific Highways.

DOUBLE-DECKER COMMUTER TRAINS

It is a case of 'train projects unlimited', including smaller but no less expensive capital-city commuter rail and light rail projects crying out for implementation, especially in Sydney, Melbourne and Adelaide. There is no true metro system as such anywhere in Australia, and one such project for Sydney has just been canned, after many millions had been spent on feasibility and early planning. The Sydney daily rush hour, especially in the morning, goes from bad to worse, but few Sydneysiders realise just how much worse it could have been except for the brilliance of two of its citizens: John Bradfield and Roy Leembruggen.

Bradfield dominated his chosen career of civil engineering after graduating from Sydney University in 1889. He laid out a huge network of underground railways for Sydney, and proposed a bridge across Sydney Harbour. World War I postponed things but Bradfield eventually produced one of the greatest bridges in the world, affectionately nicknamed the coathanger, and the second longest of its type. It was built with two tram tracks, two heavy rail tracks and six road lanes, at a width decades ahead of its time. The Sydney Harbour Bridge leads the world each New Year with spectacular fireworks, helped by the early time zone of Sydney.

Bradfield proposed many schemes, including some fantastic detailed water schemes for Far North Queensland to divert water inland and make the rivers flow permanently from Queensland towards South Australia.

It was his attention to detail, laced with vision, that led to the masterstroke of tram and train approach tunnels to the Sydney Harbour Bridge. By raising the vertical loading gauge to the height of 14 feet 6 inches (4.4 metres) clearance, he laid down a generous height that was then applied across the Sydney suburban system. It was a vertical clearance over 15 per cent higher than that applying to the British loading gauge — higher even than that of the then NSWGR country network — and it worked.

The advantage of this height was that it created scope for design engineer Roy Leembruggen's trailblazing idea. Leembruggen was an outstanding guest on episode 22 of the ABC's *Great Train Show*, and during the interview he showed in his humility yet determination how he won out against inevitable opposition to change. I have often said it should be a case of Saint Roy of Collaroy, as he lived near there, north of Sydney Harbour, but his contribution to boosting rail-commuter efficiency was worldwide, if almost by accident.

The Sydney suburban railway system was facing huge congestion around 1961. Quadruplication of vital sections of the suburban system was far too expensive and yet more trains or bigger trains with greater capacity were required. Roy Leembruggen and his employer Tulloch Engineering went into bat with the then emperor of NSWGR, Neil McCusker, a wiley Scot who delivered the last-ever fair-dinkum profit of the NSWGR, just before he retired. An upgrade to the Sydney fleet was needed; and maybe bigger automatically opening doors would help.

In a famous conversation, the young Roy Leembruggen went for the jugular, saying why not double-deck the new fleet and lift capacity of the eight-car train set from about 1000 passengers to 1900 passengers, without having to lay one extra kilometre of track. Neil McCusker agreed and the prototypes were soon running. By 1968 Tuscan-red-coloured consists were providing greatly improved capacity with their double-decker configuration and large automatic doors at platform height.

At the time, Roy's design led the world and was eagerly sought by the world. Then Roy or his company made a mistake that belongs to an era of graciousness. When the German DB and the French SNCF and eight others asked for a copy of the design of the Sydney double-decker, they were kindly sent off by post without copyright or intellectual property protection.

Ouch, as the 'on sale rights' to Europe and the USA might have solved the NSW deficit, but it was too late. Years ago, on my first visit to Versailles and Chartres in France, I looked out of the carriage window of my single-decker heading from Paris to Cholet to see nearby double-decker carriages that looked very familiar. In fact they were an almost exact copy of the Sydney double-decker. So by accident and Australian generosity, Sydney's Saint Roy Leembruggen helped rail around the world.

Melbourne experimented with two double-decker carriages on the Ringwood line but did not persevere due a lack of foresight, as the commuter numbers on these corridors in peak time have exploded; Southern Region in the UK likewise experimented just after World War II, but found them not workable and unpopular with the commuters, not least because of the length of time it took to get everyone on and off. Sydney's sorely stretched system today owes much to John Bradfield and Roy Leembruggen; otherwise things would be much worse.

HIGH-SPEED RAIL

Australia's three big projects of the future I have listed in an order of probability, I guess; certainly the first project of HSR has much to commend it and should be operating by now. It is a big call to say it will be up and running ahead of other big rail projects, but with a set of airport hubs integrated and airline company involvement, it may yet be the case.

Imagine departing Platform 1 at Southern Cross, Melbourne, and diving into a long tunnel almost to Tullamarine, Melbourne's international airport and the only major airport without curfew or curfew threatening in Australia, and with space for four runways. After a brief stop at a modern intermodal hub station imagine moving either express to Canberra or via brief stops at the Benalla hub, Albury hub and Tumut–Riverina hub, before diving through the Brindabella mountains, using a mere 11 kilometres (7 miles) of tunnels to arrive at Canberra, then on to Sydney Central through the East Hills corridor.

It is a matter of supreme irony that the original maps of Canberra, including a valid town planning map of 1933, show a 'Railway Reserve' for Australia's planned national capital city exactly where the best HSR station location in the 21st century could be or should be (if not at the airport). Located between the Canberra Convention Centre and Lake Burley Griffin on the north side of the lake, just southeast of Civic, around the axis of Amaroo Street, it is close to the central hub of Canberra, has space for a mega road coach/rail transfer terminal, and it is within walking distance to and from a sizable convention centre. I thank Graeme Stanley and the *Federal City Express*, May 2010, publication for this information, and highlight that a cut-and-cover station and bus hub terminal could be

Sunrise timetable Melbourne–Brisbane

There is an art to creating railway timetables conceptually and of course they offer many temptations; a TGV-type HSR operating at a mere maximum of 330 kph (206 mph) and an average of near 282 kph (176 mph) — that is, not as fast as part of the TGV network which runs up towards 400 kph (250 mph) every day of the week — would deliver the following, approximately:

DEPARTURE DAILY		
	READ DOWN	READ UP
Melbourne Southern Cross	0700	1350
Tullamarine Airport	0710	1340
Benalla Hub	*	*
Albury Hub	0800	1250
Tumut Hub	*	*
Canberra Hub	0850	1200
Goulburn Hub	*	*
Moss Vale Hub	*	*
Sydney Central ETA / ETD	0955#	1100
Sydney Central ETA / ETD	1010	1040
Newcastle Hub	1050	1000
Taree Hub	*	*
Coffs Harbour	1200	0850
Lismore Hub	*	*
Murwillumbah Hub	1300	0750
Brisbane Roma Street	1350	0700

* Denotes that not every train would stop there but market would indicate at least four a day should, with the all-stopping HSR running on the even hour out of Melbourne Southern Cross, the non-stopping super expresses could leave on the odd hour. This is one practical type of approach, leaving the slower train that stops more often still ahead of the faster train departing one hour later.

All of this should be regarded as work in progress; however, it is a not-too-subtle futuristic stir. The ability for some trains to bypass Melbourne's Tullamarine Airport platforms by passing to the east — think Charles De Gaulle Airport at Paris and the Eurostar — would be useful from the outset, but my hunch is that non-curfew 'Tulla' is the key to the political will to get going with an Australian HSR.

\# Alert observers will have noticed five minutes extra is allowed on the sector into Sydney Central from the southwest, mainly as a margin to help build towards 100 per cent punctuality and to reflect practicalities. Arrival in Sydney from Melbourne on time would be the key performance indicator that would make or break the reliability reputation, as southerners tend to be more punctual than those of the harbour city.

The key first-morning service southbound out of Sydney for Melbourne could even be scheduled as a through express with just one stop at Canberra. With an extra five minutes loaded in to guarantee on-time performance, this 'sunrise' service would be as follows:

Sydney Central depart	0700	0945
Canberra (two-minute stop)	0800	0840
Melbourne Southern Cross arrival	0945	0700

located there, without too much disruption — but tunnels on the airport or the Sydney side would need to avoid the new ASIO HQ and its deep huge basement.

The Sydney–Newcastle–Coffs Harbour–Brisbane sectors would tap the most populous corridor in Australia, but the three obvious entry points into Brisbane and the Roma Street terminal would need careful evaluation. The options are easy to spell out; less easy is to decide which one is best. The first one is to use the existing short western Kyogle–Beaudesert rail corridor; the second is the direct, central Murwillumbah–Beenleigh option; and the third is the eastern Gold Coast option. Every extra kilometre chasing market en route means the vast majority of Brisbane–Sydney through passengers and trains pay a penalty in money, time and carbon footprint.

All of this requires careful, detailed research, but if the choice is made to not develop an HSR rail–air hub at Coolangatta, it might make sense to connect the Gold Coast market at a Murwillumbah hub by extending the QR electric from Robina and Coolangatta to Murwillumbah. Then the direct, central Murwillimbah–Beenleigh route would possibly stack up, but would require tunnelling for grade and environmental reasons.

If you have read the timetable box, you might say again: 'Pigs might fly.' But if Dr Paul Wild had been allowed to proceed with a half-even break from the Federal Treasury at the time in the 1980s, his very fast train syndicate would be operating by now on this key corridor. The current rail route Sydney–Melbourne is a huge 960 kilometres; the proposed Wild Gippsland route came in at 876 kilometres; the preferred inland route denoted here is a mere 859, and by taking out the Brindabella kink with 11 kilometres of tunnelling between Tumut and Canberra on a direct route, the distance tumbles to just 822 kilometres.

Dale Budd of Canberra has followed HSR closely for over 25 years, in Australia and overseas. His experience ranges from working with Paul Wild at VFT headquarters years ago to advising the Saudi Railways on its Mecca–Medina HSR project. His very broad rail expertise includes being a director of ARTC for six years and leads him to contend that Australia needs HSR on the east coast, perhaps starting with the Newcastle–Sydney–Canberra sectors first. Dale Budd further contends that the line should be built for a speed of not less than 380 kph, with the capability to increase to perhaps 400 kph in the future.

In 2011 Transport Minister Anthony Albanese launched the latest HSR study and it is in full swing, with bipartisan support and tight timelines. There are key people fully on board, like Bryan Nye, from the Australasian Railway Association, and a member of the Study Reference Group, so fingers crossed for positive lateral thinking outcomes.

The second project, the inland railway freight project, IRF, is being promoted by the irrepressible Everald Compton. This project would slash freight train times between Melbourne and Toowomba/Brisbane. Now, many underestimate Everald Compton who is a dynamo in many fields and lives in Brisbane but turns up at conferences all over. I last saw him in full flight at the huge Parliament of World Religions conference in Melbourne in December 2009.

The objective of his project has been refined over recent years but it is essentially to provide a less-than-21-hour freight service from Melbourne to Brisbane by an inland route which would pass through the growing hub of Parkes in central New South Wales. Later it would head north from

Toowoomba, west of Brisbane through Queensland to Tennant Creek in the Northern Territory. The global financial crisis has been no help but the concept remains solid, especially cutting through the interstate border on the direct route from near Moree, New South Wales, through Yetman to Inglewood and on to Toowoomba.

Elsewhere on this Melbourne–Brisbane route existing medium and heavy standard gauge rail would be used, including in the initial phase from Melbourne through Albury to Junee, Cootamundra and Stockinbingal, then direct to Parkes and Dubbo. This route would preclude double-stacking containers because of low over-head bridges, so the alternative Shepparton option could fly further down the track, especially if it enabled double-stacking with new rail. This would run via Seymour, Shepparton, Tocumwal, direct to Jerilderie then Narrandera and around to Stockingbingal.

One of the key companies behind the project is ATEC — Australian Transport and Energy Corridor Ltd. Certainly the project reflects the potential for a finite freight rail expansion that many argue should have preceded the Alice Springs–Darwin line, but when the political and economic constellations line up for some decent rail infrastructure in Australia, such as the standard gauge to Darwin from the south via Alice Springs, then you grab them. The opportunity was a narrow window around 1998 and it had to be taken. APT/FreightLink, which uses the north–south line, has increased tonnage fivefold into Darwin since it opened in 2004.

Also bidding to build inland freight lines is a company called Great Australian Trunk Railways (GATR) headed by Vince O'Rourke, a former head of QR and no slouch. It is pushing forward with its agenda and providing conceptual competition re the freight railway systems and key corridors in Australia.

Project number three relates to the old Lang Hancock/Joh Bjelke-Petersen railway directly connecting the Pilbara with central Queensland, and is currently being pursued by Shane Condon, also Brisbane-based like Everald Compton. Hancock staked out the early mining claims in

Nerves of steel: Adelaide–Darwin:

Major railway projects in both the planning and construction phase, and in the first few years of operation, require raw courage and much leadership from the handful of leaders involved. The world's newest transcontinental railway, from Adelaide to Darwin, was a project that nearly fell over several times, with capital funding shortfalls and a raft of other deal-breaking problems. Then on start-up a little matter of grinding almost cost the APT/ FreightLink some big freight customers. The harmony between the bevel on the steel wheels did not match the railhead grinding, and the required 1-in-20 canter on the top of each rail, conferred by the shape of each sleeper, or tie, tilted the overall rail inwards. An intense vibration resulted on the new northern section — think Monte Carlo biscuits arriving in Darwin but in a powder form.

This saga and several others required nerves of steel. The APT/FreightLink triumvirate with nerve enough to carry this burden was Malcolm Kinnaird as chairman, Bruce McGowan as first CEO and later director, and John Fullerton as second CEO. At other levels Rick Allert, Frank Moretti, Tony Aldridge and many others also performed miracles, but it was these three who more than all others carried the burden and delivered a successful outcome, with freight tonnages booming on this rail corridor.

Alice Springs in the Red Centre of Australia should create an avenue of honour along the northern entrance to Heavitree Gap, and, yes, the Flying Doctor John Flynn of the Inland, aviation pioneer Eddie Connellan, and Albert Namatjira and Emily Kngwarreye, the great Aboriginal painters, should be honoured there as 'Citizens of the Centre', along with Malcolm, Bruce and John on the southern entrance.

the Pilbara, starting with those on his old cattle property, 'Hamersley', as he knew for years that iron ore in abundance was to be had in the area. He went on to own and develop mines and became a millionaire many times over. He had a liking for the cut-through developmental style of the Queensland Premier Sir Joh Bjelke-Petersen in his brilliant early years as Queensland Premier. Alas, they both died before the Pilbara–Central Queensland project could be built, but further studies continue today. Already the cross point of the Alice Springs–Darwin line with the proposed east–west line has been pencilled in for just north of the Larapinta Grade, north of Alice Springs. This has been examined in a degree of detail, with Shane Condon submitting that the heavier trains on the east–west line could not go over the north–south line due the extra fuel costs required negotiating the grade created by a rail flyover. His point that the north–south existing line should go over the east–west line is for way down the track. At least the passengers on the Ghan at that point would get a very good horizon view on top of the flyover, as the Ghan passes this section, both ways in daylight, as it happens.

I hasten to repeat that this is all for way down the track and possibly long after I have departed the scene. Still, you read it here first so perhaps I can have naming rights for this rail flyover in the very middle of Australia. I would call it the 'Emily Flyover' after Emily Kngwarreye, the famous Aboriginal painter who lived and painted nearby.

All in all Australia has considerable rail potential but too often has made huge mistakes in policy and projects, yet it does lead the world with heavy bulk rail operations based on iron-ore movement in Western Australia. At the 'mistakes' end of the spectrum, triple gauge points at Peterborough and Gladstone in South Australia could have been avoided and indeed in the process a shortcut created from Peterborough through Terowie, where General Douglas MacArthur changed trains, then through to Gawler and Adelaide in standard gauge.

There are so many 'what ifs' attaching to the development of rail in Australia, the biggest one being had there been no break of gauge between the main states from inception of rail, would Australia be greatly different today? Certainly development would have been more seamless and efficient, especially for inland New South Wales, South Australia and Victoria.

A more specific question relates to the area south of Nowra on the rugged and beautiful South Coast of New South Wales: had rail from Sydney not stopped at Bomaderry on the north side of the river that divides Nowra, but continued through to Eden direct, would South Coast development have taken off more quickly and even matched NSW North and Central Coast developments? I suggest this would have been a likely outcome.

Even in this century the penchant for errors continues. At Echuca on the Murray River in Victoria, the RFNR committee found that a new branch line restored to the river port at the start of this century had been disconnected after just one year of operation. In an act of corporate vandalism, the points had been staked and a short section of track removed. How dare they! Especially as it happened to be the only new Irish broad gauge branch line built this century anywhere in the world. It also prevented tourist charter trains from running down to the wharf platform and beautiful, historic riverside precinct.

In Melbourne the magnificent Monash outer circle was ripped up just a decade ahead of when it would have hit pay dirt as a freight train bypass and today as a passenger commuter route. John Monash was Australia's greatest general, who should have been our first field marshal but wasn't because of several reasons including the fact he was Jewish, that he fell out with then PM W. M. Hughes, and that it was known he had a mistress. He used trains frequently, including catching four trains through Albury on his honeymoon to Sydney and back to Melbourne. So what does Australia do to the general? In a typical move we rip up his greatest rail construction project, namely the Melbourne outer circle which he engineered and which was named after him.

Likewise Sydney struggles to rebuild heavy rail back to Castle Hill and the sprawling northwest suburbs. A century ago there was a perfectly good branch line operating there but also torn up in a shortsighted move.

MacArthur never did return ... to Terowie

In March 1942 General Douglas MacArthur's forces were in full retreat from the Japanese. MacArthur had flown south from Darwin to Alice Springs with his family and entourage. He allegedly hated flying, so he switched to rail and travelled on the old narrow-gauge Ghan to Quorn then Peterborough and Terowie, where he had to switch to broad gauge for the final leg into Adelaide. A plaque at the disused station at Terowie testifies to the fact that it was at Terowie that MacArthur uttered the famous words 'I will return'. This he did, at least to the beach near Manila in the Philippines later in the war — after the cameras had landed — but of course never ever to Terowie.

The drivers of that special Ghan were Stuart Holland and Ollie McHugh. In March 2002 some 60 years after the trip, Stuart told the *Australian* newspaper that there were some advantages having the VIP general on board and these included the superior rations of the Americans: 'The Yankee tinned stuff was out of this world.'

After many changes of train due to breaks of gauge, MacArthur arrived to a welcome by thousands in Melbourne in the darkest days of the war. He then finally stopped travelling south and turned north, again by train to Sydney and met then PM John Curtin. Later he travelled by train to Brisbane and set up his HQ in the CBD to plan the fightback. Today the main floor of his HQ has been brilliantly preserved as a Brisbane museum.

Today a new line has been built direct from Chatswood to Epping and awaits extension to and beyond Castle Hill, where a million Sydneysiders currently live without rail.

Which way rail in Australia in the 21st century? In Sydney even the sounding of a horn by the train driver on departure has been prohibited as of mid 2010, so whichever way rail Down Under goes, it is going to be quieter around the suburban stations of Australia's biggest city. However, in summary, there is considerable potential in Australia for HSR, as well as further hub-to-hub freight-rail development (and the latter will happen). It would also help to take more heavy trucks out of the suburbs of the big capital cities, but on past form, the pace of rail development around the country will vary greatly. Hopefully it will be a case of getting the gauge and new routes right, without kinks, and perhaps also finally a touch of long-overdue speed.

If the new Southern Cross Railway Station in Melbourne can make it into a huge new publication *Splendid Stations of the World*, along with Gare de Lyon Paris and Berlin HBF, it shows some aspects of rail have been done well, but there is a long way to go.

Reflecting growing interest in and support of rail amongst voters, every Australian federal and state election this century has witnessed debate over rail priority and projects. In March 2011, New South Wales was no exception and the new Coalition Premier, Barry O'Farrell, is determined to build long-overdue rail connections to Sydney's outer southwest and northwest. However, will HSR — say the Sydney–Melbourne 822-kilometre route at average speed of 282 kph and delivering a less-than-three-hour service — get up in Australia? All sides currently support the big study launched by Minister Anthony Albanese in early 2011 and its remit to examine corridors et al. Watch out for how far the phase-one report goes.

I would only highlight the fact that the cost of a second Sydney airport would build a lot of HSR track, including Canberra–Sydney–Newcastle and a bit beyond. And rebuilding long sections of the Hume and Pacific highways to a necessary eight lanes in the future would cost even more again.

CHINA AND GREATER ASIA

A rail extravaganza

Railways and religion were two of the big-ticket items despatched from Europe to China over the centuries. In return oriental silk and much more was sent in the other direction. Today Greater Asia and especially China is streaking ahead of Europe, particularly with its rail expansion.

'Greater Asia' is a term that has been around for years and under the normal definition means the area stretching from Turkey to Australasia, up to Japan, and including Russia east of the Urals, all the various 'stans' and Iraq and Iran. In other words it covers from Istanbul to Indonesia, Japan to Tasmania and most definitely freezing Sakhalin in Russia to the South Island in New Zealand. It is clearly heading for huge economic development in the 21st century, if only political stability and peace can be obtained and retained right throughout.

As always it is the railways, among other things, that have suffered in recent conflicts — the mighty Khyber railway from Jamrud up the pass

The Khyber Pass is in the background. (Tim Fischer)

to the Pakistan–Afghanistan border being one victim. Sadly now its operations are indefinitely suspended. A key road bridge at the entry to the Khyber Pass from the Pakistan (or Peshawar) side was recently destroyed, plus a key rail bridge around the same time was washed away by heavy rains and flash floods.

Fifteen years ago I had the ride of a lifetime — a steam-hauled special train of the Pakistani Railways from the bottom to the top of the pass, followed by lunch in the Khyber Rifles Officers Mess overlooking a chunk of Afghanistan, then under the Taliban. At one point, the Khyber Pass is no wider than a tennis court and you stop to meditate as you look up the sheer cliffs to the ridge line and sniper points way above.

You pause and recall that through here passed the armies of Alexander the Great heading east, and later Marco Polo and his caravan. Heading west came the Mongols and their leaders Genghis Kahn and Kublai Khan; as the 'Tatars' they made it all the way to the Danube and Eastern Europe.

Lawrence of Arabia, as an anonymous member of the RAF, stood guard in the Khyber briefly, as did then Subaltern Winston Churchill about 30 years before, around 1896.

There is so much history captured in the sweeping, narrow Khyber Pass, and it continues to command world attention to this day. After the British had been thrashed three times in the Anglo–Afghan Wars, the first two times in the nineteenth century and the third in 1919, they decided to build an imperial broad gauge line entirely for defence resupply purposes, to allow battalions to be quickly shifted from the plains of Pakistan through the choke to the border barriers.

The initial leg from Jamrud to Landi Kotal was officially opened in 1925. This section involved many tunnels, some emergency sidings for runaway trains that might have lost their brakes, and two reverse stations, or zigzags. For a brief period the railway went beyond the summit plateau of Landi Kotal and descended close to the Afghan border, but this section was closed in 1932 due pressure from an ascendant Kabul which felt threatened by the railway's proximity to the border and Afghan soil; pity about this.

It was with a degree of fear, but also absolute enjoyment, I rode in one of the three carriages between the two large steam locomotives as they pulled and pushed their way up the 600-metre (2000-feet) climb from Jamrud to Landi Kotal. I remain ever grateful to a dedicated ambassador, Geoff Allen, and defence attaché, Group Captain Graeme Carroll, then representatives of Australia in Islamabad, for helping to squeeze this half day into a busy schedule.

FIRST-EVER INTERCONTINENTAL TRAIN TUNNELS

Let us switch from a railway for defence of yesteryear to the newest railway between Europe and Asia, the new US$3 billion Marmaray metro line and its tunnels under the strategic Bosphorus Strait. With eleven sinkable box concrete-and-steel sections installed under the strait at Istanbul, this 1.4-kilometre twin tunnel is nearing completion but is not yet fully operational. When completed, it will be the first-ever intercontinental tunnel anywhere in the world. The entry point on the European side of Istanbul points to the huge size of this project and is part of a massive metro and overall rail upgrade taking place in Turkey.

The beautiful and large Haydarpasa Station awaits on the Asian side. This large, lofty, Germanesque station was built in 1908 as a gift from the Kaiser. When I saw it in 2010 it was rundown and in need of a major revamp. It is in great contrast to the Orient Express terminus, Sirkeci, on the European side of the Bosphorus in Istanbul, a station of subtle, understated beauty. Both stations have huge entry halls with many galleries and offices attached; in short, they are giant edifices of a certain grandeur. If revamped properly, they would make superb hotels and maybe an opportunity exists now with Haydarpasa, as its roof caught fire and the building suffered much damage in December 2010.

Other metro developments in Istanbul have attracted a huge increase in patronage, expected to jump further when commuters can cross between continents in an earthquake proof tunnel at about 100 kph. It will take about one minute from shore line to shore line, Europe to Asia, from the Occident to the Orient, and plans are that the tunnel will be multipurpose rail, including freight trains in non-peak periods. All of this is expected to be reality by 2013, but the unearthing of an old fishing port and pottery dating back to 6000 BC near the tunnel end on the European side does not help progress towards completion. In fact the project is about four years behind schedule.

Turkey adjoins the large countries of Bulgaria, Greece, Iran, Iraq and Syria, and the dominant gauge in all these countries happily is Stephenson standard. Now this conjures up some great possibilities because the system from London through Paris to Istanbul is Stephenson standard gauge; likewise through the Asian part of Turkey and on to Iran and down into Iraq. In a peaceful and progressive time, you could have the Orient Express rebadged and redirected as the St Pancras London to Shiraz Iran Express, with the unifying name of the 'Great Abraham Peace Train'. After all, Abraham, and for that matter Moses and Isaac, are revered by the Christian, Jewish and Islamic faiths, plus the train would traverse the area once traversed by Abraham. Interestingly, there is another Jewish connection conferred by the Jewish community of renown at Shiraz, who actually elect a Jewish member each election to the Iranian Parliament.

Maybe I am overestimating, but perhaps that great travel expert and raconteur Michael Palin has the wit to put together at least one running

Great Abraham Peace Train

It is a bit of a mouthful but the express joining the Occident and the Orient does deserve a name with a difference. The Simplon Orient Express dominated a large part of this corridor before various wars literally blew up the track in many places. Then the Cold War created non-negotiable barriers for a period. By various routes but always through or around Paris and always eventually making it to the superb sea-level station 'Sirkeci' on the European side of Istanbul, the Orient Express has waxed and waned. A huge plaque and statue celebrates the Orient Express at the Istanbul terminus. Of course this train was brilliantly presented in the grand film *Murder on the Orient Express*.

Today the train by that name and with old 'des wagon lits' operates on key tourism routes, such as Calais–Paris–(Simplon tunnel)–Domodossola to Venice, where it more often than not terminates.

So a train running beyond Istanbul to Ankara and perhaps even Shiraz should have a special name, to distinguish it from the Simplon Orient. If not the Great Abraham Peace Train then the Occident–Orient Express, but do not expect to make bookings anytime soon. Maybe the MÁV Nosztalgia Kft group will come up with a special train first, namely something like the Danube–Damascus Express — I wish.

of such a special through train as a peace-train gesture, with the artist formerly known as Cat Stevens, Yusuf Islam, on board. Somewhere in the Balkans, where peace is a fragile concept to this day, Cat Stevens could pick up his guitar in the lounge car and give a vibrant rendition of his timeless 'Peace Train'. After that the company, Serco, could take up the train's running and have it depart St Pancras every Saturday for the 'down' journey, and depart Shiraz every other Saturday for the return 'up' journey.

Turkey is also developing a new set of relatively high-speed rail tracks between Istanbul and Turkey's capital, Ankara, but sadly there have been some derailments involving fatalities over the last couple of years. Yet Turkey is developing a pivotal hub role between East and West, Europe and Greater Asia, and it should continue to develop rail as part of this equation, especially seamless freight rail.

Two other smaller countries that Turkey adjoins are Armenia and Georgia, both with badly rundown Czar broad gauge systems. Due to this and regional politics, nothing is likely to happen quickly with international rail across the borders between Turkey and these countries, especially as it is less than three years since Russian forces bombed a key railway bridge in Georgia.

The big action in railway development in Greater Asia is in China, India and Japan, both with freight and also high-speed rail. These are the big hitters, so to speak, but also putting in huge rail upgrade efforts are Malaysia, South Korea and Taiwan. The Australian railway realm we have already put in a special category with its own chapter. Then there is the other end of the spectrum, such as Bhutan and Nepal, with zero railways but the odd, very old and often broken rope-tow for carrying light freight over mountain ridges. Still, the Indian railway system is heading closer and closer to its northern border and by mutual agreement there are plans for it to cross the border into Bhutan within five years.

CHINA RAIL BOOM

Let us now focus on China and start with the opening of a huge new, stunning high-speed rail route at the end of 2009; namely, the HSR from Guangzhou, Guangdong province, to Wuhan, Hubei province, offering travel over 1100 kilometres (690 miles) in less than three hours while breasting 394 kph (245 mph) along the way on its opening run. It is called the Harmony Express, a dreadful name, I think, but very Mandarin, and no worse than the Great Abraham Peace Train.

The Harmony Express is brilliantly engineered in Stephenson standard gauge, basically patterned on the Siemens ICE system, however, it runs à la left-hand (British) style on double track. It cost US$17 billion to build — yes, about AU$20 billion — one GFC stimulus package, approximately. The average speed is less than 320 kph (200 mph) following a snap decision to cut HSR speeds in China in early 2011. It would be wrong to expend huge amounts of money on HSR projects and not have the capacity to bring them up to this average speed, if not from inception then down the track.

Large new stations geared for HSR at both Guangzhou and Wuhan are about one hour from the centre of these huge dynamic Chinese hub cities. This, it has to be said, is one weakness with the system, but even the Chinese have to weigh the rail benefit with the social disharmony attached to people dislocated by inner-city train corridors. They would not want it nicknamed the 'Disharmony Express'. The new Wuhan station has a gigantic all-glass roof designed to resemble the yellow crane, the mascot of Wuhan city. It is sweeping and spectacular — in more ways than one a touch of the new Berlin HBF station.

Wuhan Station is a very long way from the Barlow train shed of St Pancras, but perhaps one day they might be connected. For the record, at the average speed of the Harmony Express, St Pancras, London, to Beijing West Station (on the London side of Beijing which lacks an overall central terminal) would be 36 hours, and then due south to Wuhan another five to six hours, if no shorter direct route was available. On that comparison and over that distance, aviation has not too much to worry about. As mentioned before, it is at around the three-hour point-to-point mark that HSR is successful enough to eliminate short-haul flights almost completely, for example Paris–Lyon and Paris–Brussels. London–Singapore, if ever an HSR standard gauge were built, would be about two and a half days, or 60 hours, unlikely in the extreme.

It is expected that over the next few years China will build another 18,000 kilometres (12,250 miles) of HSR rail track, in part driven by a

Xian and the Terracotta Warriors

One of the great Marco Polo cities along the old silk route is beautiful Xian and, just to its east, the fabulous Terracotta Warriors Museum and its three excavation pits. On an official visit around 1994, our liaison officer said he had good news for the morrow: a morning free to shop and an afternoon to see the Terracotta Warriors. It did not help when one backbencher (not me) piped up and said loudly: 'Good. Who are they playing?'

To overcome this minor diplomatic incident and create a distraction, I asked if I could forgo the shopping and make a morning visit to the local Xian Railway Station, a major hub station. This was agreed to and I was warmly welcomed with red carpet (actually, very embarrassing). Then I was ushered into the VIP lounge once used by Mao, and informed of this fact in hushed tones.

After due protocol, at last I managed to persuade my guide to take me outside so I could see the rail action. It was a few years ago now, but to see massive steam engines going about their work on a fresh Saturday morning was an absolute delight. Sadly almost all steam action in China has been now been done away with.

What I did closely observe was large-scale freight congestion with consignments had obviously been held up for months in places like Xian. I vividly recall noticing loads of timber on large railway wagons with weathered dockets showing that their journey had commenced about five months before, in fact in the previous year.

stimulus package of gigantic proportions, so far as rail is concerned, to ease the burden of the GFC and related economic downturn. China had been urged by many countries in the West to keep its economic engine going strongly and so maintain or even increase imports, thus helping Australia and many others who export to China in a big way.

The size of the Chinese Railways, all government owned, continues to expand every which way. On the freight score there is some extraordinary growth in tonnage statistics, helped by an increase in the number of hub rail-freight depots of size and consequence being built. In 2002 there were 118 hub 'hump' depots hills (from which wagons roll to a particular loop); in 2007 this had grown to 130. These depots are yards that allow efficient sorting and distribution of freight wagons at key locations.

Similarly, trackage in China has jumped over the same five years, from 72,000 kilometres (45,000 miles) to 78,000 kilometres (48,500 miles), and today there is much more. This has also involved massive increases in double track and electrified track. Coal dominates the freight task, but many other minerals and now container traffic to and from the hinterland, such as between Chengdu in central China and the coast, have taken off.

As comparisons are made between the USA, Japan and now China, as the leading three APEC economies, history will record that one of the many factors in the relative decline of the USA relates to its failure to develop rail in the main, especially passenger rail, whereas massively proactive rail policies and priorities have been pursued in Japan and China. These have not exactly saved Japan from a period of decline and stagnation over the last decade or so but I would contend Japan's situation would have been far worse if it did not have the Shinkansen as well as modest freight-rail progress.

China, meanwhile, has survived the GFC and also geared for the future with an enlightened and large commitment to rail overall; a wise approach and — damnation — perhaps helped by the remaining degree of command economy and centralised control mechanisms pertaining.

JAPAN: 50 YEARS OF SHINKANSEN

Japan currently remains the world's third-largest economy but the GFC, the 2011 giant earthquake and tsunami, and nosedives like the Toyota saga involving huge product recalls are having an overall negative effect. Still, nothing can take away from the fact that Japan led the world with the Shinkansen, as discussed in previous chapters, and is a respectable rail performer on most other fronts as well.

Rail first arrived in Japan quite late, specifically in 1872, and was for years under the control of Japan Railways (JR). The golden 1960s and '70s of economic growth without break led to complacency in JR and for once the long-serving government of the day took action, in the 1980s dividing the huge entity into six major groupings, later floating some of these. These groups still tend to be lumped into a single reference, the JR Group, but broadly stated, the result was a more energetic and efficient template for rail in Japan, with usage trending upwards. In some parts of Japan, passenger usage is among the highest in OECD countries.

Several gauges are used in Japan, but the whole Shinkansen system is in Stephenson standard gauge. The now-modernised original non-high-speed-rail system and the freight system is Anglo Cape narrow gauge, and there is a parcel of Scottish gauge (4 feet 6 inches or 1372 millimetres), a rare gauge long-gone from Scotland, but only over a distance of 117 kilometres (73 miles).

Japanese politicians through the powerful Diet (parliament) intervene often enough in railway matters but sometimes get outfoxed by wily JR CEOs and line managers. In one case, Diet members from the Gifu prefecture were determined that the Shinkansen line from Tokyo and Nagoya to Kobe and Osaka should go through their beloved and, I might add, beautiful prefecture. After a standoff, a compromise was agreed; no kink in the Shinkansen main line towards Gifu, which would have added around 40 kilometres (25 miles). Instead, one extra station, namely Gifu-Hashima Station, was to be built in the middle of just about nowhere on farmland at a point where the main line was nearest to Gifu. Last time I boarded a Shinkansen at this station it looked as lonely and out of place as ever, but the principle of straight and fast tracks for the Shinkansen had won out.

It is a long time since Shinji Sogo led Japan Railways for two terms, retiring at age 80 in 1963, but he delivered the ticket to the future that counted — the adoption of Stephenson standard gauge for future Shinkansens — and they have been operating smoothly ever since 1 October 1964. For a look back over the history of rail in Japan and its extraordinary rolling stock, a new rail museum opened in 2007 on the edge of Tokyo at Saitama. Officially known as Tetsudo Hakubutsukan, the museum has both historical displays and a learning unit, all in a modern setting.

The long-serving Liberal Democratic Party Government hopelessly favoured public works of dubious real value, building bridges to nowhere and tunnels between islands which have resulted in the longest overall length (given the long approaches under land to get low enough to go safely under sea), but not longest undersea railway tunnel in the world, at 53.85 kilometres (33.46 miles). The Chunnel under the English Channel holds the record for the actual section under sea, but when the new super Gotthard Tunnel in Switzerland opens around 2015 it will hold the world record for length, albeit under the Alps.

The Japanese Seikan Tunnel opened in 1988 in narrow gauge but is now dual gauge with both narrow and standard added, so it is Shinkansen-capable. It connects the mainland of Japan to the northern island of Hokkaido and the large city of Sapporo. Undoubtedly after a slow build-up in usage this tunnel now stacks up, if not all the tunnels and bridges scattered around Japan do so.

INDIA INVESTS IN HUGE RAIL EXPANSION

The title of the biggest employer organisation in the world goes to another country and its giant railway; namely, Indian Railways with about 1.6 million employees — but who can be sure, as they paid one employee for over two decades, while he was serving a long term in jail. Only this century and many years on was he removed from the railway books as a paid employee.

Indian Railways is so big it has its own national budget, generally presented in the parliament in New Delhi about one or two days before the main national budget. I digress to add that also in New Delhi is a masterpiece of a railway museum, in a garden setting alongside a main line and next to the Embassy of Bhutan. It has a collection of rolling stock for several narrow gauges, including Indian zero gauge of one elevated steel rail on which the carriage runs but with a deep overhang on each side to maintain stability. There are many smaller museums, including one at Mysore, and a museum with attitude at altitude at Ghum near Darjeeling, on the World Heritage-listed Toy Train route.

China is far outstripping India in growth in rail track, but to be fair the Indians have had to go and revisit the question of gauge and convert most of the narrow metre gauge system to the dominant Indian one of imperial broad at 5 feet 6 inches (1676 mm). This particular agony goes back to Lord Dalhousie and British rule and some very bad decisions made to go multi gauge in India and walk away from Stephenson standard.

The so called 'Unigauge' project has rolled out over recent years and led to massive conversions and upgrading, but still four gauges operate today: imperial broad, supreme metric, Suez narrow and cane narrow. The last two are in mountainous areas and are a sight to behold. The Indian rail system now has 83 per cent of its network in imperial broad gauge; the split was about half and half back in 1951 when the overall giant Indian Railways was created under government ownership just four years after British rule had finally ended.

Passenger trains vary enormously in standards. The specially named expresses aimed at the international tourist are superb and outdo most other named trains in the world. The classic art-house film *Darjeeling Limited* was close to the mark in its portrayal of the average Indian distance-train experience. Many regional and regular short trains will commonly carry people on the carriage roof and authorities think nothing of it.

Given that there are eighteen million passengers daily on about 9000 trains in India much can go wrong, but it has to be said much has been improved this century. Sadly in May 2010, rebels lifted a section of track in West Bengal, causing an express to derail at exactly the moment a heavy freight train was passing on the double track. The result was more than 90 people killed and a sharp reminder of the exposure of rail to sabotage, if huge preventive security steps are not implemented.

On the freight front, the Indian Railways hauls millions of tonnes of freight a year but has not yet sorted intermodal and double-stacking of containers. Several key fast-rail freight corridors are being created to really boost freight efficiency and competitiveness, with provision for double-stacking of containers. However, Indian Railways is a long way behind best world practice with regard to fast unit train loads of freight, yet, in some ways it is ahead in making a fair-dinkum profit in recent years.

For a few years in the first decade of this century, the Indian Minister for Railways, Lalu Prasad from Bihar (a former Bihar head of government and one steeped in controversy), took an unusual but simple approach: he actually allowed the divisional rail managers and the senior management at HQ in New Delhi to do their jobs without excessive ministerial interference. The result was some sound decisions with application in the short, medium and long term, and these are already delivering profitable returns. This was particularly so in rolling out super rail freight corridors. May the momentum be maintained.

If the Chinese and Indian railway networks ever meet, it will be near Sikkim and Siliguri. The Chinese will bring their Stephenson standard gauge through from Lhasa, Tibet, down through the Sikkim gap to the Indian border just west of Bhutan. The break-of-gauge problem between the two systems might just be regarded as a plus by both countries; after all, it constitutes a useful impediment in case of hostilities: trains from either side with munitions, missiles or troops on board would not be able to run straight through.

ASIA BEYOND

Malaysia, South Korea and Taiwan (or Chinese Taipei) are next in line in rail size and modernity. All three have systems which have enjoyed big investment in upgrades over the last two decades, and also the addition of HSR. The Pusan (or Busan)-to-Seoul HSR is a superb train service that rolls along at about 250 kph, but with some high-speed sections not yet fully completed. When travelling, the trick is to plan ahead and use these trains in daylight if possible; it is a great way to see a large chunk of the country, with the added convenience of centre-of-city departure and arrival.

Singapore remains the world leader, or at least equal leader perhaps with Paris, in the very best of metro or suburban systems for commuters. There is no graffiti at all; on the big stations there are glass double doors as in the type for a modern lift and located on the edge of the platform to prevent anyone falling on tracks, and of course all train sets are fully air-conditioned. Stations are modern and clean and well planned, for example, with big new schools being built in close proximity to new stations on new lines.

In the middle of high-rise downtown Singapore there is a quaint, old-looking railway station building: the terminus of the trains to and from Kuala Lumpur and actually Malaysian-leased property under a 999 year lease with over 900 years to run. The modernisation of the locality around it and the rail infrastructure itself has now been agreed to by Malaysia and Singapore. When running, the luxury Eastern Orient Express departs from this terminus for a superb trip through Kuala Lumpur and Hua Hin to Bangkok and beyond.

Indonesia and New Zealand have extensive Anglo Cape narrow gauge systems, and in recent decades some curious upgrading and revamping has occurred in New Zealand which we will leave for a later chapter.

From a shaky start in 1874, the railways of Indonesia, mostly located on Java and Aceh, have had their ups and downs, most notably due to World War II, but also some cruel own goals, such as ordering 100 steam locomotives as late as 1950 when the big switch to less costly diesel had already commenced elsewhere in the world. Today there are many colourful passenger trains but no sleeper compartments on the few night trains. Other gauges were changed last century to the one Anglo Cape narrow gauge, so break of gauge is not a problem this century.

On Java, the electric train trip to the Summer Palace of Bogor, just south of Jakarta, is a great way to go. It makes for a good half-day outing to see the superb gardens that surround the Summer Palace, and the old terminus station in the older part of Jakarta is a blast from the past. For years the bohemian Batavia café nearby, where the late-night crowd and young diplomats used to hang out, was an even louder blast from the past, I have to say.

Taking photos around key railway stations

The best advice I can give from harsh experience is simply don't. That is, do not bother trying to take photos around colourful, vibrant railway stations in Myanmar or Iran or even Saudi Arabia. If American and British trainspotters are often cautioned these days post 9/11, then I was nearly deported pre 9/11 when trying to take a happy snap at the then-new Ad Dammam Railway Station in Saudi Arabia. Back in the 1980s, I was visiting with a friend, Steve Goudie, and we had driven across the giant causeway from Bahrain to have a look at this part of Saudi Arabia. I had noticed that BHP rails (as stamped on the side) had been used in building the six platform tracks and they were shining in the late afternoon sun.

As soon as I started snapping, guards came from everywhere running and gesturing in a menacing way. They demanded the camera, removed the film (it was pre-digital days) and then stomped on the film before handing back the camera in a non-polite way. Much the same happened in Myanmar, and also Iran; however, not at the beautiful and underused new railway station at Esfahan. The officials there were happy to show off a largely empty station, one which I understand to this day handles about one or two trains on a big day, mainly the overnight seven-hour express running down from Teheran.

Moving further west, I cannot bypass Myanmar (or Burma, as I knew it when growing up). In the days when people bypassed Bangkok to shop at Rangoon and soak up the sights of a pagoda-dominated skyline, a major narrow gauge railway system operated on metre gauge, with the Rangoon–Mandalay main line being the spine of the system. Alas, it still takes about fifteen hours by comfortable but slow train between these two colourful cities.

The hilarious or most interesting aspect for me on the long overnight trip was on return to Rangoon (or Yangon) from Mandalay, when I noticed the train suddenly slowed even more about 8 kilometres (5 miles) from the main station. Bags full of goods from China appeared near the doors of the train, apparently from nowhere, and were carefully slung to the ground outside. There fast-footed and fit-looking locals collected them and dashed off into the teeming streets on either side. It is clearly one of the last great smuggling train routes of the world.

Further west again and the mixed-gauge Bangladesh Railway is encountered, now offering fully air-conditioned intercity trains between Dhaka and Chittagong. I happily recall giant pots of tea coming frequently along the corridor and big free cups of tea being offered and poured expertly in the swaying conditions.

The newest development in this region is the advent of the Maitree Express, or Friendship Express, between Dhaka and the old capital of Bengal, Calcutta, now called Kolkata. This is just what the South Asian Association for Regional Cooperation (SAARC) was invented for, and at last there is a direct international train between India and Bangladesh. The only problem is that this journey of around 400 kms (250 miles) takes ten to twelve long daylight hours. Why? Because there are very slow border stops for customs clearance on each side of the border. There are now plans to rectify this by having border clearance on board. So what might otherwise be around a six-hour train trip on a good day is instead around twelve hours, with almost one-third of that time stationary, going through clunky border customs and immigration clearances.

Needless to say, this Maitree Express is a portent of what the future might hold if the political and economic situation allows, including a resumption of international trains between India and Pakistan and one day between India and China, but the old Talgo sets from Spain will be needed to allow the train at the border on the southern edge of the Himalayas to change gauge while in slow motion. The Talgo bogies were engineered to allow the axle to widen or contract on a special section of track and in slow motion switch from one gauge to another.

The various countries that border on to the Persian Gulf, especially those big ones that are members of the Gulf Cooperation Council (GCC) are looking at rail, and in the case of Saudi Arabia expanding their standard-gauge network a great deal. The Saudi Landbridge project — a freight line connecting Jedda and Riyadh — is proceeding but also an electric high-speed train between Mecca and Medina, where a 320-kph (200-mph) service is planned to facilitate the travel of pilgrims, in particular. So another country is venturing into HSR and of course doing it in Stephenson standard gauge.

Curiously Mongolia, or to be correct Outer Mongolia, decided in 2010 to upgrade its rail systems, mainly to enhance connections from major mining projects now opening up. Against the trend, the government decided on doing this in Czar broad gauge, not Stephenson standard, so creating a seamless route back into Russia but a break of gauge south into China. It is the one standout on gauge — in a sense going the wrong way in the 21st century.

Likewise Israel is planning an upgrade to a form of high-speed train on the Tel Aviv–Jerusalem corridor, in Stephenson standard gauge of course, ending at a new underground station beneath the current Jerusalem bus and coach terminal. Both Israel and Saudi Arabia lead the region in rail revamp and development.

Syria still operates in both the old Lawrence gauge of 1050 mm (3 feet 5⅓ inches) and standard gauge, notably from Damascus northwards to

Aleppo and into Turkey. Alas, the picturesque line direct from Damascus to Beirut has not operated for 40 years, but some remnant lonely snow sheds with roof and half walls — protecting the track from snow and ice — can be seen in the Bekaa Valley or at least on the ridge lines, where the Lawrence gauge line has weathered the elements.

The famous London-to-Cairo railway was completed and had a brief life towards the end of World War II but was wiped out during subsequent incessant local wars. This line came down the coast from Turkey through Syria then Lebanon and the Palestinian mandate. The line then traversed the length of the Gaza Strip. I remember stepping along a disused section somewhere near the Gaza–Egypt border years ago to establish that it was standard gauge.

Earlier on the same working visit to the Middle East I had taken a half-day off from the schedule and walked up Dog River, just to the north of Beirut in Lebanon. There there is a section of the riverbank with many plaques, including one saluting the fact that Julius Caesar had visited the area. However, close by is a more recent plaque celebrating the completion of the London-to-Cairo railway and saluting the work of Australian army engineers for their efforts in its construction. Sadly those efforts were largely wasted and this railway has been mostly obliterated.

Ironically the most likely next incarnation of a London-to-Cairo railway will be through Spain, under the Gibraltar Straits and down through Morocco, Tunisia and Libya to Egypt.

Greater Asia on the railway front has much to show the world. It has a huge diversity, ranging from magnificent busy stations, like the 100-year-old Haydarpasa in Istanbul, to the brand-new Wuhan HSR station in China; from the fast and very fast trains to some of the slowest in the world. The reality is that it is this railway realm which will produce the greatest length of new track each year for several decades to come. The railway expansion in Greater Asia will make previous railway mania periods look very small by comparison.

AFRICA

Ever-changing but
no Cape-to-Cairo

Westminster is a long way from deepest, distant Africa and the famous Mombasa-to-Nairobi railway, the main trunk route inland across Kenya and the Rift Valley. Yet it was a House of Commons debate in 1896 that took the cake in relation to the good and bad of early railway development within the African continent.

As part of it, Henry Labouchere read out to the honourable members a stinging attack on a railway bill providing for the Mombasa-to-Nairobi railway project by way of a poem that has currency to this day, perhaps the best poetry ever written about a railway:

> *What it will cost no words can express;*
> *What is its object no brain can suppose;*
> *Where it will start from no one can guess;*
> *Where it is going to nobody knows.*

What is the use of it none can conjecture;
What it can carry there's none can define;
And in spite of George Curzon's superior lecture,
It is clearly nought but a lunatic line.

Nevertheless, the railway legislation was assented to and British engineers and navvies arrived in Africa, only to encounter the Tsavo River and a group of large man-eating lions. A temporary bridge and then a permanent structure had to be built to conquer the river obstacle, as the line headed west and began its long climb, but the lions were having little of this intrusion.

The 1996 film *The Ghost and the Darkness* portrayed with great drama and skill the difficulties at Tsavo River before eventually both the large river and the large lions were conquered — but not before many deaths had occurred. Eventually this railway made it to Nairobi and on to Lake Victoria with many connections by ferry and extensions to central Africa. It was a huge achievement, built in supreme metric gauge, and while dubbed the lunatic line, it actually worked and has on occasions even returned a profit due to the vital access it conferred from the rich inland to the Port of Mombasa.

It is often said that this particular railway created the core dynamic of the nation of Kenya in the same way that the advent of the railway was used to unite Belgium, Germany, and Italy in particular. Further, while the choice of gauge was supreme metric gauge and not Anglo Cape, common throughout the rest of Africa, considerable effort was made to establish a large set of seamless networks throughout most of the countries of the central-eastern section of the African continent.

Thinking about it, if much of the freight involved rail connection with ferries on the many and large lakes in Africa, gauge was of less concern, provided that from the last inland ferry port to seaside port, there was no break of gauge.

One of the out-of-kilter lines in the area was built by China between 1970 and 1975 and recently revamped and upgraded by that country. The

Gauge unity

If ever a break-of-gauge split was on, it was in South Africa, where at first the British meddled with Stephenson standard gauge and then decreed Anglo Cape narrow gauge as the way forward for visionary Cecil Rhodes (1853–1902), who opened up much of southern Africa by establishing diamond mining and rail tracks, including the Cape Town-to-Kimberley-and-beyond railway. Meanwhile, as that railway gathered pace towards Johannesburg and Pretoria, Afrikaan President Kruger (of Boer War fame) was building a railway from the coast at Maputo up to Pretoria.

This was driven by a desire to bypass the British stronghold on Cape Town, and Kruger's teams followed through with an order for all equipment for this railway from Germany; it was a case of order anything but British-made equipment. In the mix-up that followed, a large number of small-capacity tank steam locomotives were produced near Stuttgart for the 370-kilometre (350-mile) corridor that climbs from the coast at Maputo up 1500 metres (5000 feet) to approach the central hub area of South Africa from the east.

However, counterintuitively it was not supreme metric narrow gauge but most fortunately Anglo Cape narrow gauge that Kruger chose for his railway, perhaps thinking the Boer War would ultimately go his way and the connections to the Rhodes railway network would pay big dividends for the Boers. Instead the dividend was not so big and was collected by the Anglo interests after their victory.

Eventually, some years after the Boer War in 1910 the three big railways dominating the southern part of Africa merged; namely the Cape Government Railways, Natal Government Railways and the Central South African Railways, to form the mighty South African Railways, or SAR, and 100 years later, this giant railway network continues to power the economies along.

With Stephenson standard in the northern part of Africa, supreme metric in the east, but also pockets elsewhere, such as in dual-gauge Tunisia, Africa can boast large-scale usage of three gauges to this day.

line from Dar es Salaam travels up various escarpments and over plateaus and ranges to service Zambia, ultimately with a connection ending at Lake Victoria and the Victoria Falls. It was built in Anglo Cape gauge during the time of apartheid in South Africa when every effort was being made to avoid having to send and receive produce and product via the then-hated South African regime.

Trade sanctions existed officially in the so-called frontline states against South Africa, by far the most powerful economy in the continent with excellent infrastructure to match. Furthermore, for decades it had had good connections with most of its neighbours, physically both with key rail links and some good highways, if less so politically. Until South African President F.W. de Klerk bravely released Nelson Mandela from prison and piloted through big changes that swept the African National Congress to power in South Africa, effectively ending apartheid, officially it was in a state of war with its neighbours, with no commerce crossing certain national boundaries.

At the height of this standoff in the 1980s, a curious strategic railway meeting was happening every quarter: the various railway managers of the so-called frontline nations would meet discreetly with the giant South African Railways (SAR) executives, generally in Johannesburg at the SAR HQ. They would then plan the broad pattern of train movements for freight between the ports of South Africa and the frontline nation states, many of them landlocked, such as Zimbabwe.

Even huge South-West Africa, now Namibia, had a railway system enmeshed with the SAR's, and while Namibia had its own coastline and ports, the big freight volumes were by rail to and from South Africa. In fact, all of the surrounding nations adjoining South Africa except Mozambique had railway networks underpinned in various ways by the SAR.

In other words, as political leaders railed against doing business with apartheid South Africa, and many Western countries beyond Africa wrestled with adopting various trade and travel sanctions, the railways were in full swing with trains reliably and regularly crossing the mighty

Zambezi River, just below the Victoria Falls. This famous bridge is 198 metres (650 feet) long, and links Zimbabwe and Zambia. It was built in 1905 under the umbrella of empire, as existed at that time, and was opened by the son of Charles Darwin, Professor George Darwin.

Now showing signs of wear and tear, various upgrades for this truly international bridge have been considered, and where crucial to it remaining open for business, these upgrades have been implemented. In recent years it has become the place of a 'rite of passage' — the place to bungee jump in Africa, deep down into the gorge, ending up a few metres above the fast flowing water. This is a sacrilege, I feel; an undignified use of a bridge that created history and international connection.

There is no doubt that the African continent has enormous economic potential, and abundant agricultural, mineral, oil and gas resources which should see it boom and its railways take off in the first half of the 21st century. However, a legacy of years of colonisation, civil war and lack of strong governance with confident vibrant institutions of state, makes predictions of this kind risky, to say the least.

The railways of Africa will be ever-changing; alas, some of them from fully operational, with good ballasted tracks and efficient freight and passenger trains, to total disuse and decay. The jungle, if not the desert sands, stands ready to take over any remnant railway that has fallen out of use, and quickly.

Examples of this can be readily found in Eritrea, Ghana, Madagascar and Sudan; but against considerable odds, some sections of former lines are being dusted off and refurbished, to resume operations. This is being driven by the high cost of building good roads in much of Africa; single rail track can be cheaper and, if operated properly, just as efficient.

The most incredible decaying remnant railway is way out in the Atlantic Ocean on the Azores Islands. It is technically a part of extended Europe, nevertheless not far from the northwest coast of Africa. Here the Brunel broad gauge track can be seen rusting away, along with some steam locomotives that as late as 50 years ago assisted in the redevelopment of

Civilisation is at the Victoria Falls

One Sunday afternoon I arrived hot and dusty from a long trip by road to Victoria Falls, and after avoiding real live elephants and inspecting these superb gifts of nature I repaired to the local railway station to survey the recently arrived Rovos Rail luxury express. It was much like the exquisite, luxurious Blue Train, which links Pretoria with Cape Town, I have to say.

Then I crossed the road and entered the grand Victoria Falls Hotel and terraced garden, relaxing with friends and drinking while consuming lamingtons and cream. After a while, as sunset approached and we gazed along a reach of the Zambezi River to the great rail and road bridge, gin and tonic and, yes, fresh cucumber sandwiches were served.

I thought to myself: now, this is living it up; a great experience at a location steeped in history and natural beauty, a privilege to experience before a heavy work schedule resumed. Alas, no train appeared on the bridge to top it off, but, still, I have memories to this day of the pleasantness of it all, which led to further research and a discovery of the ultimate railway perk.

For years the president of the Southern Africa Railway mission, a mobile Anglican outreach to the railway settlements of southern Africa, (later called the Rhodesian Railway mission), was the then Anglican Bishop of Matabeleland, Zimbabwe, Bishop Robert Mercer, based at Bulawayo. Until the Victoria Falls Hotel was sold by the Rhodesian Railways, he had the right to railway travel in the 'mission carriage', which came complete with mobile chapel. He also had the right to free accommodation at this famous hotel at any time, along with use of the hotel chapel. Perks like that are long gone; ruthless efficiency has removed them in the name of 'accountability'.

the local harbour. Executives of the UK's Great Central Railway today will be interested to know that a Brunel broad gauge locomotive built at their Falcon works at Loughborough still exists in the Azores but looks a little forlorn.

The economic future of the world belongs to the African continent after the USA, India and China have peaked — remarked one boffin in 2010 — but if this is to be realised, there needs to be some major sorting out on the rail front, both with gauge and broader harmonisation.

To digress, the ghost of the legendary Mahatma Gandhi lingers on. Gandhi once famously rode trains in Africa, sitting in carriages reserved for the white population, until arrested. He was banned as a coloured under the by-laws in existence at the time. His leadership powers, which brought non-violent protest and eventually independence to India, at least non-violent in relation to his own personal approach, are needed once again in the continent of his first stirrings, namely Africa.

Indeed a combination of the vision of a Cecil Rhodes, the early tenacity of a Benito Mussolini, who ordered narrow gauge railways to be extended in Italian colonies in Africa, such as in Eritrea, and the leadership of a Mahatma Gandhi would work wonders, if it could emerge in one of the current crop of African leaders. Ironically a few of these leaders have held Rhodes scholarships, others have just enriched themselves beyond belief and in the process sapped their economies of any capacity to modernise any transport infrastructure.

AFRICAN PRIORITIES FOR THE FUTURE

In 2002 there was a major African rail conference in Johannesburg which saw a review of priorities within and between nations. The conference accepted that there will always be three dominant gauges — Anglo Cape in the south and west of Africa, supreme metric gauge in the eastern parts of Africa, anchored by the lunatic line from Mombasa to Nairobi, and finally Stephenson standard gauge in the north along the Mediterranean. The

Egypt-to-Morocco corridor is a northern subset of Africa and all of the countries along this corridor have good terrain for railways, so an east–west main line is doable, and would connect Rabat, Morocco, to Alamein, Alexandra and Cairo.

The bigger challenge is in middle landlocked Africa, especially Mali, Niger and Chad. These three large countries are a long way from the sea; they are very poor countries with little development and yet they need rail more than most for vital access to sea ports. I am assured by ambassadors from these three countries, albeit not those accredited to the Holy See, that it will happen one day. Imagine the Timbuktu Express to Timbuktu from, say, Tripoli, but do not hold your breath.

Benin on the Gulf of Guinea is well placed to provide some connection from the coast to the inland. Furthermore, it has entered into negotiations with Indian interests about upgrading its north–south Anglo Cape narrow gauge line to Stephenson standard, as part of a major revamp. Actual construction has not commenced but the interesting point is the decision to switch gauge — the spirit of George and Robert Stephenson surfaces again.

Where there is action and new international rail connection planned is between Angola and Namibia, the two most southern and western countries of Africa. This part of the world in the last half of the 20th century has seen more than its fair share of guerrilla war, civil war and wars of independence. Everyone from Cubans to wayward sons of European prime ministers have been involved, one of the latter rescued from Angola in a midnight raid by the South African SAS.

Bit by bit today, the Anglo Cape gauge railway is heading north from Namibia to the Angolan border, from Tsumeb to Ondangwa and beyond, with the ultimate objective of linking all three of Angola's long-separated and never previously connected east–west railways. Enthusiasm for this connection extended to cabinet level in Namibia, with all ministers heading out to help with initial working bees. A visiting British parliamentary delegation in 2004 could not meet with ministers at the capital of Namibia,

Windhoek, because they were away that weekend on the orders of then President Sam Nujoma working on the railway.

The Namibia–Angola rail link concept is about right, but a couple of big mining projects generating ore freight from Angola into South Africa are needed to secure or anchor this huge rail investment.

Inland from Namibia, Botswana's first railway was opened quite late, in 1897, as part of a through route to Victoria Falls and beyond. Ninety years later the Botswanan Government finally came to own and operate the rail track in Botswana when it purchased it back from the National Railways of Zimbabwe (NRZ). Ten golden years followed before a new line opened to the east (direct from Bulawayo to Pretoria) causing through freight to bypass the nation, but against the odds, both Botswana and its railways have done well and have even been profitable.

On April Fool's Day 2009, a tough decision was implemented by the Botswanan Government: all passenger services operated by Botswana Railways would cease that day. Perhaps this sort of decision-making to hive off the loss-making passenger service helps explain why Botswana Railways is viable and actually running at a profit.

It was a giant iron-ore mine in Mauritania at Zouerate that created the need for a 704-kilometre (440-mile) Stephenson standard gauge railway on the northwestern side of Africa, which opened in 1963. It efficiently hauls millions of tonnes of iron ore to the coast for export from the port of Nouadhibou, but takes a route south of the shortest line due to the colonial boundary of West Sahara, now under Moroccan hegemony. Until the Choum rail tunnel closed, this line was entirely within Mauritania but today it nicks the southeast corner of Western Sahara, saving a few kilometres along the way for each huge train.

Further south it is huge phosphate deposits that need to be mined and moved to the coast that has led to approval for further rail construction in Mauritania.

During the last decade, Libya has decided to get serious about rail development and entered into three big contracts. It is a case of long-haul lines being done by Chinese and Russian companies, the Tripoli Metro being done by Italian companies, and all was going well until the 2011 Libyan revolution intervened and construction ceased.

There is a short test rail track near the main Tripoli airport and it is in standard gauge — the gauge planned for all Libyan 21st-century rail projects — but Libya faces so many challenges that have to be dealt with before any modern trains commence running.

It is an international troika, then, that is seeking to revamp and develop rail in Libya, just 40 years after the revolution by Colonel Gaddafi, and on his express orders. I had to represent the Australian Government at the 40th anniversary celebrations at Tripoli in 2009. I shared the experience with Cardinal Martino, who represented the Holy See, on a very hot and dry day over a long set of colourful celebrations. I digress to say the lobster

Scavenger gauge at Leptis Magna, on the Libyan coast east of Tripoli. It was built by Italians to ship artefacts back to Italy. (Tim Fischer)

was good, the no drinking or eating before sunset was not so good, as it was Ramadan, but it was a chance to see and learn much. It was also a chance to promote Australian priorities and policies.

The bonus was discovering some remnant railways from the Italian colonial period, including some scavenger gauge at the big Roman ruins at Leptis Magna. The Italians built short sections of this narrow gauge railway to run Roman columns, statues, arches and anything else of value to the sea for loading for Italy. I trust the Italian companies will make amends by doing a first-class job with the Tripoli Metro which also links up with work by some Australian companies seeking to plan super-connected suburbs of the 21st century in Tripoli. In short, the metro is an attempt at city infill with the best layouts and public transport and buildings where once there were scattered slums.

What is unlimited, as far as Africa is concerned, is the capability of having the best travel conversation of a random nature on board a passenger train.

(I should say that I mean conversation in English, French, Spanish or German, most notably, and I say this with the experience of visiting over 72 countries, of which around 60 have operating railways and passenger trains.)

Why is this so? In short, those on board African trains are rarely business people in a great hurry. They have time to slow down and engage in conversation and like to do so while gazing out at captivating scenery, heading along at a sedate pace and knowing that much can be learned and enjoyed from words with a fellow traveller or two.

I cannot speak of sea travel or canal barge travel; yes, there is some capacity for conversation on board a coach or bus, but nothing as compared with that offered the train traveller. With air travel, short haul or long, rarely is there a chance for conversation of value up in the crowded cabin in the sky. If in first class, it is de rigueur to avoid eye contact and not talk casually; if business class, it is only form to converse with your keyboard and no interruption will be brooked (additionally, you have to work out if you are sitting next to a competitor with big ears and angle vision). If in economy, the proximity helps, but the overall cabin mood is to get the business over with as fast as possible, and silence is golden.

None of this applies on rail. Further, there are no pesky announcements about ensuring seat belts are done up due to approaching turbulence, and life-jacket-wearing instructions on every sector. There is just a soothing clickity-clack — although this is no longer the case in Europe and North America where the railways are all welded, but is happily still the case in many parts of Africa.

As the sun rises on this enigmatic great continent of Africa in the second decade of this century, there will be more rail development but not the unlimited mix of European-style HSR and USA-style double-stacking rail freight. The Gautrain will hit its straps as a new Stephenson standard gauge fast-commuter system Pretoria to Johannesburg and the international airport they share.

Meanwhile, Rovos Rail, with its Pride of Africa and other clever rail tourism trains will flourish, at least while the baby boomers continue their determined spending, leaving to their children a sum for their parents' funerals and not much more. But beware: disaster can strike as happened to the Pride of Africa on 21 April 2010 when two electric locomotives were detached in order to attach a steam locomotive for the home stretch into Pretoria. In the manoeuvre, the seventeen carriages which had not been secured started rolling away down a long grade, derailing at speed and killing three people.

The African train I leave you with is another of the best and unique: the Apple Express tourist train from Port Elizabeth along part of the fabled Garden Route corridor to Loerie as part of the Avontuur cane narrow gauge railway. You will enjoy the scenery, you will enjoy the conversations, you will even enjoy the apples, and you will muse how once upon a time a coloured man like Gandhi would not have been allowed aboard.

The Avontuur is the last of the cane gauge regional lines on the African continent and possibly the last in the world used for passenger movement over some distance, (along with the World Heritage-listed Darjeeling Toy Train in northeast India). About a century ago the first line down into Beira, Mozambique, on the African eastern coast was built in cane gauge, but within a decade this was converted to Anglo Cape narrow gauge.

Looking at Africa today, other than rail development driven by big mining ventures, it is difficult to see a huge harmonised network unfolding across the continent within the next 90 years. It is neither gauge-simple, as noted, nor economically justified, so out goes Cecil Rhodes' Cape-to-Cairo vision, at least for the immediate future. Still, there are bursts of rail activity unfolding across Africa, and with South Africa itself becoming a BRIC member (Brazil, Russia, India, China) to make it BRICS, the rail potential will be unlocked.

Avontuur line in South Africa.
(courtesy John Browning)

Blue Train v Trans Karoo

Once upon a time in 1989 I ventured to Africa, mainly to visit the Australian army units then serving in Namibia and help to supervise the first presidential elections. All went well. The Australian diggers did a great job and President Sam Nujoma was elected to what is known as the Ink Palace. I did manage to squeeze in a ride on TransNamib Rail, in the locomotive cabin of a noisy diesel, as it growled under the load of a freight train climbing out of Windhoek.

We were heading south; it was a steep grade up to a short tunnel and on to the top of the grade. The train had a brief rest. I was allowed off and collected by the army in time to fly out the next day for South Africa, where I had bought tickets for a long-promised ride by rail from Pretoria to Cape Town and return.

I then made a big mistake. I went one way on the Blue Train of absolute luxury and returned on the non-air-conditioned Trans Karoo Express after just one day in Cape Town. In both directions the conversations were splendid; a bunch of holidaying German frauleins southbound and a group of young South African soldiers, in fact conscripts, heading north.

The problem was that a heatwave had begun and it was unbearably hot on the Trans Karoo; even long visits to the one air-conditioned carriage, the buffet dining carriage, provided only brief relief, although the half hour underground in the mighty Hexton Tunnel, not far past Stellenbosch, did help.

At De Aar there was additional agony in the middle of the night. The Trans Karoo was placed on an outside platform and we watched both northbound and southbound Blue Trains sweep through, with just one-minute stops. Luxury in cool air-conditioned solo apartments was alongside but not reachable.

The lesson: always do the second-class train first and then the first-class train, as (1) you will have earned it; and (2) you will doubly appreciate it. Also, always avoid young soldiers determined to drink their way from one end of the country to the other — all seven of them in a cabin with eight seats, made for a boisterous, long day and night.

SOUTH AMERICA

with the mighty Panama and Porta

The Panama City-to-Colon railway, connecting container ports on both sides of the isthmus, and technically speaking located just on the South American side of the great canal, is by far the most successful short-haul railway in the whole of South America. It has a profitable passenger train service, mainly carrying commuters from Panama City to their work stations in Colon, and of course freight generated by the ships that are too big to pass through the Panama Canal and disgorge their containers on one side for quick movement by rail on double-stacked container trains to ships waiting on the other side.

Ship owners carefully calculate that it is cheaper to unload, use the railway across the isthmus and reload than travel by ship via Cape Horn — it is about 12,530 kilometres (7880 miles) shorter through Panama from, say, ports on the west coast of North America via Panama to ports on the east side of the North American continent, than via Cape Horn and the Magellan Straits.

The Panama railway was the world's first-ever transcontinental railway when it opened in 1855, using Czar broad gauge for its 74-kilometre (47-mile) length. Like the Panama Canal itself, the railway had several ownership phases.

Built originally for US$6.5 million it was owned first by US interests. In 1879 the French paid US$25 million for it, when the great canal engineer Ferdinand de Lesseps took on building the Panama Canal. He had already built the superb Corinth Canal in Greece and the Suez Canal in Egypt, but the Panama project proved too much for him and the USA had to return to Panama to get the canal project finished.

Eventually the consortium that took this historic Panama railway into the 21st century invested US$80 million and switched gauge to, yes, you guessed it, Stephenson standard, and now millions of containers roar across this railway, along with a commuter train from Panama City on the southern or Pacific side to Colon on the northern Atlantic side. Since re-opening after the gauge change on 27 November 2001, the railway has shown how savvy engineering and investment can deliver a successful new operation, with high productivity and revenue flowing from the many daily double-stacked container trains, in both directions.

It is a case of good investment and good management, but also location, location, location, helping ensure at last huge success for the Panama Canal Railway Company and the world's first transcontinental. It had come through periods of bad management, awkward gauge for purchasing rolling stock and route alteration over the decades to make way for various previous canal expansions and is now bigger and better than ever.

There are not one but two rail systems alive and well in proximity to that mighty engineering feat, the Panama Canal. As well as the Panama City–to–Colon railway there are the twelve sets of mule trains — electric trains with there own form of grip traction. These mule locomotives help tow the huge container and cruise ships through the six locks involved in passing through the Panama Canal between the Atlantic and Pacific Oceans.

Over the years since the canal became operational on 15 August 1914, these mule trains have been upgraded, and of course use electricity created by the hydro power generated by Gatun Lake water flowing through the locks to the sea, a vertical fall of about 26 metres (85 feet) on an average tide.

It is the size of the Panama locks and the size of the huge steel gates that control the water in the locks that govern so much of the transport logistics of the world. By 2010 about 40 per cent of world container shipping in operation was too big for the Panama Canal, and this percentage is increasing every year. Anticipating this trend, Panamanians voted 80 per cent in favour in a referendum in 2006 relating to the Canal's expansion and the big deepening and widening project now being undertaken.

The expectation on this US$5 billion dollar expansion project is that the Panama Canal is going to remain viable and in demand for decades to come.

The new sets of locks being put in near the existing locks (which will continue to operate) are of course wider and longer to allow bigger ships to pass — bigger than the current maximum size known as Panimax size — but are also designed for maximum water capture and reuse.

The new larger locks alongside the existing locks will swing into action in 2014 and 2015 and a twofold impact on railways will occur. Firstly, in the USA volume through the huge ports of LA will reduce, but for US railroads as a whole, it will not be a loss situation. More likely it will be a case of a subtle change in rail freight flows as the big container ships on the run from China and Japan switch to east coast US ports. Rail once again will have to step up and help distribute bigger volumes out of those eastern ports to the hinterland. As there has been much warning of this, planning can start early.

Secondly is the impact allowing more freight through the canal will have on the Panama Canal Railway Company, now owned and operated by Kansas City Southern in joint investment with Mi-Jack Products, an intermodal container freight company. The calculations are no doubt being made, but even with the expansion of the canal, it will not be cheap for shipping companies to use the canal. Fees are on the rise and so the freight rail link between two giant oceans of the world I am confident will survive. I am certainly happy to wager it will, albeit with some necessary adjustments from time to time (triple-stacking containers maybe) but nevertheless with an ever-continuing viable role into the future.

One cheap passage

In the late 1920s a young Richard Halliburton became the first person to swim the Panama Canal through each and every lock. He had to sign an indemnity accepting full responsibility for any injury that might befall him and also for any damage to the canal.

The fee for his passage through the canal was less than a dollar, in fact 36 cents — he was the lightest or smallest ship/object/person through the canal — and while others had also tried, the Halliburton venture is considered as the first all the way through.

A colourful US travel writer and hellraiser, he lost his life attempting to sail across the Pacific in 1939, but his record for paying the smallest Panama Canal fee will keep his memory alive forever.

LIVIO DANTE PORTA

Although we have met him before, Livio Dante Porta is not exactly a household name, not even in his home nation of Argentina, but he should be. Livio Dante Porta was born in Parana near Rosario, upstream of Buenos Aires, in 1922, and in 1946 graduated in civil engineering from the Rosario University of the Litoral. He then decided to concentrate on locomotive development and sensibly, before the internet, he set about learning English, French, German, Portuguese and Romanian, with a smattering of several other languages. Of course he maintained his mother tongue of Spanish and second language of Italian from his migrant parents. His immense capacity for language was to ensure he could communicate with the best in his field right around the world. He was also a patriotic Argentinian who lost his own daughter during the regime of the generals, taken away in the night at gun point. She was never to be sighted again, and I acknowledge the biography by Martyn Bane in relation to this aspect. It was a cruel blow to a proud and dedicated Argentinian who deserves to be denoted as the Brunel or Stephenson of his country, with a practical brain to match almost anyone.

Had Dante Porta been born and educated in the great steam locomotion nations where ample project capital funding existed, such as China, the UK or the USA, then I venture to suggest hundreds of solid-fuel-powered modern reciprocating and steam-electric locomotives would be hauling ore trains today (see Chapter 2).

These would have an overarching winning efficiency and have no worse, if not better, environmental footprint than many diesel-electric locomotives today, with the steam-generated driving 'through turbines' (not pistons), which in turn would drive electric generators, powering the electric engines that drive the axles.

Earlier in Chapter 2 on locomotives, the contribution and life of Dante Porta were covered but it would be remiss not to put Porta's work into context with regard to his home continent of South America.

There are few railway engineers, and even fewer steam-locomotive design engineers, who contributed as much as Dante Porta did to the wellbeing of the world's transport systems. Here was a giant of a man whose work spanned two centuries, and whose ideas and processes are set to play a role in the future.

His creation of new streamlined locomotives, along with facilitating various mining railways, was one thing. His passing on to others his knowledge and templates for getting locomotive design right was another. Shaun McMahon was his leading disciple and friend, a determined and dedicated Welsh-speaking (Manchester-born) engineer, now residing in Buenos Aires. He has taken up the cudgels in more ways than one to see the Dante Porta templates further explained and utilised. Shaun McMahon has a continuing active role with railways in Argentina, but its mining railways have a patchy record, due to straight-out difficulties with the mine deposits and their extraction but also due to the world global financial crisis and the various Argentinian economic meltdowns, even before the GFC.

Other disciples of the Porta template include Nigel Day, Phil Girdlestone, David Wardale and, from Puffing Billy, Melbourne, Don Marshall. None of them matched Porta in an outright sense but all have used the Porta inventions with steam locomotives to great advantage.

The first locomotive ever built in Argentina from go to woe was built by engineer Porta and called simply *Argentina*. It was a slick, streamlined racehorse, made for supreme metric gauge. In all white with blue trimmings, it emerged from the workshops in 1949 but, alas, at the time when dieselisation was taking off around the world, so it cannot be said that it was a progenitor of a batch of like locomotives, although certainly the technology involved was utilised in the last generation or two of steam locomotives in many ways.

In 1981 Dante Porta produced the very best design for steam locomotion, later offering it to the A1 Trust in the UK. This Trust was formed in 1990 by some very dedicated enthusiasts in Great Britain, and formally known as covenators, a form of controlling trustees. Their objective was the building from scratch of a new locomotive capable of being cleared and certified for main-line operation. However, they knocked back the chance to go with Dante Porta's 'new world' steam locomotion and went on to develop the conventional No 60163 Pacific Class *Tornado*.

Many argued that the *Tornado* Project was a chance to build a steam locomotive incorporating all of the Porta methodology with water and ejectors and so forth, in other words to create a top-of-the-range performer with efficiency maximised.

This Ferrocarril Austral Fueguino (FCAF) locomotive No. 2 (originally named Nora) was built in Buenos Aires, Argentina, at Tranex Turismos workshops at Carùpa during 1994. After a complete mechanical breakdown in February 2001, it was fully rebuilt and modified to 21st-century standards by then railways Engineering and Operating Manager Shaun McMahon. (Courtesy Shaun McMahon)

It was not to be, as the key British decision makers wanted to stay true to the Pacific Class of British domain and design, with all its (now better understood) inefficiencies.

The *Tornado* was developed as a brand-new but conventional working steam locomotive, launched in 2008 and now making star performances on all the key lines in the UK, including the steep gradient Shap Bank in Cumbria and on the nearby famous Settle–Carlisle line, the highest main line in the UK, in both directions. It has already crossed the mighty Ribblehead viaduct, in October 2009, on the southern section of this famous main line.

But it was the steam-electric locomotive that remained the gleam in the eye of Dante Porta and many others; he argued that the ultimate maximum-efficiency steam locomotive had not yet been built. This is the case in terms of a large production run, but some engineers still tinker with the concept, so watch this space is a good axiom, I think.

Turning to actual operating railways in South America, a good place to start is south of the Beagle Channel and the Magellan Straits in Ushuaia, at the southernmost tip of Argentina. Here you will find brightly coloured, spotless steam locomotives in full power on the railway known as the 'End of the World Train'. Officially (and originally) it was known as the Southern Fuegian Railway (FCAF) when it commenced operation in 1909,

Sunday steam-up in Buenos Aires

Operating under great difficulty with the downturn in the economic fortunes of Argentina are several steam train groups, including one on the standard-gauge run into the suburbs of Buenos Aires itself. It is the only national capital in the world with three gauges in full operation and grand terminals attaching to them all.

One hot Sunday I was taken for a great run on this standard-gauge system. I was given a seat alongside the local steam heritage group's president and two vice presidents, but, alas, I could speak no Spanish and they could speak little English. The result: a chance to ride up front on the footplate was lost in the translation — now, where was the multilingual ambassador when I needed her? I think busy enough getting the program ready for the next day, if not recovering from another midnight 'Tango Dance club' session. I soon learned midnight in BA is not the case at all. Everything starts after midnight and ends around dawn.

No matter, and after a while the president and I were able to exchange some information using a hybrid form of Esperanto, to the extent it could be denoted a language at all. I hope to return to BA one day, especially now that the superb opera house, the Colon, has reopened, in May 2010, after a major revamp, but also to survey progress with high-speed rail from BA to Rosario.

mainly to transport prisoners to go out into the woods and gather timber for their large prison camp and the local township.

An Argentinian transport businessman, Antonio Enrique Diaz, known simply as 'Quique', stepped up and delivered progress at Ushuaia in the 1980s, especially with developing shipping and the local port. In his early years he had visited Liverpool and nearby North Wales, absorbing the delights of the Ffestiniog Railway, and when the remnant convict railway just west of Ushuaia was pointed out to him, he swung into action and invested in its restoration.

Enter again Shaun McMahon who was appointed by Quique as the technical and operations manager of this railway, the southernmost railway in the world. Shaun has greatly boosted productivity of the steam locomotives that draw tourists to this part of Tierra del Fuego, a region originally 'discovered' by Westerners way back in 1520. Ferdinand Magellan sailed through these parts in that year, then, like Captain James Cook 250 years later, met his end in violence on islands in the giant Pacific Ocean.

Today local industries are gas, tourism and some fishing, with the odd heavily subsidised factory, such as that operated by Amcor in Ushuaia. Over the decades, Tierra del Fuego has been claimed in its entirety by both Argentina and Chile, and now that peace and the border between Argentina and Chile have been firmly anchored in a treaty signed in 1984, international railway connections await. The treaty, brokered by the Holy See and then Pope John Paul II, laid down once and for all some 900 border adjustments between Argentina and Chile, including a north–south border line through Tierra del Fuego.

Today a short extension west would see the 'End of the World Train' cross into Chile, but of greater market value would be a short extension eastwards into the town of Ushuaia to catch the tourists from the big cruise liners that now call there as part of a summer loop to Antarctica — tourists fly into Ushuaia to board their chosen ship for a fortnight around Antarctica.

Perhaps the perfect, affordable compromise would be a light railway, a tram of some form of uniqueness, to provide the link from the CBD of the city and also the wharf area to the modern and comfortable terminal station of the End of the World Train. Given the inventiveness one Shaun McMahon could bring to the project, I would urge the creation of the world's first all solar-powered tram, complete with a large flywheel to assist acceleration, and people could catch the first solar tram to connect with the last train in the world, so to speak.

Argentina is once again considering new international linkages by rail, following the cessation of previous passenger linkages, such as from Antofagasta in Chile through Salta in Argentina to Buenos Aires. One big proposal is to consider boring below the Mendoza Pass to create a much lower imperial broad gauge double-track rail tunnel, and thus a more direct link between Santiago and Buenos Aires. This would make a seamless connection between the two big networks of Argentina and Chile, both of which are in imperial broad gauge.

Again the global financial crisis has hit hard, along with other sharp economic downturns around the turn of the century, effectively delaying the finance of any robust tunnelling under the mighty Andes. However, it is food for thought that when done it might be called the 'John Paul II Peace Tunnel'.

After all, it was his initiative that brokered the treaty that brought peace to the region — and just in time, as the crazy generals of Argentina were within twelve hours of bombing Santiago in the early 1980s when, instead, the deal was struck to commence negotiations.

On the subject of gauge, the first railways were built in Argentina in 1857 and the story goes that surplus locomotives built in the UK and meant for India had somehow ended up in Argentina, so they had to build their first tracks in imperial broad gauge to match. Chilean railways developed a little later, basically with two systems of imperial broad in the south and supreme metric narrow gauge in the north, where the job is often to handle mineral traffic.

Further northeast of Ushuaia, on the same latitude south as London is north, lie the disputed Falkland Islands and an incredible wind-powered

Atacama Desert Railway

There is a really weird place in the world with next to zero rainfall. It is the Atacama Desert to the east and northeast of Antofagasta, along the Pacific coastline. Inching inland and uphill from the busy port at Antofagasta is the Antofagasta Escondido–Salta railway main line, built originally by two brothers, Juan and Mateo Clark.

Now because of next to zero rainfall and because of the granular composition of the Atacama Desert, a great deal of this railway was laid without discreet ballast, indeed some without ballast at all. The Clark brothers ordered a shallow scrape-up of the desert sands and then laid the track, knowing there would be no moisture from rainfall to rot away timber ties or sleepers.

The story goes that if in fact the Clark brothers had dug just a little deeper, like only another metre, then they would have discovered the world's largest and most readily extractable copper deposits. BHP Billiton has for years operated the giant Escondido copper mine, and in recent years has enjoyed high copper prices.

railway operated during World War I and for a period afterwards. It was built in cane narrow gauge at Port Stanley on the Falklands, mainly to carry coal up to the big generators that powered the large radio transmitter station there. The railway ran for a distance of about 5 kilometres (3 miles).

This tiny Falklands railway was unique in a special way. As renowned author Trevor Rowe has pointed out, the morning steam train would take the coal westward to the boilers and generators of the station, along with rostered staff on some small passenger carriages. At the end of the various shifts, the locals would jump on an empty carriage and erect a sail. Soon they would be hurtling engineless downhill and home thanks to the strong westerly trade winds.

* * *

Moving north, it is Brazil that has a huge railway system of renown, which started back in 1852 in Rio de Janeiro, and for obscure reasons in Irish broad gauge. However, like most South American countries, Brazil soon ended up with a dual-gauge system, which it is now seeking to harmonise.

The real headache in the early decades was building a line from Santos, the nearest port to São Paulo, up a huge escarpment to the mega city of São Paulo. It was no easy task, with malaria also being part of the deadly equation.

The solution was some winching stations with cable haulage. The trains would be attached to the various grips on the cables and helped up the steep grades. (Such haulage was considered and rejected for the original Liverpool & Manchester Railway.) Eventually stronger locomotive power obviated the need for fixed winching stations. Their use is always a slow process but one old way of getting trains up escarpment grades. Generally extra tunnelling or even zigzags are preferred by engineers around the world today for this purpose.

All of this is a far cry from the 21st-century rail projects under consideration and in some cases development in Brazil today. The high-speed rail project at the top of Brazil's list is from Campinas to São Paulo and then on to Rio de Janeiro. Once again the indications are that it will favour Stephenson standard gauge for this project in a country that has over 28,000 kilometres of rail but until now only 194 kilometres in Stephenson standard.

In other words, the pathway dependency factor wins again, driven by commonality of design of HSR rolling stock built for standard gauge, and so saving money, at least on the rolling stock score. (This is forcing country after country to steer away from their dominant gauge to go to the definitive gauge for HSR, namely good old Stephenson standard.) The race is on to see if this project can be up and running for the 2016 Brazil Olympics, having missed the time slot for the 2014 World Cup — the football or soccer World Cup for the uninitiated.

* * *

Guyana was the first country to establish rail in South America, way back in 1848, and it followed the opening-day precedent of the Liverpool & Manchester Railway eighteen years before. On 24 January 1848 a key guest, indeed one of the directors, Alex Wishart, was riding in an open carriage up front when a cow wandered onto the track. The impact killed Mr Wishart and another passenger named Butcher. The event was not unlike the one involving poor old William Huskisson, MP, who was killed by the Stephensons' *Rocket* on the Liverpool–Manchester opening day. The fate of the cow is not recorded.

This first South American, indeed Latin American, railway was a relatively short hop from Plaisance to Georgetown. Now if you think Mexico was first, it was first only in planning a railway as early as 1837, but political instability ensured there was no operating Mexican railway until 1873, 25 years after tiny Guyana had trains rolling!

Near neighbours French Guiana and Suriname are about the only two countries with zero or next to zero railway development in South America, having closed down previous railways due to dam and highway developments. The larger countries of Bolivia, Colombia, Ecuador, Paraguay, Peru, Uruguay and Venezuela all enjoyed early rail development, mainly for the movement of ore from inland mines to coastal ports or in some cases large river ports. There was also considerable sugarcane-network development, to get the bulky cane to the local mill, then in some cases to get the sugar product from the mill to markets.

In recent years Ecuador has examined switching its remnant railway to operate entirely as a tourist attraction and sought advice from the UK and Wattrain, an emerging worldwide heritage and tourism railway organisation, as to the best way to do this. Certainly Ecaudor has the scenery and some historic rolling stock and locomotives awaiting restoration. The trick will be to proceed in a way that attracts large numbers of wealthy international tourists to a partially revived system.

The overall problem of rail in South America is that the dominant colonial powers of Portugal and Spain, and much more modestly Britain and France, were so otherwise distracted and in competition with each other (if not outright war) that there was no 'whole of South American continent' approach with regard to rail. If there had been, then the narrow-gauge systems should have all been built in supreme metric and the heavy-duty systems all built in Stephenson standard. Ironically the gauge least used in South America to date is likely to be the gauge of choice for all HSR development in this vibrant continent — namely Stephenson standard.

For decades South America, in particular Peru, was able to claim the highest railway in the world at 4829 metres (15,843 feet) on the line west of Lima, which included some nine zigzags. Now the new line in China which opened in 2006 to Lhasa, Tibet, has taken this title. At the point the Lhasa train crosses the Tanggulla Pass it reaches 5072 metres (6,640 feet) and without zigzags on the way.

South America anticipates a vibrant century of development, and the role of rail is now emerging once again in the thinking of leaders and policy makers, and hopefully they will sort out once and for all the many miles of rough and bouncy, indeed non-harmonised, rail tracks. The next international connection in this giant continent just could be on the Rio Turbio railway near Ushuaia, from Rio Gallegos on the Atlantic coast, past the coal mine at Rio Turbio, to Puerto Natales, where, true to form, a break of gauge awaits, from 750-millimetre to metre gauge.

Enter once more Shaun McMahon, for many years the operations manager of the Rio Turbio railway and a great regular guest on ABC Radio's *Great Train Show* because of his leading-edge rail knowledge. I confess that Shaun and I have conferred about this connection, even agreeing on a name for a new international express of about 320 kilometres (200 miles) length — the 'Dante Porta Unlimited'. This would be in salute to the greatest railway contributor ever from South America, deserving of commendation and adulation, one giant of a railway design engineer, Livio Dante Porta.

PART THREE

YOU THE
PEOPLE
AND RAIL

HERITAGE RAILWAYS

boom with the baby boomers

Is there really a heritage and tourism railway boom happening at the start of the second decade of the 21st century? The answer is an emphatic yes! From New Zealand to North Norfolk in the UK, heritage and tourism railways are in business.

Comprehensive patronage analysis around the world points to this, perhaps driven by people clipping back on distant holidays by ship or plane in favour of the heritage and tourism experience within easy reach. The global financial crisis has reduced holiday budgets for many in OECD countries, and on top of all of this the mid-April 2010 shutdown of aviation over Europe, as Icelandic ash drifted across aviation lanes, possibly helped.

While it is always dangerous to quote particular examples, a pointer to the buzz of the boom can be found in the UK where 10,000 people turned out on 11 March 2010 at Sheringham, Norfolk, as witnessed by my friend and chair of FEDECRAIL (European Federation of Museum and Tourist

Railways) and North Norfolk heritage railway, David T. Morgan, who was present. This was for the mere reopening of an ordinary level crossing in an ordinary location in a nondescript seaside town on the North Sea, a long way, in more ways than one, from a Brighton or an Eastbourne.

The steam locomotive *Oliver Cromwell* was on hand to be the first locomotive to cross this ordinary level crossing — admittedly a locomotive that is a bit of a drawcard — but 10,000 people for a level crossing opening is amazing.

The level crossing in question reconnects the North Norfolk railway to the British Rail network and will allow seamless transfer of locomotives and rolling stock from time to time. Eventually there may be even be a through special from London to Holt in Norfolk; certainly this is now possible in theory. North Norfolk is one of 115 UK heritage and tourism railway operations that have sprung up over the last six decades. It has a good variety of activities and equipment, along with pleasant scenery, and is a big tourism drawcard for the region.

HERITAGE RAIL ROLLS EVER ONWARDS

Europe and the euro may get the wobbles from time to time, but in each of the last six decades, more and more C Class rail operations have commenced, and many of these are outstanding in their uniqueness. At the FEDECRAIL meeting in Budapest in 2010 a list was tabled showing 277 active operators of heritage and tourism railway units, either on their own track or connected to main line and accredited to operate.

The UK leads the way with 115, then France with 62. Surprisingly the country that led the world with magnificent Marklin model railway equipment, namely Germany, has only 20. Still, almost every European country is having a go. As for the renowned Marklin, it turned 150 years old in 2009 and sadly filed for bankruptcy in February that year.

Take the renowned Ffestiniog railway in northern Wales, technically owned and operated by the Festiniog Railway Company (note the

Europe country by country

Excluding tiny countries such as Monaco and San Marino, which simply do not have the space, almost every European country has units of heritage and tourism railway of one kind or another.

UK	115	Belgium	6
France	62	Norway	5
Sweden	29	Hungary	3
Germany	20	Switzerland	2
Poland	11	Luxemburg	1
Netherlands	8	Rumania	1
Austria	7		
Finland	7	Total	277

anglicised spelling), which is a trailblazer in many ways and a delightful experience. As a slate-carrying railway decades ago, it made a contribution locally, but today it is internationally famous as a heritage and tourism operation. It generates 375 jobs and pours millions into the local economy. While for a period privately owned, it was an early heritage operation to emerge from the British Rail cutback-and-closure phase, helped by the fact that the 1947 British Rail nationalisation bypassed taking over the Festiniog Railway Company. With good overall grades, splendid scenery and a record of good performance, the Ffestiniog is often the benchmark narrow-gauge railway against which other heritage operations are judged.

The Ffestiniog also does not hesitate to go into legal battle with rail neighbours to maintain its patch, so to speak. It even has a direct connection at Blaenau Ffestiniog (a break-of-gauge station) to regular

British Rail passenger services and these passenger services are now delivered by one of the franchise services. From Blaenau Ffestiniog you travel to Llandudno Junction and then pick up a fast-service Holyhead-to-London train, however in total it is still about five hours with a change or two en route before reaching London.

Steam through the dining tables

On Thursday 22 April 2010 delegates and visitors to the FEDECRAIL Budapest 2010 Annual Conference attended a welcome dinner at the MÁV Nosztalgia Kft Railway Heritage Park, located broadly on the left bank of the Danube and northern side of Pest. Dinner was served on formal table settings in the glorious old Roundhouse, still standing and in good shape.

Suddenly a live steam locomotive burst through the improvised false door and doorway arch to slide narrowly past some of the dinner tables and patrons, coming to a stop safely and unloading from the footplate some dancers and musicians, mainly MÁV Nosztalgia Kft staff volunteers, to perform for the dinner patrons.

After unloading, as if by magic, the steam locomotive withdrew and the proper undamaged door was closed against the mild evening elements. There was a huge round of applause for the enterprising MÁV Nosztalgia Kft team and the dinner resumed. The French delegates were immediately overheard planning to adopt the idea. The British delegates were bemoaning OHS restrictions preventing any such delightful nonsense occurring in the UK. Other delegates from countries closer to Russia were reflecting on the plight of Tolstoy's Anna Karenina, who of course in fiction ended her life under a train wheel or two.

Closer inspection revealed there was a diesel shunting locomotive attached behind the steam locomotive, conferring a reasonable level of safety and ensuring a very enjoyable and memorable heritage railway dinner.

Hungary has followed a different template for its heritage and tourism operations. Two years after the Berlin Wall came down, a smart decision was taken to hive off MÁV Nosztalgia Kft Ltd from the main MÁV Railway Company and place a key Budapest roundhouse railway museum and considerable heritage rolling stock with MÁV Nosztalgia Kft, along with other operations.

Despite the difficult times faced by the ex-communist Eastern European countries, Hungary has emerged as a hub of kinds, and MÁV Nosztalgia Kft has proved to be a very successful template, today employing over 60 personnel and providing product with flair and profit potential. Indeed, I am advised many of its products are operationally profitable and the organisation is planning ahead with some dramatic new, attractive long-haul product.

Currently the luxurious Danube Express mentioned previously and run by MÁV Nosztalgia Kft saunters down the Danube, or at least parts of the left bank of the Danube, operating from Budapest to Istanbul and return. Plans are in place for a new product for 2014, one that will attract worldwide attention — the Danube–Damascus Express or some such name. Ultimately this train will use the two new tunnels being constructed under the Bosphorus, offering a seamless same-gauge service from Budapest to Damascus via Dracula's Castle, Ankara and Aleppo. Maybe there will be a chance to step off the train at Aleppo and see the famous Citadel and sip tea in the Hotel Baron, where Churchill and Lawrence once stayed, not to mention the feisty UK envoy Gertrude Bell.

Conversions to rail on the way to Damascus, as passengers add it to the list of must-do great train journeys of the world, are greatly anticipated.

It is possible MÁV Nosztalgia Kft's Danube–Damascus Express will be in operation ahead of any London- or Paris-to-Damascus luxury train-travel product, but we will see. Let us hope there is enough peace in the Middle East to allow these developments to build momentum and in the process offer very low carbon-footprint tourism on a sustainable basis, with numbers at manageable levels.

As opposed to Hungary's centralised, partly government-owned but unusually progressive, approach, most countries have gone in the other direction. Their templates for heritage and tourism rail development have adopted a private-enterprise or voluntary-enterprise approach, also at times a very haphazard approach.

Britain arguably led the way with trusts and foundations on a not-for-profit basis. These were designed to shoulder the huge tasks and liabilities of operating railways with the public and cover all occupational, health and safety (OHS) aspects. These are usually very complex and must be dealt with unless heritage railway directors want to be exposed to devastating negligence claims. As momentum has built, many have switched to, or developed as, limited liability companies, and much the same has followed in most OECD countries, with some government grants and peppercorn rentals or long-term leases helping greatly.

The USA has a number of outright individual- or family-company-owned operations, including the flood prone at one end but impressive Black Hills Central Railroad in South Dakota. This railroad climbs through the scenic Black Hills in sight of Mount Rushmore, where the visages of four ex-presidents are carved in rock. I might add it is a worry that there is space for some more faces to be carved in, but not for all 44 ex-presidents or incumbent.

Large states dominate the count of heritage and tourism railways but the quality of each one varies and is always difficult to assess. Perhaps the formidable *Trains* magazine could introduce a definitive one- to five-star rating system, as they have the credibility to do this and maybe even the courage. This courage would be needed, given the litigation such a rating index might unleash in the USA.

All in all, there is no doubt the USA is the largest heritage and tourism railway provider in the world. Most of the large museums in each state are government owned, such as the Californian State Railroad Museum brilliantly located near the Sacramento River in the state capital of California. It is a museum with a very dramatic entry foyer and theatre to

State-by-state USA heritage and tourism railways

In 2010 *Trains* magazine published its pre-summer guide to heritage and tourism railways, including the big and small museums. An interesting spread of train operations and museums around the country emerged from this list:

Alabama	6	Maine	9	Oregon	10
Alaska	4	Maryland	12	Pennsylvania	37
Arizona	10	Massachusetts	8	Rhode Island	2
Arkansas	5	Michigan	24	South Carolina	3
California	55	Minnesota	14	South Dakota	2
Colorado	23	Mississippi	1	Tennessee	14
Connecticut	8	Missouri	14	Texas	21
Delaware	1	Montana	4	Utah	5
Florida	12	Nebraska	6	Vermont	3
Georgia	10	Nevada	5	Virginia	12
Hawaii	5	New Hampshire	13	Washington	2
Idaho	4	New Jersey	8	West Virginia	7
Illinois	16	New Mexico	4	Wisconsin	18
Indiana	12	New York	32	Wyoming	3
Iowa	8	North Carolina	10		
Kansas	7	North Dakota	6		
Kentucky	9	Ohio	25		
Louisiana	3	Oklahoma	10		

Grand total, not counting the Smithsonian, Washington, DC, as much has been transferred to the nearby and magnificent Baltimore Railway Museum: 542

welcome patrons, and while it lacks a Big Boy giant steam locomotive, it has just about everything else. Further, all locomotives and rolling stock are glistening and well laid out.

Canada is no slouch on rail-related displays and operational activities, with a total of 57, but some caution must attach to this number, as some are full-scale operators, such as Via Canada, and others are restaurant dining-tram or single-carriage operators.

HERITAGE RAIL SUCCESS KEYS

What makes an operational heritage and tourism railway worth visiting and profitable? What are the factors that build success on success instead of a drift towards closure and the lifting of tracks for bike trails or new road corridors — the latter always a matter of anguish?

(1) Firstly, as in everything, it is vital that there be good leadership, whether the railway venture is government owned and operated or volunteer run with one or two paid staff in some location at the back of beyond.

Jack Welch, former head of General Electric, had a pithy summary of leadership needs, despite his spectacular exit from the company, and he was not without some railroad equipment knowledge (manufacturing rolling stock and locomotives), so I quote: 'You should always upgrade the team, exude positive energy, see and live and be the vision, establish trust, be curious, have courage, set the example and celebrate.'

My own army-related PR drivers are also useful; namely, be positive, precise, prepared, proactive, presentable, polite, punctual, passionate and pragmatic. Above all else be of high ethics or probity. And to this I add these five directives: refresh, review, resolve, reward and repeat. Confused? Then read again slowly!

One of the big problems with volunteer-run operations is: how do you sack or shunt around well-meaning volunteers without a major split into factions and a collapse of central focus and positive dynamic with the particular operation involved? I say again that good leadership comes to the fore, and there are millions of textbooks on leadership and management to help with this.

Another problem often encountered in units run by volunteers is that while they may have the best of intentions, they may also be simply incapable of meeting the complexity of the requirements involved. The biggest failure with many volunteers and professionals in the railway heritage and tourism business is to realise that there is no automatically guaranteed level of support and revenue streams based on the notion that everyone should be prepared to salute part of our past transport heritage. The raw reality is that each leisure dollar and each hour of recreational activity is finite, and there is huge competition to attract and win those dollars and hours; nothing is guaranteed.

Good leaders and managers understand this and know the levers to pull to boost the operations and revenue. Take the Great Central Railway from Loughborough through Quorn to Leicester North in the middle of the UK, by way of a good example. In fact, the CEO of this railway can demonstrate Royal Mail train operation of yesteryear, where mailbags are exchanged at speed (collected and dropped off trackside) and just about everything else — I refer to one William (Bill) J. Ford, and his background is a good pointer on management. For years he was the head of a huge motor vehicle importer and distributor in the Middle East, mainly Saudi Arabia. He knows how to handle challenging situations and how to extract maximum traction. Where to site a turntable along the route of the Great Central Railway, thus maximising the uniqueness of the railway in offering steam locomotives passing each other on double track, was just one of the sensitive issues on the boil in recent times. Bill Ford and his Chairman David T. Morgan won the day for Quorn, and so it is all systems go with fine-tuning and boosting the attractiveness of the Great Central Railway product.

(2) This leads nicely to the second rule of success, namely the quantum of operations and in particular the length of track, which must be carefully considered. Believe it or not, but available evidence suggests that a mere

Dorrigo: a crying shame

Perched on top of the coastal range near Coffs Harbour, on the wet and wonderful NSW Mid North Coast, surrounded by rainforest and often in fog and mist morning after morning, there is something called the Dorrigo Steam Railway and Museum. When the museum was formed last century, Dorrigo was connected via a branch line to the Sydney–Brisbane main line at Glenreagh Junction through two superb short tunnels about halfway down the coastal escarpment.

Four decades ago official NSWGR operations withdrew from the line but it remained available for tourism operations. However, the controllers of policy and strategy at Dorrigo Museum allowed — or dare I say resolved — stubbornly to allow the branch line to go into disuse, and to deliberately not allow tourism trains to operate through its superb vistas. To be fair they wanted to direct all energy and monies into collecting steam locomotives from the NSWGR system for storage largely in the open, exposed to the heavy rainfall the area receives.

Eventually a brave group at Glenreagh secured permission to start using the bottom portion of the branch line, and with difficulty they have begun to operate the Glenreagh Mountain Railway. It may be that a run-through operation with a tourist train special, leaving from the big regional city of Coffs Harbour at, say, 0900 each morning for a three-hour run to Dorrigo, two-hour lunch at Dorrigo on the plateau, and a two-hour return was a concept not doable — but that window did once exist. However, short runs might have worked and added to the diversity of attractions in the large tourist region, but, alas, it was not to be.

If you want to see steam locomotive after steam locomotive rusting away in open air in the delightful mountain-top town of Dorrigo — over 30 of them — the journey awaits, but you will have to do it by car or coach. Such a journey should not be too long delayed. I commend the Dorrigio Railway Museum website, complete with aerial photographs illustrating of the saga, last time I looked.

16 kilometres (10 miles) is close to the optimum for a tourist/heritage operations, in more ways than one. It helps keep maintenance costs down; it allows about the right length of time for the train experience; and above all else it lends itself to special events and repeat business.

In this I am guided by the aforementioned David T. Morgan, current chair of FEDECRAIL in Europe, and involved directly with three railways in the UK. He is also the leading light behind moves to launch the worldwide heritage and tourism railway organisation going by the name of Wattrain. David knows his stuff and is no shrinking violet at tourism railway conferences. He readily concedes you can simply have too many locomotives, too much rolling stock, and too long a distance of track, with the result that too often the association or trust or heritage company goes bust. Rather than shortening track and operations, too often groups involved have held on in the belief a solution is just around the corner. Inevitably this leads to total death of a railway, sadly too many gone forever.

As a success story, the Prairie Dog Central Railway in Winnipeg, Canada, has had a start-stop history, but today does well with a length of track it bought in 1998 from Canadian National of 26 kilometres (16.5 miles). I would observe this is long enough!

(3) The third key factor making a railway tourism venture successful relates to the attitude of the relevant rail regulator on issues. That, of course, assumes that there might be the luxury of just one universal regulator — oh, to be so lucky! More often than not there is a tapestry of regulators and authorities involved, and if their starting point is to regard the business of heritage and tourism rail as conveying the wrong image for the area and a wasted effort, then they can lay many barriers along the track to prevent approved operations.

From time to time leadership has to be exercised, a conference of stakeholders must be called to workshop problems and get things sorted, with day one for the operators and day two an all-in, including the regulators, so the issues identified the day before can be sorted. A good starting point is to involve and also highlight the number of government authorities who are players or stakeholders. To pick three examples, in Australia, India and the USA there are three levels of government, namely local, state and federal or national, and too often all three are duplicating effort and creating costly confusion. The number fifteen comes to mind re separate clearances and certificates and all to operate a 'Thomas the Tank Engine' event Down Under — to be fair, a few years ago.

(4) The fourth key requirement where use of a main line is involved relates to the attitude of the owner-operator of the main line or through line to which the heritage and tourism railway connects. In the case of the Great Central Railway in the UK this is currently not a problem, as it is within sight but disconnected from the main line. It needs one bridge and 400 metres of track to reconnect to the main line that runs north from St Pancras through Loughborough eventually to Leeds.

Pity about this, as a UNECTO (federation of 77 European heritage train museums) steam train running from Paris or Lille (with steam shut down through the Chunnel) to Loughborough and Quorn, at least once a decade, would be sensational. Many might point out it would have to be a small SNCF steam locomotive due to the UK loading gauge, but then again the Great Central Railway was built with the largest loading gauge in the UK (equal to applicable Continental loading gauges), in anticipation of an eventual successful direct tunnel link being completed between the UK and France.

However, in so many railway realms the attitude of 'big brother' (the main-line owners and operators) can make or break a tiny heritage and tourism rail unit. In 2008 on the old broad gauge corridor from Seymour, Victoria, to Albury, New South Wales, a raft of problems including 'unhelpful attitudes' by key operational personnel ensured a return arrival of tired and cranky passengers well after midnight back into Melbourne, worse still by bus. The special train itself lost its slot and was stranded at Seymour because of these attitudes, including an excessive 'work to rule ' outbreak just at the time it would cause maximum delay. This had nothing to do with ARTC, the huge successful federal government-owned interstate main-line network operator. Over the years the ARTC has expanded greatly, at most levels maintaining a fair attitude to the heritage and tourism operators, but also with an eye to revenue priorities.

It could be said even enlightened track owner-operators can vary in their attitude to heritage rail units down the ranks — just as human nature dictates. Therefore leadership also has its role, in particular the ultimate quality of leadership I once cited in an army lecture I gave: leadership is communication, communication and communication.

In Tasmania the various incarnations of main-line operators and owners, at least so-called main line but very rickety in places, have not helped heritage and tourism operators at all. The terrific small rail museum at Glenorchie, a Hobart suburb, is barred from the main line that sweeps past right alongside. In more recent times, the Redwater Creek railway near Sheffield in Tasmania has the potential to rival the mighty Zig Zag railway near Sydney in vista, and outdo that of the Barron River falls on the famous Cairns-to-Kuranda railway. It has built a kilometer or more of track towards some local water falls, but, alas, for various reasons it has been stopped by a form of Nimbyanna Wall — you know the type: namely 'Not in my backyard and not at all!' May I borrow from former US President Ronald Reagan and say 'Tear down this wall, in the real interests of all'.

⑤ The final factor that deserves highlighting is the ability to plan, market and execute special events to build momentum and revenue success. Evidence during and after the global financial crisis suggests that special events can boost business by 30 per cent, and not just 'Thomas the Tank Engine' events but 'Wizards' Expresses', 'Steam Galas' and even 'Ashes to Heaven' (funeral) activities. Regularly scheduled events work well if closely managed and monitored, especially in building a reliable product for regional tourism operators to incorporate into a group tour schedule, and they often lift patronage through the roof.

In the UK, the A1 Trust development of the *Tornado* steam locomotive project and its star appearances obviously help boost attention and patronage. Anniversaries rate highly in this regard as well, such as when the A4 *Mallard* 50 years on, in 1986, carefully re-enacted its record-breaking steam run near York in the UK. Incidentally a railway workshop supervisor at the time said the *Mallard* was 'almost a complete wreck after its 126 mph run'.

The visit in 1988 and 1989 of the *Flying Scotsman 4472* to Australia resulted in huge crowds turning out and paying to ride on the train it hauled, and also on trains running alongside on double and in places a triple and quadruple track. It was a huge success but less successful in the USA, where it had to spend a period in limbo at Fisherman's Wharf in San Francisco. In his comprehensive book on the *Flying Scotsman* and its various owners and adventures, Andrew Roden details how things can go right but also how things can go quickly wrong, on the financial front in particular, even with this rolled-gold locomotive.

There is much in a name, it has to be said, especially with railway train product. Take Great Southern Railway which has its HQ in Adelaide. It operates the Indian Pacific Sydney-to-Perth and the company's newest famous train, the Ghan, between Adelaide and Darwin. It is said this name came about because of the Afghan cameleers who for decades provided transport with their camel trains to and through Central Australia.

The Ghan is the shorthand version that has stuck and has become a strong brand name, not to be confused with the Afghan Express that the Pichi Richi Railway operates between Port Augusta and Quorn — the other Quorn in the Flinders Ranges in South Australia. In more ways than one Quorn, South Australia, is a long way from Quorn, UK, but I hasten to add, both host good watering holes for humans, along with successful heritage and tourism rail products chugging along nearby.

So special events go best when there are strong brand names and marketing handles to be had. The Grand Canyon Railway (GCR) in Arizona is now burning cooking oil waste, or to be more correct vegetable oil waste, collected from all the local fast food outlets. There is a big difference in, say, the GCR calling its main morning train to the scenic rim

The Mallard *on the 70th anniversary of its steam speed record in the UK.*
(Courtesy Michael Kemp)

the 'Fat Express running on fast food fat byproduct output', and calling it 'True Green Canyon Express running on recycled retail-food vegetable-oil waste product'.

I accept, of course, there are a hundred factors at play in bringing about and sustaining successful heritage and tourism operations — from ambulance and medical staff being available on big days, right through to the auditors; however, the five critical factors above are the most important, all things considered.

The baby boomer generation, namely those born in the decade after World War II, has about ten more golden years left of giving something back. Federal Treasury of Australia studies show they were the lucky ones in relation to asset value growth, jobs, generous superannuation and now free time with dollars to spend. Some plan on leaving just enough for their funeral and ten dollars' safety margin at the end of their lives, so they are travelling big time. In the meantime there are now so many different rail operations in each continent, except Antarctica, that, even if going flat out, boomers will not be able to ride every named train of fame on every major continental train corridor.

At least some are putting real effort into giving back to the community — wisely so, as US studies show the act of giving extends life span and greatly reduces heart attacks. Among those giving something back is the small army of volunteers helping in a thousand ways the heritage and steam rail operations of the world. It is this support that has allowed so many railways to start up in recent decades and now many are moving to a more professional footing.

If I was to add another factor in heritage and tourism rail success it would be transition, a subset of leadership but often overlooked. Planning transition of key directors and managers and qualified drivers is an increasingly urgent task, as baby boomers also start to head in large numbers to the nursing home. Unless turnover of quality personnel is carefully managed, many railways will grind to a halt for lack of capable and trained operators.

TWELVE BEST OF BEST

Meanwhile, enjoy the diversity of heritage and tourism rail product on offer while it lasts, as there are some incredible experiences to be had and which can be enjoyed by all ages.

Here are the twelve best passenger trains of any kind and any length, by my estimation, taking into account a degree of uniqueness. After six decades, but not yet ten, I can personally vouch for these, selected from right around the world. They consist of four heritage, two modern half-day tourist, four long-distance involving overnight on the train, and two very high speed railway trips.

(1)   The order is not an absolute determination of priorities but deservedly it starts with the shortest. The *Fire Fly* Brunel broad gauge locomotive and open carriage operates along a kilometre or less of 7-foot ¼-inch track within the Didcot Railway Centre, UK, and is special. It is the only Brunel broad gauge operating anywhere in the world and is both the shortest and widest rail product in the world. It is also conveniently placed, about 30 minutes west of Heathrow.

(2)   Next I go for the world-heritage-listed Toy Train from near Siliguri up the Himalayas to Darjeeling, a climb of some 2000 metres on cane narrow gauge. At Ghum, near the summit, there is a delightful museum at the station. Further along, the main spine of the Himalayas is readily visible and the carriage *Mark Twain* commemorates the fact that he was once a passenger in 1896. The line was built by a certain Lieutenant Napier, ultimately Lord Napier, who went on to achieve military conquest and fame in Africa. The Toy Train is part of the huge governmental heritage and tourism train operations in India.

(3)   Puffing Billy makes it as a makeover of an old Suez gauge steam-train service that mainly hauled vegetables towards the Melbourne markets from the Dandenong hills just east of Melbourne. Great scenery, superb timber viaducts and new bridges, a diverse set of locomotives and rolling stock all help to make this Australia's most utilised heritage and tourism narrow-gauge railway.

(4)   The 'End of the World Train', namely at Ushuaia on the southern tip of Argentina, has to be ridden to be believed. Location helps make this train service enthralling and the fact it was once a prisoner-worked railway for bringing in timber supplies gives it an eeriness as well. Snowcaps abound in the distance, and for a pleasant morning or afternoon before returning to that conference or cruise liner, you could not do much better.

(5)   The Bernina Express from Italy to Switzerland is a superb train and vista experience, as detailed in Chapter 5, operating very reliably on narrow supreme metric gauge with its bright red carriages standing out against the snow. A great escape in both directions from the hassles of the world,

and it also parallels one of the great escape routes of World War II. It runs not far from where the von Trapp family crossed over the Alps to safety in neutral Switzerland. The Grosotto escape route out of Nazi-controlled Italy can also be sighted through the Bernina Express windows

6 For diversity of vista in one half-day, the TranzAlpine across the South Island in New Zealand rates a high place. The New Zealanders arguably have the greatest train vistas to offer the world: the Auckland–Wellington, North Island, daylight trip has everything from spirals (where the track does a 360 degree circle to gain or lose height) to volcanos, but the South Island is even better, with the TranzAlpine Express between Christchurch and Greymouth.

Until the earthquake that shook and wrecked Christchurch in February 2011, almost everything could be seen on this half-day trip: the old steeples of Christchurch, then the rich Canterbury Plains of the South Island, the spectacular gorge country (Waimakariri Gorge) and the bare foothills of the Southern Alps, then the snow caps and Arthur's Pass. On the western side of the Otira 8.55-kilometre heritage tunnel (built with great accuracy from both ends, as it happens, during World War I and one of the longest in the world at the time) there is the lake-country section, followed by the sub-tropical forests and finally a run down the river valley to the Tasman Sea coastal plains and the Port of Greymouth.

The large windows on the comfortable rolling stock help greatly as the TranzAlpine speeds along on the Anglo Cape narrow gauge. The only disappointment is that there is no regular steam locomotive haulage. A ride up front in the diesel locomotive cabin is to be commended, if offered, as you dive through tunnels and across bridges over deep ravines. The cuisine may not be the very best, but the experience and vista are very much deserving to be rated best of the best. Better still, this train operation survived the 2010 Christchurch earthquake with only one short section of track impacted and this was quickly repaired. It was a sad case of déjà vu in 2011 but again the TranzAlpine is now back in service.

7 The Ghan deserves its place on this list, with its scheduled four hours at Alice Springs in the centre of Australia and four hours' stop at

spectacular Katherine Gorge near Darwin. The rolling stock reflects massive revamping and refurbishment, and the dining and lounge cars are very stylish. Wonderful private carriages are also available for hire and attachment if travel is sought as a group or large family.

(8) Along the West Coast of the USA there is an underrated Amtrak train, the Coast Starlight, which operates between Los Angeles (City of Angels or fallen Angels) and Seattle (city of the morrow with Bill Gates in residence). The range of scenery is unbeatable, including being right down along the beach, about 10 metres (30 feet) from the surf between Los Angeles and San Francisco. In 2008, while riding it with my family, we watched the dolphins diving through the surf as if pacing along with the northbound train. Throw in the Cascade Mountains and reasonably good-quality double-decker rolling stock and all is very commendable.

(9) The fabulous Blue Train of South Africa is unadulterated luxury amid good scenery, as it tracks between Pretoria and Cape Town. You do notice the Anglo Cape narrow gauge versus, say, Stephenson standard gauge rolling stock, which can provide larger sized bedrooms and so on. Through clever design this does not become an insurmountable problem. The Stellenbosch wines are readily available on board as you meander through wineries near Stellenbosch and up to the Karoo Plateau.

(10) The MÁV Nosztalgia Kft Danube Express has much to offer and behold, especially the trip taking in Dracula's Castle in Transylvania. The rolling stock I have encountered is comfortable and conveys understated heritage luxury with a bonus of actually working showers. So you do not have to rely on perfume and male cosmetics alone as you sweep along parts of the Danube from Budapest to Istanbul and return. I happily completed this journey in reverse from Istanbul, in fact to Pest, the left-bank side of Budapest, where you arrive at the Eiffel-designed Budapest Nyugati Station and are welcomed into the Royal Waiting Lounge with a glass of champagne.

(11) Eurostar from Paris to St Pancras, London, for a range of reasons is one of the best of the best, and is very comfortable. Having had so many horrible ferry crossings and delayed short-hop flights from Heathrow, to

sit back and do it in just over two hours, city centre to city centre, is a privilege each and every time. Against considerable odds it is now high speed on both sides of the English Channel and hitting its straps in more ways than one, although as mentioned, its shutdown due to snow is unacceptable and should be completely preventable.

(12) Finally, the original high-speed Shinkansen from Tokyo to Nagoya hurtling past Mount Fuji deserves a place on this list, especially as it was the very first of its genre way back in 1964 and has not missed a beat since. Of course rolling stock has been upgraded over the years, including double-decking on JR East (one of the companies of the JR group) lines and the installation of the super pointy nose for streamlining and reducing the wall created by air pressure at high speed. It is the Liverpool–Manchester of high-speed rail and it is a great pity many OECD countries did not quickly follow the exemplar it set.

The best of best: the twelve greatest, most extraordinary train journeys in the world:

1 *Fire Fly*, Didcot, UK
2 Toy Train, Darjeeling, Himalayas, India
3 Puffing Billy, Dandenongs, Melbourne, Australia
4 'End of the World Train', Tierra del Fuego, Argentina
5 Bernina Express, Tirano, Italy–St Moritz, Switzerland
6 TranzAlpine Express, Christchurch–Greymouth, New Zealand
7 Ghan, Adelaide–Darwin, Australia
8 Coast Starlight, Los Angeles–Seattle, USA
9 Blue Train, Pretoria–Cape Town, South Africa
10 Danube Express, Budapest–Istanbul, Eastern Europe
11 Eurostar, London UK–Paris France
12 Shinkansen, Tokyo–Nagoya, Japan

So the list is a combination of heritage and commercial, short and long and, I concede, reflecting personal whims, inspections and experience.

Finally I admit to one or two omissions of significance and I am working on booking trips on these one day. They are the Trans-Siberian from Vladivostock to Moscow, preferably in comfortable sleeping-berth class, plus one of the big window trains from Cusco to Machu Pichu in Peru, using the Inca route. On evaluation of reliable feedback from others, I do commend both as being special; they are one long and one short train experience of grand vistas.

If the World Heritage-listed Toy Train at Darjeeling is the highest route on the above list, the lowest above-ground railway in the world has to be the Stoomtram operation between Hoorn and Medemblik, a distance of about 20 kilometres (13 miles), in the lowlands of the West Frisian countryside, in the northern part of Holland, and all below sea level, protected by dykes.

Perhaps Stoomtram should promote itself as offering the only regular 'Submarine Steam Train', that is, a steam train operating entirely below sea level.

The Stoomtram, which dates back to 1879, is one of many runners-up to the top twelve. Others include the mighty Pichi Richi in South Australia and the Zig Zag in the Blue Mountains of New South Wales, the Durango and Silverton Narrow Gauge Railroad Train in Colorado, USA, and many more mentioned elsewhere in this book.

In terms of 'best value for train ticket purchased', let me be decisive and nominate just one train and one route: it is the morning train that operates between Sarajevo and Mostar for which US$7 will cover the cost of sitting in a first-class carriage and gliding down the valley past the Sarajevo Airport and on through a set of tunnels and magnificent high-level bridges before a steep descent into Konjic then past a lake into Mostar. At famous Mostar, you will see the large, high single-arch (rebuilt) Roman bridge. Diving from this bridge is best left to the local professionals, but it is great to watch the local exhibitors after the three-hour train trip and is a wonderful start to adventure in the Balkans.

In surveying the railway museums of the world, let me dwell on one which is a standout in many ways — new and bold and located on a busy corner of the megacity of Tokyo, Japan.

The East Japan Railway Museum in Onari near Omiya, is the largest rail museum in Japan. Like all things Japanese, it is both meticulously designed and elegantly executed, and it delivers a first-class experience to the visitor. With its own railway station, and easily accessible from the JR network at Omiya, the museum is a major drawcard for both young and old.

It preserves and presents the past, but also educates and looks to the future. You can test your skill at driving on one of a number of train simulators — an electric around the suburbs of Tokyo, a Shinkansen at speed, or the most exciting — a steam engine bouncing along the tracks. Climb aboard railway carriages, inspect the imperial and royal cars, and see a cross-section of Japan's locomotives and rolling stock through steam, diesel and electric days. The museum boasts an enormous model railway, where, in about 30 minutes, an eighteen-hour one day (or to be more exact the most interesting eighteen hours of a day) in the life of a train of East Japan Railways is presented, with perfect models of most of the currently operating trains of the network.

You can learn about what new technology presents for future rail, and the younger ones among us can ride on model trains around an outside track that illustrates the basic principles of trains, tracks and signals to the curious. With two excellent souvenir shops, a range of eating places, soaring ceilings and space, changing exhibitions and displays, all located next to the 'live' railway outside, it sets a benchmark in heritage and education in rail.

Greatest railway museums in the world

This is really a work in progress because I have visited many but not all the key railway museums and, alas, not many in the northern parts of Europe, where I have never found the time to get past the superb art galleries that dominate. So I beg off creating a definitive list but do mention in despatches the following:

- National Railway Museum, York, UK (greatest standard gauge)
- Didcot Railway Centre, UK (greatest broad gauge)
- National Railway Museum, Port Adelaide, Australia (greatest multi gauge)
- Workshops Rail Museum, Ipswich, Australia (greatest narrow gauge)
- California State Railroad Museum, Sacramento, USA (greatest loading gauge)
- Italian National Railway Museum Pietrarsa, Naples, Italy (greatest gold-inlay dining carriage)
- Baltimore & Ohio Railroad Museum, Baltimore, USA (greatest restored roundhouse)
- National Rail Museum, New Delhi, India (greatest zero gauge)
- Railway Museum, Omiya, Tokyo, Japan (greatest high speed)
- La Cité du Train, Mulhouse, France (greatest cutaway steam locomotive)
- Swindon Steam Railway Museum, Swindon, UK (greatest foundry presentation)

One short of a dozen, I know, but my inspections continue for the lucky number twelve. Having been to all the above, except one which I have studied closely by IT, I do say not only railway buffs but the broad public will find them all interesting.

STEAM SHANGRI-LA

Way up north in Italy, on the edge of the section held by Austria for decades at Primolano, east of Trento, there is a 'Steam Shangri-la in the Sky', namely project 880.001 to revamp a superb heritage steam-locomotive depot in the mountains and restore a special steam engine which was first in its class.

The Associazione Societa Veneta Ferrovie is driving the project along, led by Pierluigi Scoizzato, his brothers and a young team with a vision. It is an example of a new steam heritage and tourism venture with the rising generation to the fore, a rare example, but nevertheless an example of renewal. The effort has been helped along by just one or two mentors, including Bill Parker of the key Flour Mill engine works in the UK. All strength to their project and to the cause.

In July 2010 further progress was made on this project when the actual locomotive 880.001 was safely delivered by truck to the HQ depot for this project, ready for restoration work to commence. The depot is located on a bend in the regional rail track just south of Primolano Station and I predict one day it will be as dynamic a steam rail centre as Didcot in the UK. Further, on a one-day course you will be able to learn how to drive a steam locomotive and then be allowed to do so.

Meanwhile, just 31 minutes by train south of Rome on the Cassino line you come to Statione Colonna and the new narrow-gauge 'La Ferrovia Museo', also under development by a team of young locals. These include several descendants of the last great stationmaster when the line was fully operational right through to Termini, namely Giuseppe Arena. It is a jewel of a blending of history from both early days and the last days of operation, and with the troubled Nazi-occupation period of World War II when the station HQ was used as a radio signal station well covered.

Italian rail heritage is full of surprises today, and full marks to a younger generation in stepping forward to ensure all is not lost for future generations.

....

The Valletta Express: been and gone

It was 1 March 1883 when the Malta Railway Company commenced commercial operations from Valletta to Notabile. The train was never known as the Valletta Express, as it struggled along taking about 40 minutes on a good day to complete the 24-kilometre journey. On a bad day it derailed, started fires or merely slammed into herds of bulls. As detailed in Joseph Cassar's book on the Malta railway, 34 imported bulls were killed at a level crossing on 22 July 1923, but no humans were harmed.

On 31 March 1931, the axe fell on what would today be a perfect low-cost diesel or steam tourist railway across the main island of Malta. Pity about that, as Malta, full of superb remnant forts and churches to die for (many knights of Malta did just that), is congested today with bus and car traffic, not to mention taxi and truck traffic, especially near the magnificent harbours.

Some aspects of the Malta railway are pure British railway culture and style. The timetables always showed the curious terminology of 'Up Trains' for those in fact running broadly downhill to the capital city of Valletta, and of course the 'Down Trains' for the opposite direction to Notabile.

....

I leave you with the Sierra Leone Railway Museum rescue, necessitated by the turmoil of the rebel war, and led for a period by one Colonel Steve Davies as part of a process of building connectivity and progress in this African country. This project was an extension to the vital International Military Assistance Training Team UN peacekeeping role, and involves creating the new revamped museum, located near Freetown. While to some extent it is a work in progress, it is a great example of using all tools at one's disposal to turn a situation and create positive worthwhile projects. I am assured it is a gem of a museum, growing in popularity.

In fact Steve Davies has advised that today the Sierra Leone Railway Museum is a source of real national pride, due in part to the normality it has helped engender, and the fact it was done with little government help. 'All of this has helped to bind the project to the hearts of the majority of Sierra Leoneans,' Steve Davies added in a comment dictated on the run, in his busy role as the head of the National Railway Museum, York, UK.

Gustave Eiffel's Garabit Railway Viaduct

There is a bonus with rail heritage and that is the potential to use grand spirals, brilliant bridges and extraordinary viaducts, not to mention zigzags, as both marketing tools and revenue magnets. In other words, railway engineering efforts of the nineteenth century can be and should be saluted in the 21st century in a win–win way. Ribblehead Viaduct, UK, and the Zig Zag Railway, New South Wales, are good examples, but let me reveal one of the best of them all: the Garabit Railway Viaduct built by Gustave Eiffel and hidden away in Cantal, central France. This highest arch or span in the world at the time opened for trains in 1888, after over 3000 tons of iron had been brought from Paris and hit up with 678,768 rivets. Engineer Gustave Eiffel learned from this huge effort just ahead of his next project, which you may have heard of or even climbed: the Eiffel tower in Paris.

A trick for French rail might be to develop a special summertime train project called the 'Great Viaducts Express', leaving Paris, Gare de Bercy, pausing for lunch at Garabit and overnighting at Millau. By which route you would steam over Garabit, then proceed under the huge new freeway viaduct at Millau, which is also an incredible sight. All of this stands a good chance of happening if local historian and dynamo Deputy Mayor Patricia Vergne-Rochès holds sway; further, such an express would be a rare experience and helped along by the superb local produce available en route!

LOBBY LONG AND HARD

the case for rail

Domodossola is the last big town in northern Italy on the main line from Milan to Brig, Lausanne and Geneva, not far short of the mighty Simplon Tunnel. Between the Swiss border and Domodossola there is, or used to be, a tiny station just south of the Simplon twin tunnel portal, Mine di Trasquera. Here the great raconteur Peter Ustinov failed in his lobbying of a railway official, the feisty local stationmaster. It did not help that the stationmaster was a proud member of the Communist Party of Italy and a one-day strike had been called.

Ustinov wrote of his encounter in his aptly named book *God and the State Railways*. He detailed how he had departed on the overnight sleeper train from Rome to Geneva and beyond, when the one-day strike was called to commence at midnight. Against the odds the train made it right through to Milan and was allowed to depart for Switzerland, helped by a sweet-talking train guard, or controller. The train put on a burst of speed through Domodossola but, alas, at the next station the signal was thrown to red and the stationmaster was adamant the train would have to wait out the remainder of the strike, about another eighteen hours.

The train guard remonstrated, Ustinov remonstrated, both highlighted the train was just a few kilometres from the border but the stationmaster was having none of their argument. After several hours' standoff, the deputy stationmaster emerged from the telegraph office to announce there had been a landslip between the station and the border. A bridge had been knocked out and it was realised that if the train had been allowed to proceed, it would have crashed down a ravine and almost certainly all would have been killed.

Ustinov was forced to concede and travelled on to Geneva by road coach, where two days later he read an article about the hero Mine de Trasquera stationmaster whose judgement had saved the day, and who received a medal from the local mayor. This caused Ustinov to concede with mutterings to the effect: 'Well might the card-carrying member of the Communist Party, the officious stationmaster be labelled a hero, but he will never know whether in fact there is a God or not.'

Yes, I would have loved to have interviewed Sir Peter Ustinov on the *Great Train Show*. Alas, he has now departed the trains of this world to enjoy those in the next, no doubt regaling all with his fabulous tales from a rich life on earth.

Direct action and lobbying by passengers on trains generally does not yield results; however, strategically planned, targeted lobbying can work wonders in support of rail. It has to be done properly. Impossible, you say, unless you are a cabinet minister or a billionaire, but in fact it is quite possible for a member of the public to have big say, and also for a backbencher or junior MP in opposition to obtain breakthroughs for rail.

THE CASE FOR RAIL

What then is the case for rail and how is it best to lobby for same? In many ways the case is laid out in the previous chapters but extrapolating from these, it is time to apply discipline and simply and concisely state the case for rail in the 21st century.

Rail as a mode of transport versus all others requires less fuel per passenger and tonne-kilometre, and less space on the ground than cars, coaches and trucks. Rail uses less space for major terminals than airports and contributes less carbon to the atmosphere. It generates less in greenhouse gasses than all other modes. Overall only rail can deliver the energy efficiencies and transport capacities required in this century for short distances (passenger and some freight), medium distances (all passenger and all freight) and long distances (some passenger and all freight) over land — of course when operated efficiently.

SPEED AND ENERGY EFFICIENCY OF RAIL

I mentioned in the Introduction the core reason for rail's efficiency over other transport means: that a steel wheel on a steel rail has one-seventh of the friction of a rubber tyre wheel on a bitumen surface. This is worth considering carefully. What it means is that if a loaded truck on a road and a loaded rail wagon on rail at the top of the same rise both roll downhill entering an absolutely level road and rail track respectively at the bottom with the same momentum or speed, then the train wagon will roll seven times further than the truck. Unit train loads of freight or passengers have massive energy savings compared to the truck or car because of this 'less friction factor'.

This is also the very central characteristic that delivers the following, taken from the UK Department of Environment, Food and Rural Affairs (DEFRA) 2008 Guidelines and the International Energy Agency (IEA):

CO_2 emissions per passenger-kilometre in Britain, on broad equal criteria:

Air	191
Road	131
Rail	53

* * *

It gets better: 77 per cent of world emissions are due to the transport sector, and of that the split is chilling, or, in fact, warming, to the core:

Road	72 per cent (of the 77 per cent)
Rail	1.6 per cent (of the 77 per cent)

* * *

Finally, there is the aspect of land usage in a more crowded, congested world. An average one lane of freeway/autostrade or one railway track occupies 3 to 5 metres width, but delivers the following movements — to be exact, passengers per hour:

Motor vehicle or car	2000
Coach or bus	9000
Tram and modern light rail	22,000
Metro and modern heavy rail	50,000

* * *

To deliver all of this, you need fast, fuel efficient locomotives for passengers and strong ones for freight, both of which the world can now produce.

On the speed score, it is the French well out in front again, reaching the world speed record of 574.8 kph (357.2 mph) in the TGV over a test run on 3 April 2007 with special wheels on standard-gauge track but also with considerable sparking between locomotive gantry and overhead wiring, although secret research has found a solution leaving a tiny gap between overhead cable and pantograph (more to be revealed in time). This will never be the average speed of the TGV or VFT station to station, but it does show how a 300–360 kph speed station to station is not far around the corner … so long as the corner or curve is not too sharp.

Maglev as a form of non-rail electric-magnetic mode of transport is faster again, but hideously expensive with track construction. It does operate from Pudong International Airport into part of Shanghai in China, and the German and Japanese have been experimenting with it. In Japan a speed of 581 kph (361 mph) has been reached with a maglev test vehicle on pathway, or magnetic track, but it remains beyond reach for most countries and is never likely to match TGV, ICE, Shinkansen and other trains.

SAFETY RECORD

Modern rail is the most energy efficient, safest and most effective land transport method around, essentially because, as I have said, a steel wheel on a steel rail is fundamentally very efficient and has one-seventh of the friction of a rubber tyre wheel on a bitumen surface. At true cost reckoning to the user and the community and nation, it is more beneficial than all alternatives.

For the record on the safety front, here is a statistic worth learning: in 1995, according to the American Railroad Association, in the USA there were zero train accident deaths (specifically passengers killed on trains); on the roads there were some 41,817 fatalities. Aviation and gun deaths in the USA are another matter, especially gun deaths which annually exceed 30,000 and are at least five times greater per capita than in Australia, due to the divergence between Australia and USA gun policy. 2001 statistics show total gun deaths per 100,000 in Australia at just 1.68, and in the USA that year, 10.26. A 2010 postscript on this is that Amtrak has commenced fitting special gun-carrying lockers for the transport of guns safely on US passenger trains — in the circumstances a necessary and a good thing.

Back in 1905, a total of 9703 people were killed in train accidents in the USA, including collisions and derailments. This figure encompasses passengers, employees and even trespassers. Rail has come a long way in terms of safety performance over the last 100 years or so, both in the USA and worldwide.

Now, how do you take the case for rail and argue it loudly in the community and especially in participatory democracies? With difficulty, is the response, especially, say, in the birthplace of democracy, namely Greece, where the Hellenic Railways were over 10 billion euros in debt in 2010, and losing over 4 million euros daily. Yet, it is worth arguing the case for railways in democracies, even worth trying in dictatorships, given the gains to be had for the people.

The four keys to this are simple enough. Firstly, go for an objective that is practical and obtainable; secondly, add in a win–win dimension to get stakeholders on board; thirdly, be incessant in clever working of the media; finally, never give up. If the cause is sensible railway revamp and enhancement, the tide is in and in fact massively in favour for many reasons. Sadly, not every seat of power in the world recognises this but many will as the 21st century further unfolds.

OBTAINABLE OBJECTIVES

(1) First things first, and do not ask for the moon — for example, do not ask for new branch lines to towns of less than 1000 without any rail freight demand, or an extra stop of an express train or a TGV when clearly the overall timetable dynamic will not allow it. Asking for such things generally leads to disappointment and defeat. In the case of Taiwan's high-speed rail service, many contend that in fact each service has far too many stops, due to too much local lobbying. It is best to assess what is achievable, work out what might be obtainable, and if need be take advice from someone working on the inside of a giant transport agency to gain more knowledge.

From time to time governments will call for select committees or set up task forces to investigate various transport matters, generally with a carefully crafted set of references, in part to produce a pre-ordained result. Often this is the moment for Joe or Josephine Citizen to strike with a submission that is well argued and strong enough to register on the radar screen of the committee. In turn this can lead to hearings at which you can be called to give evidence.

If, for example, you are arguing for immediate duplication of a suburban line that is single track for the last six stations farthest from the city hub, you do so intelligently and with stakeholders on board. Your most compelling argument is generally that the extra duplication would eliminate constant delays when peak hour trains get out of kilter or delayed. Of course you tic-tac with local chambers of commerce or commuter associations to gain backing for your submission.

A smart way to proceed is to suggest a two-phase implementation, initially double track between the fourth-last station and the second-last station, then a second phase completing double track to the terminus. Trust me, there is method in this approach, but study the local timetable and the pattern of delays to determine where extra capacity would help the most.

In other words, argue in a practical way for what is achievable, perhaps at times going further in your demands than really necessary to allow the government to clip back and be seen to be in control.

This, in fact, leads to the second key aspect of win–win dynamics — making everyone feel a winner and minimising losers, thus enhancing chances of favourable recommendations and quick government action.

A WIN–WIN STRATEGY: SWITCHPOINT

(2) When I was chairing the Victorian Rail Freight Network Review (RFNR) investigation into freight rail in Victoria in 2007 we received some 100 submissions from organisations and about 25 individual submissions, the majority of which were well argued and helpful.

Switchpoint report

My initial urging was for a sharp name for the RFNR report, for example, 'Last Chance: Avoiding rail to rust' and 'Nerves of Steel: Which way the Victorian freight railway?' Both sent the senior departmental support staff in the committee secretariat nearly apoplectic, but at least one staffer thought I was on the right track. I persevered for as long as I could, held out for a month, just to make everyone sweat all the way up to and into the minister's office, but I had a fallback in mind, in one sense so attractive it knocked out my previous suggestions.

Once I floated the fallback name, it was quickly adopted unanimously by the committee, and so we went with: 'Switchpoint: The template for rail freight to revive and thrive'. My fellow committee members, Peter Wilson, John McQuilten, Bruce McGowan, Kerry Murphy and Rob Spence, were massively helpful in, firstly, keeping me on track and, secondly, adding greatly to the worth of the deliberations and outcome.

I confess the cause was greatly helped by a bonding night with magnificent McQuilten's Reserve Shiraz, supplied by committee member John McQuilten from his nearby winery. The wines were served at a glorious dinner in the magnificent old central Victorian Maryborough Station dining room, where Mark Twain once changed trains. Perhaps the excellent wine and the writing spirit of Twain helped keep our freight train report on track. There is no doubt that the name of the report added to its momentum.

Months later, after then Transport Minister Lynne Kosky announced the millions for upgrading the Gold lines we had designated, I arrived at state parliament on a sitting day with a bunch of twelve gold roses to say thanks. The security guards and ministerial-office outer ring all stonewalled me until finally the message reached the minister, and on a busy sitting day I was ushered in and greeted warmly, with the pronouncement this gesture broke new ground.

I took just ten minutes of her time and I commended the decision. As mentioned, it never hurts to say thanks, and a few months later, the Silver line upgrades were announced also.

Quambatook is a small town in western Victoria and its Silo committee (an elected local committee to help promote and coordinate grain storage) presented well at a public meeting we held one afternoon in the town. The result was that it had a breakthrough in the recommendations — a favourable Gold category outcome and rail capability boost in anticipation of the return of decent grain harvests in the area, as well as some prospect of nearby mineral sands being developed and eventually requiring rail.

Our activity was geared to the second key: always endeavour to create a win–win situation and the Bronze category of railway lines we created — those recommended to be placed on a 'weed-clearance/maintenance-only' basis, pending developments (see Chapter 7) — was certainly this: a way forward but avoiding total closure and the political pain involved. The RFNR was of the view with the Bronze lines that it was well worthwhile protecting the corridors involved for any eventuality in the future.

In other words it was a win–win situation, but if we had recommended wholesale closures of the Bronze lines, then all hell would have broken loose and further, future options would have been cut off, such as with the mineral sands developments, especially if requiring rail capability to refineries and ports. The shrill may get the evening news headlines but the shrewd can win out. The people of Quambatook are in the shrewd category, and they and so many other places can be proud of their influence and most of the RFNR outcomes.

If only the ugly Beeching close-down period in the UK had been subject to an overarching Switchpoint-type task force or Westminster committee review, then in this railway realm many very costly mistakes might have been avoided. If only the will of parliaments and the various congresses of the world had maintained a balance in their land transport approaches in the last half of the 20th century, then rail would have bounced into the 21st century in better shape, and more importantly far better placed to take up the ever-increasing demands of this century.

USING THE MEDIA FOR ADVANCING THE CASE FOR RAIL

③ Thirdly, the media in the 21st century can make or break good causes. They are all-powerful in many ways but also always on the lookout for good causes. The trick is to feed them well and not break the implicit rules. In this regard note the following:

- Never ring a radio-station newsroom in the last ten minutes before the hour, wait until a quarter past the hour.
- Never forget the name of a journalist or interviewer; above all else never muddle the first name mid interview — retribution can be fast and cruel.
- Never write and distribute a media release longer than one page, and never begin it with the word 'the', as it will always lead to extra subbing or tampering.
- Never ask to do a TV interview grab a second time; get it right the first time.

There are thousands of books on how to handle the media and what approaches to use, and most apply in relation to lobbying for railway causes. Always be proactive and positive with the media and get key phrases and buzz words relating to your particular issue or set of issues up early and so build momentum.

Let us say you have a railway cause arguing for a better timetable for the morning peak hour — always the much tighter and hectic peak hour for major commuter rail systems, as evening peaks are spread over several hours and not just two. You wonder why an enlightened system of yo-yo stopping cannot be implemented on two consecutive trains an hour, saving over fifteen minutes on a sixteen-station corridor. This is when the first two trains departing after the top of the hour from the outer terminus stop at every second station, eliminating seven stops each but still covering all stations on the route.

You might put out a media release as spokesperson for your local lobby

Draft media release

Here is an example of a media release (for all media and multi media outlets based in the applicable region) guaranteed to cost little but hopefully create a huge splash for the local steam-train operation:

Ashes to Ash Template Adopted by XYZ Railway: Dignity of the dead protected

ONE PUFF AND YOU'RE GONE!

President of the XYZ Heritage and Tourism Railway announced today that XYZ Railway has adopted a comprehensive template to respond to requests to distribute ashes of the deceased.

Paramount to the approach is safety and dignity of the process. The XYZ Railway will proceed as follows:

- Secure all local authority approvals as maybe required beforehand.
- Ensure crematorium and next of kin have certification that the urn is cleared for dispersal by steam locomotive.
- Ensure that the steam locomotive vigorously departs the station within one minute of formal placement of ashes preferably in a special cardboard urn, in the ash box.
- Provide a 'Dispersal Deed Done' certificate to the next of kin and family of the deceased and maintain a journal of dispersal, with details of the date/time/location/locomotive and name of the supervising official witness.

The president added that a modest fee would be charged for this service in order to cover extra costs, with an additional fee necessary if naming rights for the train on that day are sought. As an alternative to a fee, he said, families of the deceased might consider the option of making a contribution towards a scholarship for a young volunteer to undertake extra training.

For more information contact:

[ENDS WITH CONTACT DETAILS]

The simple one-page statement should always end with contact details for follow up.

group with the headline: 'Enlightened Timetable Required for Morning Peak Hour: 15 minutes can be slashed from schedule'. Alternatively you might say, 'Seven Stations Cut from the 0702 Service in Complex Move', which emphasises non-existent negatives and reduces your message to bad news. Better still, all things considered, go with the headline: 'Accelerate Key Peak Train Times: Introduce smart yo-yo scheduling', thus introducing a hopefully interesting concept.

Above all else be incessant and on the ball with the media at all times.

This is not meant to be a comprehensive media template, but let me leave you with one final thought. If you have a win, for example, when the Victorian State Government accepted the RFNR recommendation and converted the branch line running from Benalla in Victoria (on the Sydney–Melbourne main line) right through to Oaklands in the Riverina in southern New South Wales at a cost of over AU$16 million, then remember to say thanks. Why? Because it is polite but also you never know when something else will be required.

NEVER EVER GIVE UP

④ Finally, the fourth key I say is simply never give up. In fact the tide is in for rail revamp and development. Even the most biased car lobbyists and congress representatives or MPs cannot turn a blind eye to the big breakthroughs in rail that have been made in the first decade of this century.

Shining examples are now there to behold on several fronts — trains that deliver freight and passenger services of excellence, with both an environmental dividend and in some cases an appreciable operational profit. Incredible, you say; not true, you say; but it is, and bit by bit the best examples are being highlighted.

The Delhi Metro was discussed for decades, and then in 1995 the Delhi Metro Rail Corporation (DMRC) was set up under strong leadership. Construction work commenced in 1998 and there are now five lines, each averaging around 24 kilometres (15 miles) in length as they crisscross the densely populated national capital of India. A new line to Delhi Airport has opened and further extensions are under way, although it should be noted there have been two big accidents in construction, and in fact around 100 people have been killed during construction of this huge project.

On the positive side there are now one million passengers daily using this metro; further, it is not only modern but spotless, with strict zero tolerance applying in relation to rubbish and spitting and even sitting on the floors. It has been a big cultural change for many Delhi residents, but they have come to love their air-conditioned metro. Incidentally many of the air-conditioning units were built in Western Sydney and exported to Delhi. Ironically, the biggest complaint on receipt was that the carriages were too cold, and could the experts come from Sydney and adjust the air-conditioning upwards? Please make it warmer, was the cry.

A Delhi Metro train arriving.

As mentioned in the first chapter, this metro is profitable. Indeed some interesting operational financial figures have emerged from a smart-ticket system that works and delivers. In the year ending March 2008, total revenue was US$68 million and net operating profit was US$4.5 million. At the end of the subsequent financial year, in March 2009, following the opening of more lines and stations, total revenue had risen to US$161.4 million with a nearly-fivefold increase in net operating profit to US$20 million.

Metro rail can pay its way, and if combined with a sensible congestion peak-hour vehicle tax, then you start to get a dynamic, balanced transport system. Delhi has put in a stellar performance; the DMRC has avoided huge corruption with construction, otherwise termed the 'brown paper bag' approach. This too often dominates in various railway realms and is a toxic brew against real progress with rail.

Finally with Delhi and its new metro, unusually two gauges have been used, both imperial broad and Stephenson standard. Why is this so? One reason was given in the first chapter on gauge — standard is more easily able to handle sharp curves in urban areas than imperial broad — and the detailed answer is for another time, as I figure (for once), you the reader have had enough on matters of gauge by now. So relax and book a trip to Delhi to find out more and enjoy the world's coolest, most profitable, newest metro system.

Of course many rail passenger systems in the 21st century are doing very well, specifically the German ICE system, the TGV/Thalys/Eurostar systems out of France, and the Red Arrow in Italy, and reaching further and further. Also Japan's Shinkansen continues to deliver a huge and faultless performance.

On the freight front, railways operated by private enterprise in Australia, Canada and the USA are doing very well; most are operationally profitable most of the time. On both the east–west corridor to and from Perth and the north–south corridor between Adelaide and Darwin in Australia, the rail freight share is at or near 90 per cent on competitive merit (i.e. rail versus road and allowing for the extra subsidy of road operators); in the main huge operational profits are being obtained.

Boom times for some railways are never enough to counterbalance losses elsewhere. However, right now government-run Indian Railways and Botswana Railways are profitable, along with many Class 1 private-enterprise US railroads. Given that no user of freeways or autobahns, highways or roads has ever paid the sunken cost of their access or usage of same, the fact so many railways made it into the 21st century at all is remarkable. What is more remarkable is their near-unlimited capacity to further meet demand and expand — heritage and tourism operations especially, and railways more generally — driven by technological and other mentioned improvements.

THE CAUSE WORTH FIGHTING FOR

So rail is worth lobbying for in the mix of transport modes required to take land transport forward this century. It has performed against the odds with a tax system in most OECD countries that in net terms favours road. In the mix of all of this, there is not one OECD country that has achieved or delivered tax equality between rail and road in the last half of the last century. This means competiveness is too often seriously stacked against rail versus road, and to get it right rail must be given a fair go. This is all the more so as — or if, where and when — any emissions trading schemes are introduced.

Buried away in Recommendation 64 of the huge Henry Review of Taxation in Australia, released by then PM Kevin Rudd in May 2010, is a clause that owns up to the imbalance against rail along certain corridors and the need to proactively tax to fix this. At last the mighty Australian Treasury and the dedicated economically dry or at least 'dryish' Australian Treasury Secretary (until 2011) Ken Henry has seen the light.

Rail does require big licks of capital for infrastructure, in the start-up phase especially, but if done properly at the outset, then maintenance costs are much lower than road.

Bridge lobbying: tricks of the trade

AusAID Australia built the first-ever bridge across the Mekong, between Nong Khai on the Thai side and Vientiane — or just near Vientiane, the Laotian capital — which officially opened in the early part of the 1990s. I had supported the project, especially as it involved a planned railway line down the middle, and fifteen years later, in 2008, this metre-gauge track was installed to link the two countries by rail for the first time. Trains began running in 2009.

For cars, it is the most exciting crossover bridge in the world, as Thailand drives British (left-hand) side and Laos drives French (right-hand) side. On the Laotian side there is the world's only X road arrangement, where traffic crosses from one side to the other. I asked a former Thai PM during the bridge construction how this would work. He told me no worries as we will simply build a hospital at both ends of the bridge!

To this I might add that the Mekong (Friendship) Bridge was not popular with my electors, as they waited for new bridges across the Murray River and related floodplain, many of which I was able to eventually obtain, some through the Centenary of Federation fund. What helped there was the fact that Corowa, in desperate need of a new bridge, was also the birthplace of the Federation of Australia. Many would add Tenterfield to this position as well. Corowa is where the key convention was held and Tenterfield is where Henry Parkes made his famous speech launching the concept of a Federated Australia. So there are dual birthplaces of Federation Down Under! I latched on to this aspect and from inception called it the Federation Bridge project and this greatly helped build momentum.

The state officials were miffed that the 'feds' were calling the tune, but then we were supplying most of the millions. The result is that today there is the new Federation Bridge at Corowa. Sadly, there are no rail lines any more in the immediate vicinity.

The fundamental reason for saying the time is right for rail in the 21st century is the environmental dimension. The peak Cooperative Research Council (CRC) for rail research in Australia has compiled some figures clearly showing how HSR outpaces private car, road coach or aeroplane on all indices relating to energy efficiency and CO_2 emissions. David George, the head of the CRC, contends that even on conservative estimates, worldwide studies conclude rail transport is four times more energy efficient with freight movement, and two times more efficient with passenger movement, than road transport.

The large American Association of Railroads has produced a paper stating unambiguously that moving freight by rail transport rather than road, reduces greenhouse gas emissions by 75 per cent. In addition, it argued in December 2009, one average USA freight train takes 280 road trucks off the road and saves thousands of litres (or gallons) of fuel per 100 tonnes moved 100 kilometres. More importantly, at arm's length to the rail lobby the USA Environmental Protection Agency highlights that railroads account for just 0.7 per cent of US greenhouse gas emissions, and only 2.6 per cent of emissions from all transport-related sources.

Rail is way out in front on every environmental yardstick you can throw at it, even more so when various population projections and severe congestion parameters are taken into account.

The tide has turned for rail; the drumbeat must be loud and clear with lobbying efforts to sheet home this message in the centres of power right around the world — for the sake of our children, for the sake of the world. Of course this is not to the exclusion of a proper and necessary road transport system. The truth is we need both working in harmony, and intermodal rail freight is one big-ticket item, high-speed rail the other, that if widely adopted might just help the world reach sustainability in this incredible 21st century.

YOU THE PEOPLE AND RAIL

PEAK OIL

Another strategic element in support of rail is embraced by the chilling term 'peak oil'. What is meant by this term is simply that in volume the oil production of the world has peaked and is now on an irreversible decline. Some would say this is true even allowing for a future big expansion in shale-oil production. Even the most aggressive members of various oil lobbies have to acknowledge oil is a finite resource and it would be prudent to use it carefully. The International Energy Agency has revamped its calculations in recent years with regard to future oil production but remains defensive about peak oil.

The Mexican Gulf oil disaster of 2010 adds a dramatic backdrop to the energy equation. The millions of litres of oil flowing into the waters of the Gulf were a total disaster.

Academics from Uppsala University in Sweden to Adelaide University South Australia have spelt it out very clearly in recent times: oil production peaked in 2008, and will never exceed that peak again. Michael Lardelli, who has worked at both universities, makes a compelling case for the year 2008. Many challenge his conclusion but all must accept that oil is a finite resource and must be used efficiently, for the sake of the world. Natural forces take millions of years to make oil, and once used it is gone forever.

As a striking example of the energy equation and railway operations in the 21st century, consider the fact that the new Minister for Railways in China, Sheng Guangzu, boldly announced in April 2011 that China's high-speed rail service top speed would be reduced from 350 kph to 300 kph. This will apply to the new Shanghai–Beijing HSR service as well, due to open in 2012. This was designed for 380 kph but will come back to the benchmark 300 kph, in part for safety reasons but also to help with lower energy costs. I might add that a 300-kph service can still deliver a less-than-three-hours trip between Sydney and Melbourne on the 822-kilometre direct inland route.

Meanwhile, TTG Australia has secured a big contract breakthrough with First Great Western in the UK for its key product 'Energymiser', a driver advice system mounted on the control panel and resulting in fuel savings of as much as 23 per cent on the reasonably level test routes utilised. Loading a range of dynamic factors into the calculations, such as timetable, gradient, speed restrictions and headway of other rail traffic, the Energymiser tells the driver where he can cut power and coast, and so forth, often many kilometres from traditional cut power locations and often counterintuitive to years of driver habit, but with no loss of timetable performance and huge energy savings. All strength to Dale Coleman of TTG, who has stayed the course with Energymiser and the related Schedulemiser over the fourteen years of their development, in conjunction with the University of South Australia.

Any step that takes energy saving further in rail operations helps put rail further in front of other transport modes, not only on energy efficiency outright but also with helping to lower the transport carbon footprint.

Trains do have limits of course, but by and large it is a case of '21st century Trains Unlimited'. Mark my written words, on all the available evidence, it really will be a case of smart, smooth passenger and freight trains tackling the huge expanding transport demands of this century. In the broad, it will be a case of 'on again' for rail, even if in some parts of the world it is sadly a case of 'gone again', with no trains in sight and rails rusting away.

I hope to see you on a train going somewhere quickly and happily in the not too distant future, and passing many freight trains along the way. Produce a copy of this book and I will happily sign it, any place anywhere, but preferably at a railway station or on board a greenhouse friendly train.

IN APPRECIATION

of the cult and culture of rail

In the first decade of the 21st century, the world faced economic shock, terrorism shock, energy shortages and climate change agony, to name just a few of the negatives out there. The world has become distracted and divided, with the last unambiguously bright nanosecond being the teams of North Korea and South Korea entering the Sydney Olympic Opening Ceremony together, back in 2000. It has been steadily downhill since then.

All transport modes have faced major upheavals, but it is rail as a mode of transport that has responded well to these upheavals and revamped in a timely way. Behind this has been a few very good men and women who have created some awesome outcomes, everything from high-speed rail success to efficient rail-freight success, all with environmentally friendly credentials ahead of other modes of transport.

I salute the dedication of rail managers, researchers, planners and operators at all levels who produce a London–Paris two-hours fifteen-minutes service, notwithstanding the Christmas 2009 heavy-snow shutdown; those who produce a fast refrigerated five-day fresh-fruit-and-vegetables express from California to New York, competing on several counts with road and beating it on the long haul. In particular, I salute the fact that every day large cities avoid clogging up, because of extensive metro and commuter systems that haul millions safely and efficiently, in the main.

I commend the culture of performance with rail that has emerged after 200 years of development, a culture that was not always on the front foot, but a culture which learned from many mistakes along the way. I salute the safety and OHS standard of rail performance, again well ahead of other transport modes but not perfect — certainly safety is close to perfect with high-speed rail to date, for example with the Shinkansen and TGV. Country by country, rail is much safer than road and air.

In turn, rail has spawned a culture among its users, requiring them sometimes to be more dedicated than others, as commuters bear up with more and more crowded trains due to the success of the service. Among long-term rail users the mood is different again, especially among those who wisely know how to pick uncrowded trains and the many tricks of the trade to maximise comfort. Those lucky enough only to travel on trains with full reservation systems are well in front.

It has to be said there is a certain joy when sitting back in a clean air-conditioned train departing precisely on time for the intended destination with good company or, otherwise, good reading material. As the train smoothly leaves the terminal and gathers speed, you relax, secure in the knowledge you will arrive, not wrung out, but refreshed and ready to swing into action. Yes, delays do occur; yes, a noisy mobile-phone user can quickly destroy the ambience; but odds are the freedom to move around, the fact there is no need to go through a long list of safety and other announcements, arrival often in the centre of town, and the comfort and the convenience will all add up the right way.

The British author Jonathan Coe wrote proudly of his return to train travel in 2010, adding that trains are perfect places to work. He wrote in the *Financial Times*, about how the landscape presents an ever-changing backdrop that 'occupies the eye but never compels your attention for too long'.

Many a good book has originated from a train ride, many outstanding movies as well, and at least one nationwide radio show, the *Great Train Show* on ABC Radio right across Australia in 2008.

The creator of *Thomas the Tank* engine, the Reverend W. Awdry, once compared the Church of England and British Railways: 'Both had their heyday in the mid-nineteenth century, both own a good deal of Gothic-style architecture that is costly to maintain, both are regularly assailed by critics and both are convinced they are the best means of getting man to his ultimate destination.' Let me revisit and also review by providing a final quote of my own, as follows (I accept a little biased but heavily backed by the facts emerging from a lifetime of researching rail as a mode of land transport):

> *While the world wobbles along in the 21st century, it is the modern, efficient railways of the world which help on so many fronts to ease transport burdens and provide for the movement of millions of commuters and tourists, millions of tonnes of freight and in an environmentally enhanced way.*
>
> *All of this is at a time when passenger demand and freight tasks are both set to double over the next few decades and at a time when peak oil and energy shortages loom. Where rail is off the pace, it is imperative to get it fixed quickly; where rail is setting the pace with profit and performance, it is imperative to shout it from the rafters and give credit where it is due.*
>
> *Rail is the transport wager from heaven that might just save the world from massive crippling congestion, if not trade strangulation and economic collapse. At the same time it will provide net help to*

the environment vis-a-vis all other modes of transport. Due to its
fundamental advantages, rail is the best transport way forward in
this troubled century.

So I salute rail as a mode of transport. I salute the culture of modern-day rail management and operators at all levels. And I salute you and your habit as a regular rail user. If you are not yet a regular rail user then consider taking the train, and if one does not yet exist near you then consider lobbying for same.

This book has been about the reality of the railway, past and present, and in particular the potential of the railway in the future. It has touched on the romance of trains, complete with a list of the twelve best of the best train experiences in the world. It is about the compelling case for rail to deliver land-transport services efficiently and quickly with environmental credentials second to none, in the process overcoming massive congestion and freight chokes, and even having some fun.

Please remember the core ratio of rail success, be it in the Riverina, Australia, or Rome, Italy, or beyond: a steel wheel on a steel rail has one-seventh of the friction of a rubber tyre wheel on a bitumen surface. If you are in a position to do so, it is my hope you will promulgate this ratio and spread the word. In 1978 in Perth, Western Australia, Councillor and now Professor Peter Newman started Friends of the Railway in the nick of time. Arguably it greatly helped save Perth's urban rail system from closure and contributed to its outstanding revamp and expansion. You too can become a friend of the railway (actually, if you have read this far, I am sure you already are). In locations large and small, where needed you can help start up a 'Friends of the Railway' organisation. In turn this will help ensure rail is here to stay and expand. Rail, in fact, has not yet reached its zenith. Indeed there is much to behold in the 21st century, with trains unlimited.

BIBLIOGRAPHY

Adam-Smith, Patsy, *Romance of Australian Railways*, Melbourne, 1973, Rigby Ltd

Adam-Smith, Patsy, *When We Rode the Rails*, Melbourne, 1983, Cornstalk Publishing

Ajdin Braco, Fevzija, A *History of the Railways of Bosnia and Herzegovina*, Sarajevo, 2005 Fevzija Publication

Ambrose, Neil, *Train Journeys of the World*, London, 1993, AA Publishing

Amin, Mohamed, *Railway Across the Equator*, Nairobi, 1986, Camerapix Publishers

Balkwill, Richard, *The Guinness Book of Railway Facts and Figures*, London, 1971, Guinness Publishing

Bhandari, R. R., *Exotic Indian Mountain Railways*, New Delhi, 1984, New Delhi Railways Ministry

Bonnici, Joseph & Cassar, Michael, *The Malta Railway*, Valetta, 1992, Gutenberg Press

Bright, Stephen, *The Line Ahead*, Brisbane, 1996, Catalyst Communication

Bromby, Robin, *The Railway Age in Australia*, Melbourne, 2004, Lothian

Bryan, Tim, *Brunel: The Great Engineer*, Hersham UK, 1999, Ian Allan Publishing

Buchanan, Angus, *Brunel: The Life and Times of Isambard Kingdom Brunel*, Bath UK, 2002, Hambledon & London

Burke, David, *Road Through the Wilderness*, Sydney, 1991, University of NSW

Churchman, Geoffrey & Hurst, Tony, *The Railways of New Zealand*, Wellington NZ, 1990, HarperCollins

Cook, John, *A Book of Australian Railway Journeys*, Canberra, 1985, William Collins

Davies Hunter, *George Stephenson: The Remarkable Life of the Founder of the Railways*, Middlesex, 1980 (1975) Hamlyn Publishing Group

DeBoar, David, *Piggyback and Containers*, San Marino, USA, 1992, Golden West Books

De Cet, Mirco & Kent, Alan, *The Complete Encyclopedia of Locomotives*, Netherlands, 2007, Rebo International

Droege John A., *Passenger Terminals and Trains*, Wisconson, 1999, Kalmbach Publishing

Eastlake, Keith, *Great Train Disasters*, Sydney, 1997, Universal International

Ellis, Hamilton, *The Pictorial Encyclopaedia of Railways*, London, 1968, Hamlyn Publishing

Engel, Matthew, *Eleven Minutes Late: A train journey to the soul of Britain*, London, 2009, Macmillan

Fearnside, GH, *All Stations West*, Sydney, 1970, Haldane Publishing

Fischler, Stan, *Subways of the World*, Osceola USA, 2000, MBI Publishing

Foxwell, Eric & Farre, Baron Thomas Cecil, *Express Trains: English and Foreign*, London, 1889, Smith, Elder & Co.

Garfield, Simon, *The Last Journey of William Huskisson*, London, 2002, Faber & Faber

Gilbertson, Colin (ed.), *Steam in Australia*, Sydney, 1977, ARHS (NSW)

Grigg, Arthur, *Country Railway Men*, Poole UK, 1982, Calypus Books

Gunn, John, *The Defeat of Distance: Qantas 1919–1939*, Brisbane, 1988, University of Queensland Press

Harrigan, Leo, *Victorian Railways to '62*, Melbourne, 1962, Victorian Railways PRBB

Harris, Ken (ed.), *Jane's World Railways*, Coulsdon UK, 2002, Bath Press

Holdsworth, Malcolm, *Famous Last Lines*, Sydney, 1993, Holdsworth, Bambery, Kingsford-Smith

Holland, Julian, *Great Railways of the World*, Hampshire, 2008, AA Publishing

Hollingsworth, JB & Whitehouse PB, *North American Railways*, Chicago, 1977, Summit

Hollingsworth, Brian, *Atlas of the World's Railways*, London, 1980, Rigby Ltd.

Holmes, Lloyd, *A Railway Life*, Byron Bay, 1991, Holmes

Horsford, Jim, *The Barbados Railway*, London, 2001, Paul Catchpole

Hosokawa, Bill, *Old Man Thunder: Father of the Bullet Train*, Denver USA, 1997, Sogo Way

Jackson, David, *A Guide to Trains*, San Francisco, 2002, Fog City Press

Jay, Christopher, *The Long Haul*, Adelaide, 1991, Focus Books

Jones, Mervyn, *The Essential Guide to French Heritage and Tourist Railways*, Dorset, 2006, Oakwood Press

Jones, Mervyn, *The Essential Guide to Swiss Heritage and Tourist Railways*, Dorset, 2007, Oakwood Press

Jordan, Peter, *India: No Problem Sahib*, Chesterfield, 1989, Three Counties Publishing

Kalla-Bishop P.M., *Italian Railways*, Devon,1971, David and Charles Inc.

Keenan, David, *Tramways of Sydney*, Sydney, 1979, Transit Press

Kirk, John & O'Connor, Mark, *The Forever Lands*, Australia, 2001, Beyond Images

Kirkland Ian, *Forgotten Railways of the Northern Rivers*, Alstonville, 2004, Dragonwick Publishing

Laird, Philip, *Back on Track*, Sydney, 2001, UNSW

L'atlas des Trains de Légende, Paris, 2000, Editions Atlas

Lee, Robert, *Colonial Engineer: John Whitton 1819-1898 and the building of Australia's railways*, Sydney, 2000, ARHS (NSW)

Maggs, Colin, *Rail Centres: Bristol*, London, 1981, Ian Allen Ltd

Marin, Eva (ed.), *Luxury Trains*, Kempon, 2008, Te Neues Publishing

McCormack, Gavan & Nelson, Hank (eds.), *The Burma Thailand Railway: Memory and history*, Sydney, 1993, Allen & Unwin

Newell, Brian, *Following The Old Ghan Railway Line 1878–1980*, Adelaide, 2000, Custom Press

Faith, Nicholas, *The World the Railways Made*, London, 1994 (Originally 1990), Pimlico Publications

Nock O.S., *150 Years of Main Line Railways*, Vermont, 1980, David and Charles Inc.

Nock, O.S.(ed.), *World Atlas of Railways*, London, 1978, Victoria House Publishing

Oakes, John, *Sydney's Central: the history of Sydney's Central Railway Station*, Sydney, 2002, ARHS (NSW)

Oberg, Leon, *Australian Rail at Work*, Australia, 1995, Kangaroo Press

Patterson, J. H., *The Man-Eaters of Tvaso*, London, 1907, MacMillan

Plowden, David, *Requiem for Steam*, New York, 2010, W. W. Norton and Company

Porter Anna, *Kasztner's Train: The true story of an unknown hero of the holocaust*, London, 2007, Douglas & McIntyre.

Portway, Christopher, *The Great Railway Adventure*, Somerset, 1983, Oxford Illustrated Press

Portway, Christopher, *The World Commuter*, Chichester, 2001, Summersdale Publishers

Puffert, Douglas, *Tracks across Continents, Paths through History*, Chicago, 2009, University of Chicago Press

Reed, Brian, *Locomotives*, Bath, 1958, Temple Press Ltd

Reid, Arnot, *From Peking to Petersburg(1889)*, London, 1899, Edward Arnold

Robbins, Michael, *The Railway Age*, London, 1962 Manchester University Press

Roberts, Lew, *Rails to Wealth*, Broken Hill, 1995, L E Roberts

Roden, Andrew, *Flying Scotsman: The extraordinary story of the world's most famous train*, London, 2007, Aurum Press

Rowe, Trevor, *Narrow Gauge Railways of Spain, Vols 1&2* Horley UK, 1995, Plateway Press

Rowe, Trevor, *The Railways of South America*, London, 2000, Paul Catchpole

Rozendaal, Jack, *Steam & Rail in Indonesia*, London, 2000, Paul Catchpole.

Sallis, Roger, *Australian Preservation of Narrow Gauge*, Adelaide, 1979, Peacock Publications

Sallis, Roger, *Railways in the Adelaide Hills*, Adelaide, 1998, Open Book Publishers

Savio, Tom, *Extraordinary Railway Journeys*, London, 2004, New Holland Publishers

Schafer, Mike, *Classic American Railroads*, Osceola USA, 1996, MBI Publishing

Seidenfaden, Erik, *Guide to Bangkok with Notes on Siam*, Bangkok, 1928, Royal State Railways Siam

Semmens, Peter, *High Speed in Japan: Shinkansen – the world's busiest high-speed railway*, Sheffield UK, 1997, Semmens & Platform 5

Sharma, S.N., *History of the Great Indian Peninsula Railway*, Bombay, 1990, Central Railway Bombay

Sheppard, Charles, *Railway Stations: Masterpieces of architecture*, London, 1996, Universal International

Simmons, Jack, *The Railways of Britain*, London, 1990, Mallard Press

Singleton, C. C. & Burke, D., *Railways of Australia*, Sydney, 1963, Angus & Robertson

Smith, Keith, *Tales from a Railway Odyssey*, Adelaide, 2001, Railmac Publications

Stover, John, *The Routledge Historical Atlas of American Railroads*, London, 1999, Routledge

Stringer, H., *China: A New Aspect*, London 1929, H. F. & G. Witherby

Talbot, Frederick, *Railway Wonders of the World*, London, 1920, Cassell & Company

Tayler, Arthur, *High Tech Trains: The Ultimate in Speed, Power and Style*, London, 1992, New Birlington Books

Twain, Mark (intro by Don),,

Taylor, Colin, *Train Catcher: Adventures of a rail traveller*, Sydney, 1996, IPL Publishing

Ustinov, Peter, *God and the State Railways*, London, 1993 (originally 1966), Michael O'Mara Books

Welsh, Joe, *The American Railroad*, Osceola USA, 1999, MBI Publishing

Westwood, John, *World Railways*, London, 2001, PRC Publishing

Wheaton, Timothy, *Luxury Trains*, London, 1995, Bison Books

Wolmar, Christian, *Blood, Iron and Gold: How the railways transformed the globe*, London, 2009, Atlantic Books

Wolmar, Christian, *Engines of War: How wars were won and lost on the railways*, London, 2010, Atlantic Books

Wolmar, Christian, *The Subterranean Railway: How the London underground was built and how it changed the city forever*, London 2004, Atlantic Books

Wood, Heather, *Third-class Ticket*, London, 1980, Routledge & Kegan Paul

ACKNOWLEDGEMENTS

I thank Allison Jess of ABC Radio; Karen Penning, Mary Rennie and the HarperCollins team; my mother-in-law, Mary Brewer; and my wife, Judy; along with Barry Blair, Lord Richard Faulkner, Professor Philip Laird, David T. Morgan, Shaun McMahon, Chris Le Marshall, Mike Mohan, Bill Parker and many more for their assistance with this book. I highlight and thank also the authors listed in the bibliography.

May I also express particular appreciation to some Parliamentary colleagues who, over the decades, helped directly and indirectly my study of rail and so helped along this book project. From the Australian Federal Parliament I thank the Hon. Alexander Downer, Hon. Wal Fife, Hon. Kevin Rudd, Rt Hon. Ian Sinclair, Hon. Stephen Smith, and Riverina MPs Noel Hicks and Kay Hull. From the NSW State Parliament I thank Sir Charles Cutler and the Hon. Milton Morris; and from the Victorian State Parliament I thank the Hon. Bill Baxter; as well as all those mentioned throughout the book.

INDEX

Index

Index

Index